To Sam

with all good wishes

for a Merry Christmas and

a Very Happy New Year.

Love from Margot & Percy.

THE AUTHOR

Modern Sports Edited by Howard Marshall

GOLF

BY

HENRY LONGHURST

Illustrated with 33 pages of photographs and 16 diagrams

LONDON
J. M. DENT AND SONS LTD.

Made in Great Britain
by Richard Clay and Company Ltd.
Bungay Suffolk
for
J. M. Dent & Sons Ltd.
Aldine House Bedford St. London

First published 1937
Reprinted 1937, 1943

CONTENTS

PART I

PART II

PART III

ILLUSTRATIONS

FOREWORD

THERE is no 'correct' way of hitting a golf ball. Charles Whitcombe went round Crews Hill in 59 in one way, Aubrey Boomer holed Saint Cloud in 61 in another, Henry Cotton set a new standard of scoring with a 65 at Sandwich in a third, while in a fourth Bobby Jones won all that the world had to offer.

All were 'correct', yet no one could have confused one with the other.

I have tried in this book to dissect the methods of the masters for the benefit of the everyday golfer, to weed out their idiosyncrasies and extract the elementary basic principles to which they all conform.

In some cases where in their writings they have proved to be at direct variance with each other, I have secured an alibi in advance by quoting them verbatim at the head of the chapter.

I offer the result of my labours with all due humility. Golf is not yet an exact science—and this is not the last word on golf.

One favour, however, I would ask of you. Do not read too much of this book at a time. After a while, though the eye continues to read, the brain wearies, and ceases to assimilate what is set before it.

Again I would ask you to remember that successful golf is largely a matter of practice. Though you may read, and understand, the way in which the master players perform a certain stroke, you cannot hope to perform it yourself until you have trained your muscles to carry out a task to which they are at the moment unaccustomed.

Playing golf is like learning a foreign language. You may, in your mind, have a perfect conception of a Frenchman saying ' les grandes rues et ruelles ': but it will be many weeks before you can train your tongue to say it as he does.

I have reduced to a minimum the expression of my own personal views, preferring, where possible, simply to interpret those of the acknowledged masters of the game. The principal exception is the chapter on putting. Here I have to thank Gerald Duckworth and Co. for their permission to use a number of paragraphs which I wrote in the introduction to ' The Short Game ', by P. A. Vaile. Since writing them I have seen some thousands of putts holed and missed, but my views have remained unchanged.

For the second edition I have made no changes except to add the Rules of Golf in full. These, it should be emphasised, are primarily for reference, though anyone who cares to plough straight through them will, I am sure, be rewarded by the discovery of some extraordinary gaps in his knowledge.

Now, after an interval of more than six years, another reprint is called for, and we have taken the opportunity of killing two birds with the one stone. Out go the Rules of Golf again and in their stead will be found Part III, a series of observations, hints, and suggestions addressed to the vast army of returning golfers who will soon, we hope, be mobilizing on the tee again for the first time for five, six—or is it going to be seven ?—years.

Many of them will not have touched a club or seen a golf course in all those years. For myself, I had the incredible good fortune to be posted in the summer of 1943 to a headquarters next door to a golf club, so I have forestalled them. It has been fun to analyse the hard process of golfing rejuvenation, and I hope that the record of my own experience may ease this process for some of the others.

'Will it ever be the same again?' they may have asked themselves in the deserts, the jungles, and the olive groves. The answer, so far as I can see from the point of view of an advance guard, is 'Yes, indeed it will!' I am astonished at the intensity of interest which people in general seem to have retained in golf and all it meant to them.

Of course it will be a good many years before we see professionals' shops stocked like Bond Street stores with matched sets, balls by the dozen, and sweaters at seven guineas a time, but that won't break any true golfer's heart. The game's the thing. Balls will be at a premium for a good many years, too, and we shall have to trust that the rubber controller after the war is a golfer.

The championships will return as soon as the war is over, but not, I fancy, the profusion of big-money tournaments which kept the golf correspondents so busy in the old days. It will be a long time before the game becomes 'news' again, and I for one shall not be sorry. I thought it was getting a little out of hand.

The bogus amateur, who was beginning to rear his ugly head in our midst, will be hard put to it to earn a dishonest living from his golfing proficiency, and that, again, will break no one's heart but his own.

This is no place to enter into the 'politics' of the game, but I would point out one benefit that the war may have brought to golfers. It has given us a wonderful, perhaps final, chance to settle once and for all the ball with which the game is to be played. Golf was the only game whose whole character was at the mercy of manufacturers. Imagine if cricket or football or tennis were played with balls which, year by year, flew farther and farther, so that every pitch in the country had to be lengthened and broadened to accommodate them. Yet that was the farcical state we had reached in golf, when we solemnly altered two thousand courses to fit the ball instead of altering the ball to fit two thousand courses! Now there are no more balls. We make a fresh start from scratch. By the grace of the Royal and Ancient we may at last be able to have a standard golf ball.

Many of the fine fellows who used to adorn the game are gone, and we shall miss them; but the courses they loved for the most part remain. Prince's, Sandwich, has vanished for ever and was used, I believe, as a target range (which, said Lord Brabazon, is akin to throwing darts at a Rembrandt). Bramshot is knee deep in heather, and I hear ill accounts of Turnberry. Some courses grow potatoes and many are nibbled to death by sheep, but on the whole we must confess to have been lucky.

I have never tried to persuade people to play golf. If you don't want to play golf, for heaven's sake don't. But I hope to see the game increase in popularity and become available to more people than before, because it is, after all, the only game played by adults and in its small way helps to turn us into a nation of players instead of a nation of spectators.

If this book helps anyone along the irritating, tantilizing road towards becoming a golfer, it will have served its purpose and I shall be happy. But I warn the new reader not to expect improvement to be continuous. It goes, as it were, in spasms. Golf is an up-and-down game, like snakes and ladders—and if you find the snakes a good deal longer and more numerous than the ladders, don't blame me! But it's worth it in the end.

H. L.

London,
August, 1943.

PRELIMINARY

These chapters are designed for the perusal of the novice in the true sense of the term—the person, that is, who knows literally nothing about the game. The semi-skilled player may, and indeed is invited to, skip them; the player who has yet to obtain a single-figure handicap may care to glance through them, partly for the satisfaction of reminding himself what a superior fellow he is, in that he knew most of it all before, and partly in the hope of filling in some of the many chinks that he will discover still to exist in his armour.

Let us address ourselves, then, to our novice—to you, my dear sir, who have come to the great decision that you will join that vast company, now more than a million strong in Great Britain alone, over whom the game of golf has cast its magic spell.

You may be a schoolboy, fired by the public worship of the latest amateur champion or merely anxious to understand what father is talking about at luncheon on Sundays. You may have served His Majesty for a lifetime in distant quarters of the globe and be seeking no more than a pastime for your retiring years. You may merely be desirous of decreasing your girth, or you may, to put it at its lowest, be a business gentleman anxious to establish contact with prospective clients.

Whatever your motive, you wish to become a golfer.

Buying Clubs

Your first consideration will be the purchase of a set of clubs.

The number you will ultimately need will depend upon the seriousness with which you decide to play the game (though it is fair to say that, whatever your ambitions, you will almost certainly end by carrying, or having your caddie carry, too many). For a beginning anyone may make a reasonable start with five or six.

Individual opinions might vary as to which these five or six should be. The putter and the mashie-niblick would, I imagine, be common to every list. For the rest, we should not go far wrong in adding a mashie, mid-iron, and brassie. That makes five; if you care to make it six, you might dispense with the brassie, and carry instead two wooden clubs: a driver and a spoon.

It is impossible to recommend too strongly that you should buy these clubs direct from a professional. The latter may be attached to a public course or a 'proprietary' course; in Scotland he may have a shop in the town.

In a later stage of proficiency, when you have arrived at an age of discretion concerning the choosing of clubs, you can patronize a shop or store. A bitter rivalry exists between the professionals, whose salary from the club that employs them is usually small and who depend for their living on the sale of clubs and balls, and the multiple stores; the former holding that the latter are depriving them of their legitimate living.

That is a 'political' problem that need not worry us for the moment. Suffice to say that competent advice is what matters to the beginner, and it is my experience that the club professional is a man better fitted to give advice than an assistant in a multiple store, who during the same morning may have to appear equally well informed on ski-ing, croquet, lawn tennis, rowing, and a dozen other sports.

An extremely high standard of business morality obtains among professional golfers. A novice may enter the pro's shop, a chicken ready for the plucking, and yet come out with all his feathers on. Perhaps that is why the average income of the professional is so low.

How Much to Spend

The question of expense will at once arise in your mind. How much are you to spend on these clubs? My advice—since, after all, you cannot *buy* skill at golf—is the same to rich and poor.

Start humbly, and buy a few second-hand clubs from the vast store lying idle in a corner of the professional's shop. Pay him anything from six shillings to seven shillings and sixpence each for them, and give him clearly to understand that, when you begin to feel your feet and launch out into something a little more pretentious, you will not forget him.

In the old days of hickory shafts (of which more later) they used to make some appallingly bad clubs. Modern mass-production may have seen the end of many of the fine old craftsmen, but it has also seen the end of those cumbersome instruments, with shafts as solid as unhewn oak or as whippy as a fishing-rod, that were made for no better purpose than to use up an old piece of hickory or give the apprentice a hand at club-making.

Nowadays a really bad golf club cannot pay its way in the cut-throat competition set up by the manufacturers, and, as steel does not warp with age, like hickory, the novice is perfectly safe with second-hand clubs. The odds are that they were good when they were born, and having lasting qualities not possessed by their predecessors, are still good now.

Steel versus Hickory

Now, as to the respective merits of steel and hickory. Perhaps the fact that at least 95 per cent. of first-class golfers, amateur or professional, use steel-shafted clubs, is the best answer to the question. A perfect piece of straight-grained hickory was a joy to behold and a joy to feel in the hands; but with the extraordinary growth of golf since the middle 'twenties, perfect pieces of hickory became a rarity, a possession only to be acquired by the connoisseur. In the end they became almost extinct.

'Perfect hickory versus perfect steel' is a controversy into which we need not enter. The position, as they say, does not arise. Faced with the choice between steel and an increasingly indifferent hickory, the beginner can come to only one decision. He must choose steel.

Steel has one merit that hickory never had. That is, uniformity. The manifold processes, the extraordinary machinery, the skilled hands, the time, precision, and money that are devoted to the manufacture of steel shafts can only be appreciated by one who has seen them being made. Accurate to within the tiniest fraction of an inch, they have to pass the sternest of tests before they reach the hands of the public. Thus, while it took an expert to 'match up' three hickory shafts for a set of wooden clubs—to say nothing of perhaps seven more for a set of irons—it takes no skill whatever to match up a gross of steel shafts. A glance at a branded mark—and the thing is done.

Another advantage of steel is that, other things being equal, it will propel the ball farther than hickory. I do not say that *any* steel shaft will give greater distance than *any* hickory, but the observation is in general true. The beginner will find it hard enough to get distance, without sacrificing so obvious an aid.

The veriest novice who has not yet aimed a serious blow at a golf ball must realize the importance of having the correct shafts in his clubs. Yet it is a fact that numerous accomplished golfers take not the least trouble to see that their clubs are fitted with the shafts best suited to their play.

'The head of your club may *look* good', run the advertisements, with commendable truth, 'and the grip may *feel* good—but it's the shaft that does all the work'.

The Limbershaft

Steel shafts differ not so much in quality as in specification. Some are stiff as ramrods, others bend like a reed in the wind. The whippiest of the lot, known as the Limbershaft, became violently fashionable in 1934, but has now settled down to a more normal, but nevertheless substantial, popularity.

You, as a beginner, will do well to steer a middle course during the earlier days. The stiffest form of shaft can be satisfactorily wielded by a young man like Lawson Little, amateur champion of Great Britain and the United States in 1934 and 1935 and now a professional, who has the strength of a bullock. In the hands of the ordinary mortal it will have no 'feel'.

With a limbershaft, the opposite extreme, you are apt, until you have learned one of golf's hardest lessons—namely, to wait for the clubhead—to find your hands too much in front during the downswing. By the time your hands reach the true hitting position, the clubhead, owing to the exceptional 'give' in the shaft, may be lagging as much as a foot behind.

The limbershaft is an undoubted asset to those whose wrists, either through *anno domini* or from any other reason, are not so supple as they used to be. Given its chance—that is, swung slowly and allowed to do the work on its own—it will make up in a large degree what nature no longer provides.

It has, too, another use, and one which incidentally illustrates very well its peculiar qualities. It is used by many a professional and scratch player, generally in a driver, as a check on his swing when he feels his action 'running away with him'. One of the half-dozen major golfing faults is that of 'snatching'—that is, whipping the club down so quickly at the top of the swing that the rhythm of the shot is lost. The limbershaft shows this up in such a startling fashion that the player is literally forced to slow down and 'wait for it'.

The Lie and the Weight

A point that must not escape the beginner, over which, with all due respect, I think that professionals are sometimes a little careless, is the *lie* of the club. This represents the angle at which it was made to rest comfortably on the ground. It is essential that the club should be made for the man, not the man self-adjusted to fit the club.

The difference between flat and upright lies can be seen from the diagram, and the veriest novice must at once grasp that a man who uses, say, an upright club when he ought to have a flat one—which means that he will address the ball with the heel of the club on the ground and the toe sticking up in the air—is labouring under a substantial and quite unnecessary handicap.

In order to tell whether a club has a suitable lie, you have only to rest it on a flat floor, holding it loosely in the fingers and making sure that the sole is flat along the ground. Then, taking care to keep the angle between the shaft and the ground unchanged, see whether in that position it is comfortable for the making of a shot. If there is a desire to drop the hands or to raise them, it means that the club is too upright or too flat.

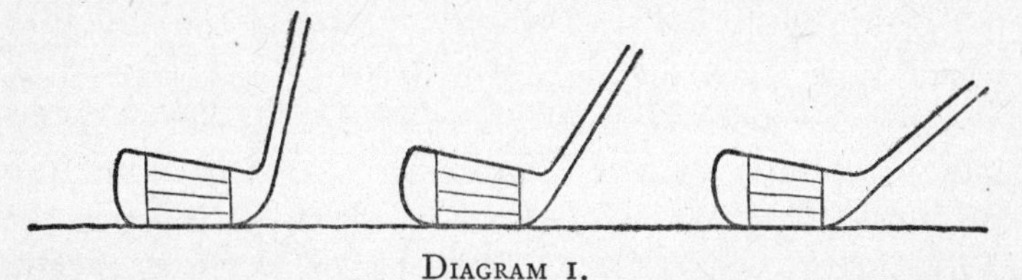

Diagram I.

Weight is another consideration that must be watched. In the beginning you will do well to make sure that your clubs are not too heavy, for you must remember that, in order to wield them, you will be using a number of muscles that are unaccustomed to the task. As time goes on, you will discern an ability, though not necessarily a desire, to use heavier ones.

It is a fact that a club, when picked up and waggled in the professional's shop, nearly always feels lighter than it will prove when wielded in earnest on the golf course. It is what we may call a kind of sensory illusion. It is so easy to waggle a heavy club briskly to and fro; so difficult to go through a rhythmical motion with it in a full swing aimed at a ball.

As a more concrete guide it is fair to say that the driver, for instance, should weigh a maximum of thirteen ounces for anyone who is not accustomed to the golf swing. Length, it must be remembered, comes from the *speed* of the clubhead, not from its *weight*.

The ideal thickness of the grip will be discussed when we come to look into the part played by the left hand in the golf swing, but it is worth while noting at once that, however delicate a sense of touch it may appear to impart to the player, a very thin grip is the cause of many a man's downfall, the reason being that when he comes to put any power into the stroke, he is unable to retain a firm and even grasp of the club throughout the swing. My advice is to make sure that there is a ' good handful ', particularly under the left hand. If the grip tapers lower down the shaft and under the right hand, so much the better.

Grips can be made of a variety of substances, leather and rubber or skilful imitations of them being the principal. For myself I strongly favour a kind of ribbed rubber grip that is usually associated with the name Whitcombe. Others, on the contrary, cannot abide it, and stick to leather. The trouble with leather—and indeed many forms of rubber grip—is that they slip so abominably in wet weather. That is why many professionals use leather grips, which can be easily ' roughed up ' with a penknife when occasion demands.

One more word concerning wooden clubs and the depth of face that is desirable. A deep-faced driver is quite in order, since you can tee the ball as high in the air as necessary, and the large hitting surface of the club may well be a means of giving you confidence; but exactly the opposite applies to the brassie and the spoon.

These are clubs which are going to be taken when the ball is lying on the ground, when the beginner's—and indeed anybody's—primary consideration is to get it into the air.

The shallower the face of these clubs the more easily will you be able to apply the striking face below the centre of gravity of the ball, and thus elevate it. The depth of face in the brassie and spoon should in no case exceed the width of a penny.

Finally, as to the putter one can only say that the number of different examples of this club must now run into thousands, each guaranteed to be more foolproof than the next. I advise you once again, if you are a beginner, to steer a middle course and start with an ordinary steel putter, preferably with a hickory shaft, and certainly with an upright, almost vertical, lie. Before your golfing career is over at least thirty putters will have passed through your hands, so you need not be concerned with getting it right first time. Further discussion on putters may be deferred until the section on putting.

Joining a Club

Among the first problems to face the would-be golfer is the choice of the club that he shall join. Fear of Doing The Wrong Thing is an inherent British characteristic, and I believe that qualms lest he shall join a club where he is not wanted or, worse still, be put up for a club and find his candidacy turned down, are among the principal deterrents of the man who has half a mind to try his hand at golf.

As a beginner you will not require a first-class golf course. Your first concern is to learn the art of hitting the ball well enough to derive pleasure from the game (which is still, despite the ballyhoo in newspapers on Walker Cups, Ryder Cups, Open Championships, and so forth, the only excuse for playing it). For this purpose almost any terrain will do. If you have the choice of two courses, one of which is muddy in winter and the other dry, your mind will have been made up for you. Otherwise, the following considerations will apply.

First comes the social side of the question. One of the principal charms of golf is that it enables a man to pass his leisure hours combining physical exercise with the company of his friends. A golf club can be, and should be, in the true sense of the word, a *Club*. And it is no use your joining a club whose members as a whole enjoy a standard of living substantially different from your own.

So many people play golf these days that it is scarcely conceivable that you should not number one or two golfers among your acquaintances. Repair to them, therefore, for information. They will know, probably, not only their own club, but also the other clubs in the neighbourhood—if not by experience, at least by reputation.

The smallest provincial town now has its golf course, but here the choice is probably limited to one, or at the most two, and the problem more easily solved.

For the Big-City golfer the position is more complicated. He may solve the problem by discovering where one or two of his friends go and then by acting on the principle that what is good enough for them is good enough for him.

Your next point will be—accessibility. If you live in London, this is a material consideration, and one that becomes, as the motor industry continues to flood the already inadequate highways with an ever-increasing tide of vehicles, more and more serious. An hour's drive is no fit prelude to a golf game.

It is useless, however many of your friends may play there, to join a club whose course is noted either for the severity of its rough or for its general difficulty. You will not be happy there and will be a burden to yourself and your friends. Choose some easy and, if possible, not too crowded course.

Lastly, you may find it worth while to consider the merits of the professional attached to the club. If the man has a reputation as a good teacher, with a 'bedside manner' and a sound understanding of the game, it may be sufficient to turn the scale in favour of that club.

On Taking Lessons

Tuition has always presented a vexed question in golf. 'Never had a lesson in my life' is a phrase uttered with smug satisfaction by a good many people. The correct reply is, of course, 'That's why you are no better than you are'.

'A natural golfer' is a common enough expression too, yet no one in the world could call golf a 'natural' game. In fact, a more studied, more calculated, and less spontaneous action than the golf swing it is scarcely possible to imagine. Is it conceivable that a man should hit upon this highly complicated process, involving a thousand muscular actions, without the aid of a guide to set him on his way?

Golf, like all other games, comes more naturally to some people than to others. They are the people with a highly developed 'games sense'—people who are liable to do things the right way because, basically, it is the easiest way. They are quick, adaptable, and readily able to co-ordinate hands, mind, and body. Untutored they will eventually learn to play to an erratic handicap of 4. If they had the time, they believe, they could soon get down to scratch. Whether they are right is another matter.

Other persons, having no natural aptitude for golf or for any other game, can often by a capable professional be moulded into first-class players.

None of the world's master golfers—Harry Vardon, Bobby Jones, Walter Hagen, Alfred Padgham, Henry Cotton—have been what is popularly known as the 'athletic' type.

For the beginner I regard tuition as a vital necessity, provided he can afford it. I cannot pose as an authority on other sports, but it strikes me that in this question of teaching there is a world of difference between games played with a stationary, and with a moving, ball.

A boy at school learns football and cricket for himself. When he shows a certain proficiency and may be useful in aiding his school to defeat others in the neighbourhood, he may find the games master devoting attention to him; but in the first instance he works out things for himself.

The movements directed at a moving ball are largely *instinctive*. Left to himself, a boy soon discovers the easiest way of kicking a football, the way calculated to give the maximum result in return for the minimum effort. In the more delicate and varied art of cricket he will soon equip himself with a range of serviceable, if not copybook, strokes. The mere instinct for self-preservation may assist him in flourishing his bat at the ball in the manner most calculated to despatch it elsewhere.

It is not suggested, of course, that he will automatically learn the correct strategy of these two games. The discussion is confined to the act of 'going through the motions' and making the strokes.

Now, there is no instinctive manner of hitting a golf ball, or even of holding a golf club. Not one beginner in a thousand takes the club correctly in his hands at the first time of asking. They put their hands under the club, on top of the club, even on top of each other. Sometimes their hands are inches apart, as in wielding a pickaxe, sometimes they are the wrong way round altogether—the left below the right.

Similarly, I have never yet seen the beginner who had any real conception of the golf swing the moment he started to play the game. He may be a born athlete, but his first efforts at golf will be crude, ungainly, and laborious.

'I realized more than ever', says Cotton in describing his early efforts to mould his style from observation of renowned players, 'that there is no such thing as a natural golfer'.

Miss Wethered, too, tells of how, when people envy her swing because it is so natural, she is at a loss for a reply, as the facts scarcely bear out such a view. 'The best golf', she says, 'is not natural golf alone. It is more than an instinct: it is an acquired gift. No one that I ever heard of became a Gold Medallist at skating, or first class at any form of sport, by the pure light of nature; nor can any man or lady get down to scratch at golf without giving his or her mind seriously to the problem. I believe the opinion that a natural swing is the best is answerable for a great deal.'

Thus my earnest advice to the beginner is—betake yourself to a tutor of some kind (he certainly need not by any means be a famous player) and set yourself on the right path at the beginning of your journey. You have a long, hard road to travel, and a good start will mean a lot to you as time goes on.

Your tutor, as I have said, need not be a man with a famous name, and for three reasons. Firstly, because champions, as is true in all branches of life, do not always make the best teachers; secondly, because, good or bad, they have earned the right to be more expensive; and thirdly, because it does not require a champion to remind you to keep your head down, to follow through, or to obey the rest of the accepted elementary principles of the game.

Their Cost

The ideal man for the job is a not-too-young and not-too-well-known club professional, a man who no longer has personal aspirations in the golfing sphere, but has had time to acquire the experience and patience that go to make up a first-class teacher.

His fee will be anything from three shillings and sixpence to five shillings per hour, and he will accompany his pupils in the coldest and most violent weather with a cheerfulness that never ceases to astonish. He represents one of the finest types of man known to sport.

As to how many lessons are necessary, that is a question that each individual must solve for himself. His pocket may have a large say in the matter. 'The more you can afford, the better' is a fair generalization.

Once again—it all depends. Practice—that is, simply standing and hitting one ball after another—is an essential for the beginner, and providing you can retain a good mental impression of what the professional has told you, you will be well advised to spend two or three hours alone for every one spent with your instructor.

Learning to play golf is largely, in its elementary stages, like learning to play the piano—a matter of attuning your muscles to perform a series of movements to which they are unaccustomed. And this can only be done by 'putting them through it' time and again, until they settle down comfortably to their new routine. You can teach someone what scales to play on the piano, but you cannot teach that person's fingers to play them. That is a penance he must perform for himself.

In the same way, golfing 'scales' are a performance that the beginner must face and carry through. You may take courage, however, from the fact that they are by no means so dull as the scales you had to practise on a piano at school.

Golf Schools

This is perhaps a convenient moment to discuss the merits of the various golf schools whose popularity is rapidly increasing up and down the country. They may readily be divided into two classes—indoor and outdoor.

An indoor golf school can perform a number of useful functions, but the persons for whom it can perform them are strictly limited. Broadly speaking, it is useful to the novice, useless to the expert. It is useful, in fact, for 'playing scales'. Hardly anyone but the schoolboy or the undergraduate has the leisure to repair to the country whenever he wishes to practise his golf swing. If he could do it in the town, he would be willing to devote half an hour to it almost daily. The indoor golf school answers that problem.

You can walk round dressed in your business attire, take off your coat, exhibit your braces with impunity, and settle down to schooling your muscles in their new duties. Furthermore, you can hit a real ball—an advantage not to be enjoyed while club-swinging in the office or bedroom.

You can also have a lesson at the same time, since nearly every golf school employs one or two professionals. But there the matter ends—for unfortunately you cannot see where the ball has gone.

Hitting a ball into a net a few yards distant is a most deceptive proceeding. Firstly, although you should not have time to see the ball hit the net, in actual fact you are tempted to look up just in time to see it do so—and that means that you have looked up too soon. Secondly, having seen it hit the net, only the skilled exponent can tell where it would have finished if the shot had been played in the open. Of all the various kinds of slice that finish on the right, some start straight and fade away at the end; some start out towards the left and curl round later; while others start to the right and never look like going anywhere else. And *vice versa*, of course, with the 'hooks' that ultimately finish on the left. So few yards separate the player from the net that it is impossible to tell whether a ball that starts, say, to the right, was going to continue on its journey and become a slice, or change its direction, veer round, and end as a vicious hook.

Again, a further disadvantage of the indoor golf school is that a very bad shot often makes the sweetest 'click' on the clubface, thus luring the player into a false sense of proficiency. 'The harder you hit', is my experience of these places, 'the sweeter the click'; whereas when you come to the golf course the truth is nearer to 'the harder you hit, the less far it goes'.

Nevertheless, the indoor golf school can and does

provide a very real service to the golfing beginner. Only by long practice and experiment can you begin to get your swing acting in anything like a reliable groove, and this practice can as well be accomplished indoors. You save yourself the bother of picking up the balls, which, owing to your inexperience, you would have 'sprayed' on all sides, and this alone represents a substantial saving in time and trouble. It means, in fact, that you can hit just about three times the number of shots in the same time.

As to observing the fate of your shots, all you need to know at the moment is whether you hit it in the centre of the club or thereabouts, or whether you hit it off the heel or the toe or the sole or the socket. And that can be felt as easily indoors as out on the practice ground.

The indoor school, apart from its accessibility, has a further advantage which in this country can scarcely be exaggerated. It is available in every kind of weather. In Britain there are days at a time when practising is actually impossible: weeks at a time when it is nothing short of purgatory. During these periods indoor practising loses the terrors it holds for the average mortal and becomes almost attractive, representing his nearest available approach to the real thing.

So much for indoor golf schools. Now, the outdoor establishment is a very different proposition. It is an institution which is highly popular in the United States, and is destined in my opinion to find a great deal of favour over here as time goes on.

It consists of huts, enclosed as to three sides, from which the pupil, warm and dry, may drive the ball out into the open and observe the whole course of its flight. These shelters offer, except for one thing, the ideal form of practice. That exception, which need not concern us overmuch, is the fact that no one has yet been able to invent an adequate substitute for turf, with which to construct the floor ; they have tried everything from fixed mats to loose sand, but all to little avail.

Apart from this failing these open-air schools have everything to recommend them. Every hut is often booked for hours in advance at the St. Andrews establishment, while London has its counterpart in the Kensington Country Club. Henry Cotton and Archie Compston owe some of their popularity as teachers to the fact that their pupils can play their shots from shelter in every kind of weather.

Discussion on the merits of golf schools ought perhaps to have come under the heading 'Practice'. It is included here as having a special interest to the beginner.

PART I

CHAPTER I

GRIP

FRANCIS OUIMET: 'I have for years pinned my faith to the interlocking grip'.

GEORGE DUNCAN: 'Being a convert to the overlapping grip, I am a great believer in that method'.

ABE MITCHELL: 'I favour the double-palm grip because it gives me greater power'.

NEARLY all the accepted masters of the game have from time to time stated or written articles to the effect that the secret of golf lies in the grip. 'The way the club is gripped', says J. H. Taylor, 'is the essential factor in making all golf shots. It is a factor that few rightly understand, if one may judge by the way the majority of players grip their clubs'.

Says Sarazen, who suffered a lean period of several years through changing from one grip to another, 'Master a good grip, stick to it, and the battle is half won'.

Unlike the golf swing, which is full of so many muscular movements and sensations that it cannot adequately be described as a complete whole, the grip is a static thing that can be both described and photographed. It is a matter of sight more than sensation, and a man can see at once, by comparing it with the pictures of the experts, whether his own grip is right or wrong.

For myself, I do not think of it as the secret of golf—or even *a* secret of golf. I regard it simply as one of the indispensable bases of the game: just as you cannot play golf at all without a club, so you cannot play it well without a correct grip.

Three grips are in current daily use, but one of them seems by common consent to be so immeasurably superior to the other two that I have no hesitation in recommending it to the average golfer. The three grips are the overlapping, interlocking, and what, for want of a better name, we may call the 'straightforward'. In the first, the little finger of the right hand rests in the groove between the first and second fingers of the left hand; in the second, the little finger of the right hand and the first finger of the left are intertwined; in the third the hands are not joined together in any way and each rests on the shaft independently of the other.

The overlapping variety is often associated with the name of Harry Vardon. He did not invent it, but he is the man who was largely responsible for making it the accepted grip for nearly all competent golfers. It says much for his perspicacity that this grip has survived the severe test of the modern passion for analysing every aspect and detail of the golf swing. If there had been a 'better 'ole', as it were, one cannot help feeling that the experts would by now have gone to it.

Eight famous men who contributed to a questionnaire in the *American National Golf Review* in 1936 were absolutely unanimous on the subject. In reply to the question 'Do you use overlapping or interlocking grip?' they answered, to a man, 'Overlapping'. It may be added that Bobby Jones also uses this grip—indeed, that I use it myself! Need more be said?

One or two qualifications are necessary before we can lay down the law that the overlapping is the best variety of grip. It takes precedence, but not a universal precedence. A man with extremely long and strong fingers may find himself getting better results from the interlocking type, whereas anyone with outstandingly small hands will probably find himself developing more power if he does not link the hands together at all.

This 'unlinked' grip is the natural one taken by every novice at the game, a relic perhaps of his cricketing days at school. It is, in fact, the natural grip. I well remember my own sensations on being introduced to the overlapping grip by my first instructor, Jack Seager. Eight fingers and two thumbs seem little enough with which, at the age of eleven, to swing a golf club, and I could not see the sense of nullifying, as I thought, the use of one of them by putting it on top of another. In fact, directly his back was turned, I used to cease doing so.

The explanation is perhaps that to the beginner power appears to be the first essential—and the old-fashioned two-fisted grip certainly gives a feeling of power. It is only later that the art of co-ordinating the hands in action is truly appreciated.

Power, co-ordination, and comfort are the real essentials of the grip: the average golfer may save himself long and wearisome experiments by accepting the verdict of the majority that the overlap is the grip by which these three essentials are most easily obtained.

This agreed, the position of the hands is still vitally important. This, again, is subject to individual variation, but it is not difficult to strike a fair average, from which the golfer should not stray until he has mastered all the first principles of the game.

HENRY COTTON uses the orthodox overlapping grip, with a glove to emphasize a firm grip with the left hand. Note the right forefinger crooked round the shaft, giving an impression of tremendous power. A dangerous position for the man whose left hand and forearm are not as strong as Cotton's.

ALFRED PERRY adopts the grip that is usually calculated to produce a hook, with the left hand right over the shaft. No doubt which is the master hand here. The right plays no part in taking the club back and, until the last moment, none in bringing it down. A grip in direct contrast to Cotton's.

ALFRED PADGHAM—an orthodox example of the standard overlapping, or 'Vardon', grip. More right hand than Perry, but less than Cotton.

CYRIL TOLLEY—the old-fashioned 'two-handed' grip without either interlocking or overlapping. The general position of the right hand exactly duplicates that of Padgham, but the left is rather more on top of the shaft.

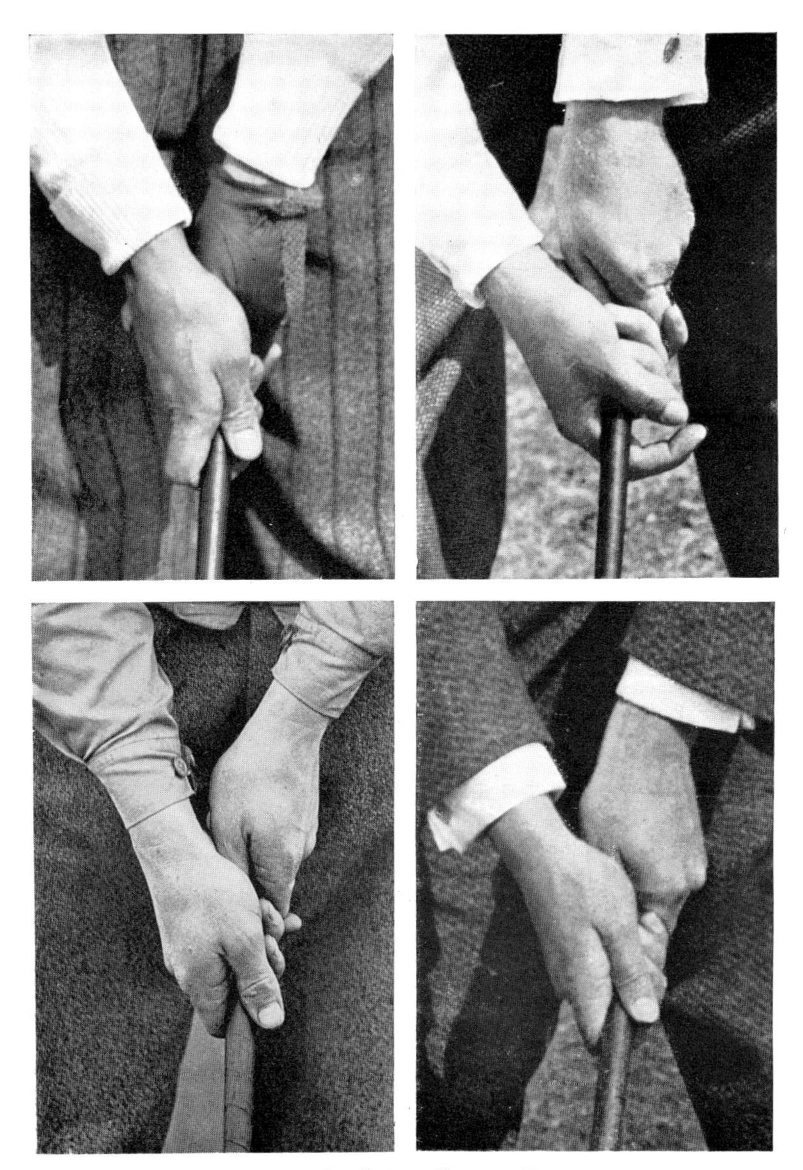

1, 3, *and* 4, *Bertram Eary;* 2, *Fox*

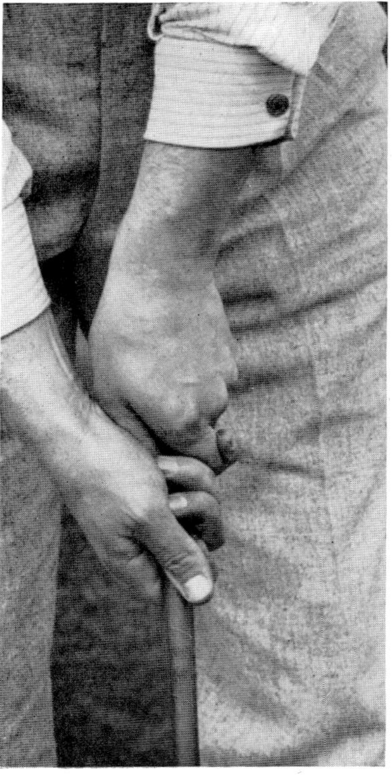

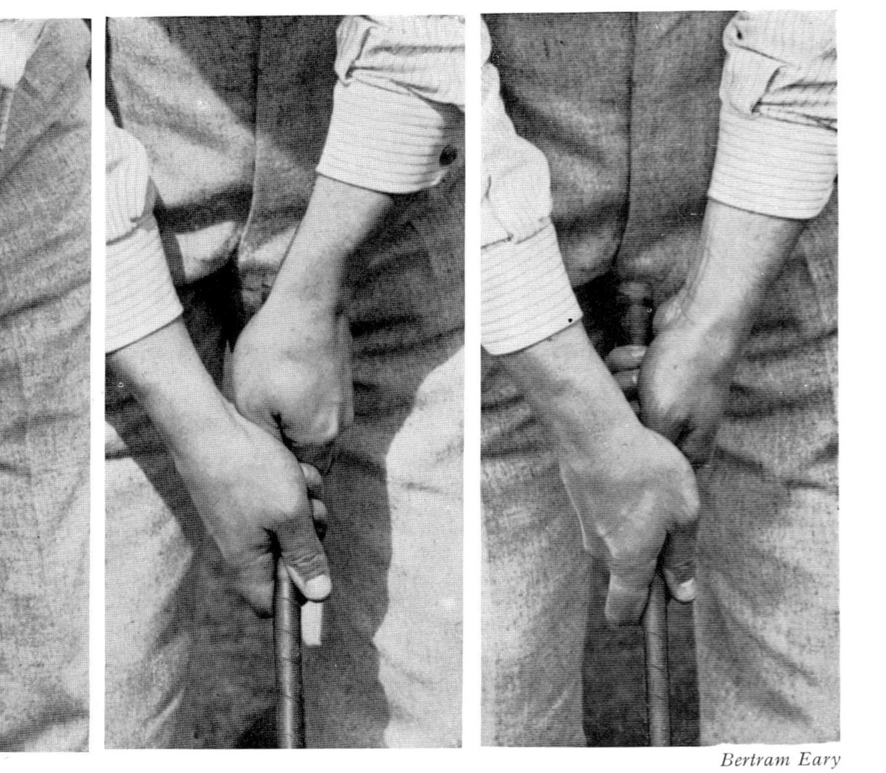

Bertram Eary

CAST YOUR EYE ALONG THE LINE

and notice the difference between these three grips. On the left is the hooker's grip—left hand well over the shaft, right hand well under. On the right the slicer's grip, the hands in reverse position.

A reasonable grip for the ordinary man is shown in the centre—a compromise between the two extremes, with each hand in a natural and unstrained position.

The best way to find this ideal position is, I think, this. The right hand is going to play a forehand stroke, the left hand is going to play a backhand. If you will make a blow through the air, with each in turn, in the direction it will take when swinging a club, you will find that with the right hand the maximum power is developed with the palm exactly facing the objective, giving, as it were, a kind of flat-handed slap.

With the left the maximum is developed not with the back of the hand facing squarely to the objective nor with it facing squarely towards the sky, but somewhere diagonally between the two.

Those two positions represent the ideal position of the hands on the shaft of the club. If you lay each hand on the shaft at the exact angle at which your previous experiments have proved it to develop its maximum power, and then close the fingers round the shaft, you will probably find yourself holding the club in the ideal manner.

This, you will find, represents a cross between a finger-grip and a palm-grip. The sensation is more of holding the club in the fingers, but examination will show that it also comes into contact with the palm. Running transversely through the left hand, the club is clasped firmly by all four fingers, and emerges at the top at a point midway between the base of the little finger and the beginning of the wrist. In the right hand it is held solely in the fingers.

The Two V's

A good check on the position of the hands is the two V's formed by the angles of the thumbs and forefingers. They should be, as near as makes no difference, parallel with each other, both pointing up the shaft, and if anything a shade towards the right shoulder. Of the left hand two knuckles should be clearly visible, and no harm is done if you can catch an occasional glimpse of a third.

The position of the left thumb causes a great deal of bother to some people. Yet in the normal and orthodox style that we are now discussing its position could not be more simple. It runs down the shaft slightly on the right in such a manner that it lies exactly under the 'life line' of the right hand when that hand is placed on the shaft in the way already described.

The Interlocking Grip

In the interlocking grip the left hand is pronouncedly on top of the shaft, and the thumb in this instance goes round the shaft *behind* the right hand. The bottom of the right palm has then to be pushed up firmly to meet the left forefinger, or an aching void will appear between the two hands—this, to my mind, being the chief disadvantage of the interlocking grip.

Nevertheless, there are those who say—and their opinion is entitled to respect—that they cannot develop real power even in the overlapping grip without thus placing the thumb round the shaft.

Leverage

The whole object of the grip is to get a good leverage on the club, and the greater the spread of the fingers (without losing the vital co-ordination of the hands) the greater will be the control they exercise over the club—or, if you prefer it, the less force will they have to exert in order to obtain that control. This is an elementary mathematical point, but I do not believe that more than 10 per cent. of the golfers who recall the days when they sat on the back bench 'taking moments about the point *O*' have stopped to realize the connection between these youthful exercises and the golf of their later years.

Perhaps Diagram 2 will recall a few boyhood memories. The fulcrum, or fixed point, was always, if I remember, called *O*, and the weight that was to be shifted *W*. One then learnt that the nearer one got to *W* the less force would be needed to shift it, a force that

DIAGRAM 2.

varied in strict proportion to one's distance from *O*. So that whereas a very small pressure exerted close to *W* might move it, it would take a very heavy pressure exerted near to the fixed point *O*. In other words, the spaces between *A* & *B* and *B* & *O* being equal, twice as much force was necessary at *B* as at *A*.

In a golf club the fixed point about which the machine moves is the little finger of the left hand; the weight is of course the clubhead. Now, it stands to reason that the nearer the forefinger of the right hand can be to the clubhead, the less pressure it will have to exert to move it—or, alternatively, if it exerts its maximum pressure, the more effect that pressure will have.

A simple experiment will clarify the point. If you thrust the two hands as close together as possible at the top of the shaft, the club will at once become heavy and unwieldy: if you put the hands a foot apart, it will become as light as a toy. In the latter position, however, the advantage is lost because the hands can no longer work as one. The ideal position is the one which obtains the maximum spread of the hands without in any degree losing the vital co-ordination between the two.

Another question that must be answered is 'How tightly do you grip the club?'. My own impression is that when addressing the ball one should grip the club just firmly enough to prevent a person pulling it out of one's hands with a steady pull, but not firmly enough to survive a sudden jerk.

A patent pressure-recorder would, I am sure, show a much stronger grasp of the club than this at the moment of impact; but that is a *subconscious* grip. There are other things to think about at so critical a moment, and we may safely trust to instinct to take care of the mere action of holding on to the club.

Once you see your opponent's knuckles whitening under the strain of grasping the club, you know that he is planning to knock the cover off the ball: a minute or two later you will probably be helping him search for it. Hold your own club just firmly enough to make sure it cannot twist in your fingers. Hold it any more tightly, and the relaxation in your wrists, and perhaps the rest of your body too, will have gone.

CHAPTER II

STANCE

GENE SARAZEN : ' My own stance is moderately open '.

MISS JOYCE WETHERED : ' A square stance to the line of play is, I feel certain, the soundest of them all '.

TOMMY ARMOUR : ' Closed for driving, square for long irons, open for short irons '.

WELL, well, well! If the professors are for the most part agreed as to what they do with their hands, they certainly show no such unanimity with respect to their feet. Indeed, they seem to be all over the place!

A study of their writings and their own personal demonstrations have convinced me that there are many widely different stances from which a golf ball may be accurately struck. My own principal golfing fault lies in the fact that no sooner do I start to play well than I find myself aiming subconsciously more and more to the right. The effort to face in this direction and yet hit the ball to the left of it—*i.e.* straight at the hole—induces the 'Beginner's Loop ' at the top of the swing; the club comes across, and the ball, feebly struck, fades away to the right. From time to time when suffering from this peculiar disease I have betaken myself to Fred Robson, a man with the bedside manner and one of England's most popular teachers. He takes one look, smiles, and then says, ' You can't hit it like that. *You're getting in your own way.*' So the stance is opened out, the left foot taken back, and all is well again.

On the other hand, I happened to come across W. J. Cox, another Ryder Cup player, one day when my iron

CLOSED STANCE

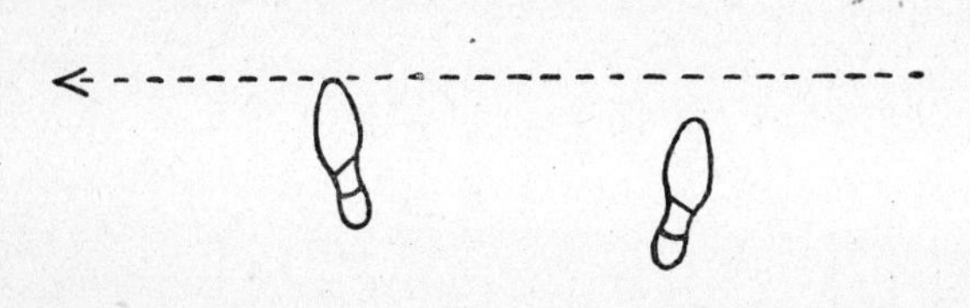

SQUARE STANCE

OPEN STANCE

DIAGRAM 3.

THE ADDRESS

The position at the moment of impact should be an animated version of the address. Note the marked similarity between Arthur Lacey standing to the ball (centre) and A. D. Locke (right) caught at the moment of impact. On the left is a 'right-handed' address position assumed, often unconsciously, by numerous golfers. The left arm and the shaft of the club should be as nearly as possible in a straight line when addressing the ball.

1 and 3, *Bertram Eary* ; 2, *Fox*

Sport and General

AN EXCEPTION TO THE RULE

Dr. William Tweddell, a British amateur champion and captain of the 1936 British Walker Cup team, aims consistently to the right and then, with a movement akin to the 'Beginner's Loop', hits straight through towards the hole. He is successful where many fail.

shots were going ' high right '. He made me put the right foot at least 6 inches farther back than the left, face out to the right, shut the face of the club, and keep it shut on the backswing. ' Now hit as hard as you like ', he said, ' and follow through. If you get the weight right through on to the left foot, you can't go wrong.' And so, for a time, it proved. It is a shot that I still value in moments of stress, when one is only too happy to find an excuse to hit hard at the ball.

These experiences have taught me that there are more ways than one in which to stand to a golf ball, but they have convinced me equally forcibly that one way is infinitely easier and safer than the rest. The stance for the average man, I am sure, is *slightly open*.

This seems to me to be the physically natural stance. If you were clasping the club with each hand equidistant from the ball—that is to say, with the right hand exactly opposite the left—the natural position would be the square stance shown in the centre diagram, with the ball opposite a point midway between the feet. To the onlooker you would present an absolutely symmetrical figure. Take up that posture for a moment, and you will see what I mean.

Now, if you shift your right hand to its normal position below the left, what is the natural instinct? Why, to advance the right foot, the right hip, and the right shoulder slightly in sympathy and to play the ball a little farther forwards—say opposite the left heel—to allow for the fact that your right arm is longer, as it were, than your left.

Conversely, it seems to me that if you choose to play with the left hand below the right, you would have to adopt the closed stance, for the same reason.

One of the basic principles of golf is, after all, that the left arm is straight at the moment of impact—*at* and *through the ball*, as Compston puts it. I know of no great or near-great player in the game's history who did not conform to this principle. (It should not, by the way, be confused with the old question of keeping the left arm straight throughout the whole swing.)

And it seems to me extremely difficult—especially for the week-end player, who is not as a rule quite so lissom as he used to be—to get into the true hitting position, with both arms straight and the left hip out of the way and the clubface square to the line of flight, unless he *does* stand slightly open.

The expert player and the student of the game will find time to experiment with every kind of stance for every kind of shot, adopting here and there his own individual adjustments. The ordinary mortal has no time, even if he had the desire, for such exercises: for him, assuming that he wishes to take the line of least resistance, I cordially recommend the straightforward semi-open stance.

Here, however, is a word of warning. The attention in this stance is at once focused upon the position of the left foot, which is slightly behind the line of play—but the right foot too deserves a passing glance. Perhaps I am unduly conscious of this because my own right foot, I have to admit, has a tendency, both when walking and at rest, to point rather outwards. Others tend to be slightly pigeon-toed. Henry Cotton is one who often adopts a pigeon-toed stance, and many a golfer has upset his game through trying to copy the great man, failing to realize that this is a position that comes perfectly naturally to Cotton.

Your right foot should be at exactly the same angle as it would take if you were standing in a relaxed attitude, facing at right angles to the line of play. If you point the toe in, it will give you a momentary feeling of solidarity, but will prevent your achieving that body turn on the backswing that Bobby Jones considers the most important single item in the golf swing. If you turn the toe out, you will fail to get the rock-like support that your right leg should supply at the top of the swing.

Another thing to consider is how far apart the feet should be. Bobby Jones, in order to achieve the body turn just mentioned, stood with his feet noticeably close together: A. J. Lacey, on the other hand, though smaller and less robust of stature, has his feet comparatively wide apart. To my mind it should vary according to the height of the player and his sense of balance. Normally the *angle* between the legs will be the same in each case: the longer the legs go on, the farther apart they will be when they end!

Every man must adjust this matter for himself, bearing in mind the dangers that lie in the two extremes. If your feet are too far apart, you cannot transfer the weight properly (at any rate without an artificial and thoroughly undesirable strain), nor can you achieve the body-turn whence flows so much of the power in the stroke: if your feet are too close together, you are liable, with whatever ease you may swing, to lose your balance. Golf may be just a question of swinging the clubhead, but a considerable amount of force must be generated in order to propel the ball a couple of hundred yards and more. That force demands, among other things, a firm underpinning.

The soundest advice is to have the feet as close together as is possible without losing balance when it comes to putting the force into the blow.

Pointing The Chin

'Pointing the chin back of the ball' was the catch-phrase that brought dollars by the thousand into the pocket of the American teacher, Alex. J. Morrison—and an excellent phrase it is, make no mistake.

The correct set of the head, for the benefit of those unaccustomed to pointing their chins, may be achieved by firstly performing half of the 'Eyes right' movement familiar to all, and then tilting the head slightly over to the left.

Such a position is of inestimable advantage in enabling one to keep the head still. The whole movement of the backswing—arms, club, weight, body, and everything—is towards the right: any movement of the head thus tilted at once rings the alarm bell, as it were, by depriving the player of the sight of the ball with his right eye. I do not say it *stops* the head moving: it simply draws attention to the fact when it does move.

Again, in some subtle way which I do not profess to understand, this attitude of the head throws emphasis, where the average golfer needs it, on the left-hand side of the body—left hand, left arm, left shoulder. It seems to give them extra strength, extra importance.

The Arms—A Warning

Before leaving the purely stationary aspect of the golf stroke and advancing to explore the details of what happens when the club begins to move, there is one more point that must be made. Such is its importance that, were it not certain to spoil the appearance of the page, I would put the whole thing in italics!

It concerns the position of the arms.

The position at the moment of impact should be, for every class of player, an animated version of the position at the address. Now, at impact it has been seen that both arms are stretched as straight as ramrods: that is a posture adopted, consciously or not, by even the plumpest of us. *The nearer, therefore, that the arms can approximate to this position before the stroke begins, the less change they will have to undergo during the stroke itself.*

That is not to say that your arms should be as stiff as ramrods as you stand to address the ball. Far from it. But they should be as nearly straight as you can make them without feeling undue strain. In particular you should take care that there is no appreciable angle at your left wrist. Push out the arm so that it and the club are as near as no matter in a straight line, and then face both of them at right angles to the line of flight. If you *must* err in one direction, let it be to face rather towards the left of the hole.

An experiment will probably convince you of the truth of this. Take up your stance with a club here and now, and get into the animated 'movement of impact' position. Your left arm and the club are in line, you are wanting to rise on your toes, there is an expression of tenseness on your face.

If you began with a bent left wrist, you will now be aiming substantially to the right of where you started. If you began with a bent left elbow, your clubhead will now be well outside the line of flight, hitting the ball on the heel—that is, unless you have instinctively drawn up the top of your body to compensate for the club's outward movement as you straightened the arm.

I believe that this simple experiment with the 'moment of impact' position will assist you more than any written explanation to achieve what is for you the most satisfactory position at the address. Find out how you are placed as the club strikes the ball, and you can work back from there to the stance that calls for least adjustment during the course of the stroke. And the less adjustment the better.

CHAPTER III: The Swing

THE 'STANDARD' SWING

A movement was once started in the United States—I believe by the Professional Golfers' Association—with a view to standardizing the golf swing and, therefore, golfing instruction. How shall the world believe us, they asked, if one of us teaches one thing, and one another? On the surface it sounded reasonable enough, but a closer scrutiny showed it to be impracticable, for our golfing masters have themselves proved beyond doubt that there are many more ways than one in which golf may effectively be played.

'By their swings ye shall know them' is as true of the teachers as it is of their pupils.

The masters both of to-day and of the past may grip the club differently, stand differently, swing differently, dispatch the ball in a different trajectory, one from the other; but two considerations I have borne constantly in mind in writing the pages that follow. Firstly, there are basic principles which are common to every first-class golfer, amateur or professional, male or female. Secondly, though there is a whole variety of ways in which golfing excellence may be reached, and though any man by constant application, study, and practice might reach it in any of these ways, there are some ways that are undoubtedly more simple than others. It is these that I have tried to discover and recommend.

The number of persons who have attempted to describe the golf swing on paper must now run into many hundreds. I cannot claim to have read every one of them, but I have read a good many; and the fact that none of them, in my opinion, has quite succeeded in his object makes me determined not to fail in the same way. And the only real insurance against such failure is not to describe the golf swing at all.

Anyone who tries to set out the myriad, intricate movements that go to make up the swing is setting himself—and, incidentally, his reader—an impossible task. I don't believe it can be done, and I don't intend to try.

There is a whole wealth of difference—and it is a point that one sees made rarely, if at all—between movement and *conscious* movement. The films have proved, in a way, to be a substantial asset in golfing instruction. They have revealed hitherto unsuspected motions in the swing, have proved the masters time and again to have been talking through their august hats in their efforts to describe even their own swings. But they possess also one lurking danger against which we must be constantly on guard: they do not differentiate between conscious and subconscious movement.

Let me give an illustration of the difference between the two. I was indulging in a favourite pastime one day, arguing golf with Archie Compston. I think the subject was the first movement of the backswing, which he said was a 'forward press' (though more of that later). We were still searching for a formula, as they say in the League of Nations' jargon, when he introduced a red herring in the shape of a comparison with the act of starting walking. Just exactly what is the first movement when a man, standing at rest with his feet together, puts himself into motion—starting, for the sake of argument, with his left foot? The reader is invited at this point to co-operate actively by making the experiment.

The first *conscious* movement, I think I am right in saying, is the forward motion of the left toe, or perhaps the left knee: it may vary from one individual to another. But supposing we analysed the act of starting to walk by means of the cinematograph. Would it show this action of the toe or knee to be the first movement? Certainly not.

Let us investigate what has taken place *before ever the toe has left the ground.* Much of it happens in a similar fashion in the golf swing. Firstly, a good deal of the weight has been transferred to the right foot, rather on the ball of it than the heel. The hips have made a noticeable turn to the right. The left heel has risen, and with it the left knee, which has also pushed forwards: the shoulders have turned slightly and the arms have begun to move, the left forwards and the right backwards. Doubtless a great many obscure muscles with Latin names have also come into action.

All this has gone on, mark you, before either foot has left the ground. The camera tells us so, and the camera cannot lie. In order purely of precedence, therefore, the forward movement of the left toe takes a very lowly place. Yet we know from experiment that, so far as we are actually *aware*, it is the first movement of the act of walking.

My contention is that it would be virtually impossible to teach anyone to walk by means of the written word. To teach them to walk *better*, to give them good *style* in walking, yes; to enumerate all its complicated minor processes, no! The preliminary stages can be learnt only by trial and error.

So it is with golf. Small wonder that the moving camera caused a revolution in golf teaching—small wonder that the experts found themselves confounded by their own words. Yet those pre-cinematograph words may have a greater value than the ones by which they were superseded, for they represent what the players *felt* themselves to do, not what the camera later showed that they actually did.

Why, then, the reader may reasonably ask, does a cursory glance show many of the illustrations to this book to be 'stills' from action pictures?

There is a good reason for this—namely, that it is beyond the compass of the average mortal to assume in a stationary posture a position that is actually reached in a state of motion. No *posed* rendering of the top-of-the-swing position, for instance, can ever show the animated position reached by the player in the course of an actual stroke. It is lifeless, wooden, and often inaccurate.

A 'still', therefore, will show the ideal position at any moment during a state of motion, whereas a posed picture will not: a 'still', on the other hand, will *not* tell the reader what mental processes the performer went through in order to reach that position. It will show where the player's hips or hands or head or feet were at any required instant, but it will not tell whether the player made any conscious effort to get them there. It is the writer's task to dissect these movements and positions, to find out whether the shoulders consciously led the hips, or the legs the shoulders, or the hands the whole of the rest of the body—or what!

No man can concentrate on more than one or two points during a golf shot. Of which, then, of the endless variety that parades itself before him is he to be specifically conscious?

Again, if he is never to be aware of the existence of certain parts of his body during the golf stroke, how is he to be sure that those parts are following the right course?

The answer to that is twofold. Firstly, he may concentrate upon getting the *conscious* actions right, for then he may be sure that their subconscious allies will follow suit. Secondly, he may learn by general imitation of other players in action. The latter will have a chapter to itself.

CHAPTER IV: The Swing (*continued*)

THE FIRST MOVEMENT (I)

Bobby Jones: 'That the first motion of the backswing should be made by the *legs or hips* there can be little doubt. To start it with the hands results inevitably in the lifting upright motion characteristic of the beginner who swings the club as though it were an axe. . . .'

Miss Joyce Wethered: 'I am quite certain that the balance and rhythm of many a good swing is often spoilt by the body moving first and causing the clubhead to begin its swing when the *arms and hands* should be beginning it'.

I do not, as I have said, believe it possible to describe on paper the multitude of muscular reactions and mental sensations experienced by the golfer during the course of a swing. Having dealt with the stationary aspects of the stroke—how to hold the club and where to put the feet—I now assume that the reader, even though he be a complete beginner, has made a sufficient number of swings to give him some kind of feeling of the motions he is going through. His swing may be faulty in many respects—indeed, it will be a miracle if it is not—but at least it is a swing.

There are numerous points at which the swing can go wrong, and an error at any one of them may wreck it as a whole. The chapters that follow do not attempt to cover the entire swing: they simply deal one by one with a number of these points.

The first step in the golf swing is to start the club back. And a simple enough operation it seems, even to the novice.

Why, then, does Bobby Jones say, 'To watch a man start his swing backward is an infallible indication of his worth as a golfer'? *Because this initial movement can make or mar the swing.*

Just as the follow-through, as will be seen, is not an end in itself, but an indication of what has gone before, so the first movement is evidence of what is to follow. Get that first movement right and you are well on the road to success.

The 'Forward Press'

A number of distinguished golfers seem to have found material assistance from a movement known as the Forward Press. This, as its name implies, is a kind of thrust forwards just before taking the club back from the ball. It is made either with the hands or with the hips or with both. It is a movement that is natural enough to any man, and in nine cases out of ten I am prepared to swear that it is a subconscious one. The best explanation of the matter is probably revealed by Compston, who reasonably suggests that it is easier to start from a state of motion than from a standstill. 'Compare', he says, 'starting off on a bicycle on a downhill slope'. With the aid of a slight forward press, the hands are given, as it were, a moving instead of a standing start.

The most easily recognized example of a forward press is to be seen in what is often known as the 'caddie swing', the exaggerated style that one sees being performed with one's own clubs behind the caddies' shed. The swing is nearly always characterized by a series of two, three, or even four forward presses in quick succession, after which the club is whisked away from the imaginary ball at a speed whose fatal nature is only revealed when the player comes to play an actual stroke. A forward press on the green, it may be added, is one infallible characteristic of the very bad putter.

My own impression is that a slight preliminary movement of the hands may well help the player to start the club smoothly on its journey and to get rid of that ramrod stiffness by which the average golfer so often handicaps himself; but it must be remembered that no preliminary forward movement can have any *direct* effect on the swing. Its sole object is to assist in getting the backswing started in a smooth, rhythmical, and relaxed manner.

Some players adopt other means to this end. Compston, for instance, taps the club gently up and down behind the ball just before beginning the stroke. His friends tell him that he does it to give himself a better lie, but in reality, of course, it is only just another method of giving him a moving start.

One thing at least may be condemned without fear of contradiction: that is, any effort to start from a complete standstill. From the moment you begin to take up your stance until the moment that the ball is struck there must be no single period of complete immobility; for, once movement ceases altogether, the rhythm of the stroke is gone for good. Countless golfers may be seen fixed and immobile as a statue carved out of stone, and gazing at the ball as if hypnotized before they find courage to start the backswing. If only they would understand that unbroken rhythm is one of the essential secrets of this tantalizing game, they would save themselves a great many strokes and a great deal of trouble.

CHAPTER V: The Swing (*continued*)

THE FIRST MOVEMENT (II)

Miss Joyce Wethered: 'The first movement is a drawing back of the hands and the clubhead without any wrist bending or turning'.

Alfred Padgham: 'I tend deliberately to leave the clubhead behind preparatory to the subsequent backward fling'.

Having established the principle of not starting from a state of complete immobility, we come to the more constructive question of what exactly constitutes the first backward movement. It is agreed on all sides that the first 18 inches can make or mar the swing. As to what should go on during those 18 inches, where the motive power should come from, and how it should be applied, there exist three schools of thought. Either of two may be right—at least in the sense that adherence to either of them may do no harm: the third is definitely wrong.

This last—practised, alas, by all too many handicap golfers—consists in whipping the clubhead away from the ball with the wrists, generally in a sharply ascending curve. An illustration of it may be seen opposite page 49, and my humble advice is, 'Look at the picture, regard with due abhorrence that which it depicts and put it out of your mind for ever'. This dastardly movement comes largely from the right hand, and concentrating on the left hand will go a long way towards getting rid of it. Its chief danger lies in the fact that, like many another pernicious disease, it can remain so long undiscovered. Indeed, a friend of mine who played to a handicap substantially better than scratch found his game suddenly in ruins, and did not discover the cause until, several months later, he had himself filmed and with the aid of slow motion detected the clubhead almost level with his hip before the hands began to move.

The first of the more correct schools of thought is exemplified by the quotation from Miss Wethered that heads this chapter. 'As your hands and wrists are in the address', she continues, 'so they should be kept over the first 12 inches. The clubhead should be swung back by the arms, not swiftly, but firmly, and all in one piece'.

'All in one piece'—those few words contain what has proved to me at any rate to be one of the most valuable condensed hints in the golf game. Personally I should simplify it a little and make it apply only to the left arm, because I believe that the part played by the right arm at this stage should be almost negligible. If you can only get the feeling that the club and the whole of your

THOSE FIRST 18 INCHES

'To watch a man start his swing backward', says Bobby Jones, is an infallible indication of his worth as a golfer'. Here (above), is how he starts it himself. Note that the relation between arms, hands, wrists and club has remained absolutely unchanged. He has neither whipped the club up with the wrists, nor gone to the opposite extreme in dragging the hands away first and leaving the clubhead temporarily behind.

The same may be said of Tommy Armour (below) and, in fact, of almost every first-class player.

'Sports Illustrated and The American Golfer'

Photos by Fox

E

A RIGHT AND TWO WRONGS

Snatching the club away from the ball with the wrists (left) can throw the swing out of gear almost before it has begun. To avoid this temptation, people sometimes go to the other extreme (right), which means that the club has to accelerate rapidly a little later in the backswing in order to catch up with the hands.

'The clubhead', says Miss Joyce Wethered, 'should be swung back by the arms, not swiftly, but firmly, and *all in one piece*'. An impression that the club and the left arm from the shoulder downwards are 'all in one piece', that there is no movable joint at the elbow or at the wrist or in the knuckles, and that the left hand can turn over neither to the right nor to the left, will help to guide the player over the first two or three feet of the swing and bring him to the correct position shown in the centre picture.

left arm from the shoulder downwards are all in one piece, the odds are safely in favour of your starting the swing correctly. Try to feel that there is no movable joint at your elbow, or at your wrist, or in your knuckles; and, furthermore, that your hand can turn over neither to the right nor to the left. Continue this while the clubhead travels, say, a couple of feet, or even as far as the level of your hips, and then, when a natural stiffness begins to make itself felt, you may be sure that the appropriate time has come to begin letting the wrists bend.

The other school of thought, represented by Padgham's words, is perhaps the more fashionable. Certainly it errs on the safer side.

'Probably a great many golfers,' says Sarazen, 'who have a vice-like grip upon their club and whose wrists are like a steel rod from the moment they start their swing, would benefit immeasurably if they would start by letting the left wrist swing back. The whole left arm goes with the same motion, and if the wrists are flexed, the hands will go back perhaps three or four inches before the clubhead starts away from the ball, practically dragging along the ground.'

One advantage of this method is that it leads towards that desirable flexibility of the wrists in the rest of the swing, which the Average Golfer often fails otherwise to achieve.

In the motion-pictures of nearly all the great players this drag of the clubhead is clearly noticeable, though to what extent it is deliberate it is difficult to say. I have noticed, for instance, in pictures of Abe Mitchell that at the moment when the clubhead is passing his right foot on the way back, his *right* arm and the shaft of the club are actually in a straight line.

Why, therefore, you may ask, have I the impertinence to suggest that a better method is to try to start the left arm and the club back as if they were all in one piece? The answer is that I believe this action will in fact lead to something of a compromise. One will retain the impression that the arm and the club are in one straight line—and if one performed the swing in deliberate slow motion, I believe that they would be.

The very speed, however, aided by the weight of the clubhead itself, ensures that in actual fact one still performs some of the dragging motion that so many writers deem desirable.

Here again, though, one must add a warning about the right hand. Having a superior power of leverage over the clubhead, any action on its part is certain to have a greater effect than any corresponding action on the part of the left hand. Keep it out of the action for as long as possible.

The 'Lateral Hip Shift'

For reasons that will appear later, I have concentrated only on the part played by the hands and arms, believing, with simple faith, that these lead the rest of the body. That is not a view that is shared, however, by a number of authorities who have expressed their opinions on the game. Some have alleged the swing to be started with the hips; some with the muscles in the small of the back; others with the shoulders. One fellow, I read the other day, even went so far as to say that it began with the legs!

Among the most popular of these theories was that of the lateral hip shift. 'Deliberate, conscious, lateral sway of the hips at the inception of the backswing I do not recommend,' says Padgham. 'Any drifting away of the body from its objective is dangerous and generally futile.'

I have the honour to agree with the Open Champion of 1936, and with that dismiss the subject.

A fuller reference to the part—and a very important part it is—played by the hips will be found in the chapter entitled 'Body Turn'.

For the moment I stand by the statement that if the action of the hands and arms be correct at the beginning of the swing, no conscious attention need be paid to the rest of the body.

CHAPTER VI: The Swing (*continued*)

HANDS

Harry Vardon: 'All golfers must realize that it is the *hands* starting the clubhead, both from the beginning of the backward swing and on the return journey which is the chief point of concentration for successful golf . . .'

I stand or fall by this chapter.

Golf, as the reader will by now have noticed, is not the sort of game in which you can lay down the law. Some play it one way, others another: how remarkably these ways may differ will be gathered from the quotations with which, in self-defence, I have started some of these chapters dealing with the swing.

I have done my best to emphasize a distinction between my own personal theories and opinions and those gleaned, as it were, officially from the masters. The latter may be taken as gospel, the former with however many grains of salt the reader may think fit. His decision may be based on his estimate of the sentiments expressed in this chapter.

Supported by the words quoted from Harry Vardon, I make the categorical statement that golf is played *with the hands*. Hips, shoulders, arms, feet, legs, and everything else play their part, I know, and a golf shot cannot be made unless they do. But I maintain that their every action should be governed and directed by the hands.

Golf is a combination of physical and mental activity. The mind decides what it wishes to do, and then, by means of the nerves and muscles, causes the body to do it. I believe that the hands, the most sensitive part of the body that plays any part in the golf shot, are the vital link of connection between the two.

Archie Compston, in answer to the question 'Why does the Average Golfer remain average ?', replied without hesitation, 'Because he has a dummy left arm'. A month or two afterwards I put the same question to Gene Sarazen His reply, with equal promptness, was, 'The great player plays golf with his *hands*—the Average Player tries to play with his head'.

'I don't know any Average Golfer', he went on, 'who does not stand up on the tee thinking of fifty different things. His brain bothers him. It is congested with ideas. In my opinion, the reason why Joyce Wethered is the outstanding player in the world is because she has such a wonderful grip. When I photographed her in America I found the whole secret lay in her hands. Her hands were the generals, the rest of her body followed every movement that they made.

'Hagen and Jones are good examples of players who let their hands lead their bodies. Both of them could have been wonderful violinists. They could have played any instrument requiring touch in the hands and fingers —though they might have finished last in a sport needing purely physical effort.'

Then he went on to relate how he had once asked Thomas Meighan, the actor, what he thought to be the most important thing in his profession, and how the latter had replied 'Hands. *Your hands create the rhythm of your body.*'

All the teaching about artificial movements of the body—lateral hip shift and so forth—Sarazen dismissed as so much nonsense. 'They're *unnatural*,' he said with emphasis.

That is the impression that he himself conveys in action. His style is the essence of simplicity. He walks to the ball, and with scarcely a shuffle of the feet raises his club in the air and despatches the ball on its errand. Yet an action photograph will show that at any given moment every part of his body has moved to the naturally correct position.

Compare, for instance, the 'swing' of a navvy driving a wedge into the ground with a hammer. At the top of the swing he is perfectly poised, almost graceful in his action. His hips have turned, his shoulders have turned, his eye is on the ball. He makes a higher percentage of perfect strokes than Bobby Jones made in his heyday.

Yet ask him where his right shoulder is at the top of the swing, or his left hip at the moment of impact, or any of the hundred and one things of which the golfer so often tries to be conscious, and he cannot tell you. He has never troubled to inquire. The reason why he produces his copybook backswing is because he is wielding the hammer with his *hands*, and has naturally and subconsciously let his *hands* lead his body.

In the words quoted above, Harry Vardon gives a meticulous and, if I may say so, thoughtful and accurate definition of the part played by the hands in golf. He does not say that they provide the power or govern the direction of the ball—he says that they are the *chief point of concentration*.

They are, so to speak, the liaison between the thinking part of the machine and the acting part. They are the only *direct* connection between your animate self and your inanimate club. You can move any part of your body except the hands without necessarily moving the club: but move the hands, and the club goes too.

The good player can tell you, without looking, the exact position of his clubhead at any point in the swing. That, they say, is the essence of successful golf. But how does he achieve this form of 'second sight'? Not by instinct, but by the sensitiveness of his hands and fingers. He feels where his hands are, and from that he is able to judge the position of his clubhead. But unless his consciousness is directed upon his hands, his connection with the club is lost.

The human brain is not so constructed that a man can think consciously of more than one thing at a time. What, then, is one to think about during the golf swing? That is a question that every great golfer is asked from time to time.

My own reply, though I am afraid I cannot claim ever to have been asked on the grounds of being a great golfer, is, '*Think of your hands*'.

It may be that you are the victim of a temporary fault that demands concentration on some individual aspect

HANDS !

'The great golfer', says Gene Sarazen, 'plays with his hands. The average golfer, trying to think of everything at once, plays with his head.' Harry Vardon, again, calls the hands *the chief point of concentration* for successful golf.

Who can doubt that Henry Cotton, caught here at the moment of impact, has made his *hands* the principal link between mind and muscle ?

Bertram Eary

Sport and General

SHIFTING THE WEIGHT

as portrayed by a golfing genius—Harry Vardon. This comparatively simple movement is spoiled by many people through the mistaken impression that the position at the top of the swing is the exact reverse of that on the follow-through. A study of these pictures shows this to be untrue.

In the top picture, showing the backswing, the left heel has only just left the ground. Although the right shoe has turned over a little, the weight is still on the inside of the right foot and the player could easily resist a slight shove from his left.

Below, on the follow-through, nearly all the weight has shifted to the left. The right heel has come right up and that leg is now taking no further part in the proceedings.

of the swing. You may, perhaps, be falling back or cutting across the ball, in which case you will find it necessary to apply some conscious correction of these faults during the swing: but in normal circumstances I am sure that you will find that the maximum control of the club comes from focusing your attention on the hands.

By doing so you will be kept ever aware that the prime object of a golf stroke is to *hit the ball*—an elementary fact that is often forgotten by the studied, artificial golfer, the man who is so busy rotating his left hip, or transferring his weight, or pointing his chin, that he overlooks the elementary consideration of delivering the blow.

If you will only let the hands lead the way and let the rest of the body follow, you will find yourself achieving something of that natural ease of movement that characterizes the professional player. Get the movement of the hands right, and that of the rest of the body will be right too, provided no artificial action is allowed to check it.

The golf swing, as we have agreed, is not in itself a 'natural' movement, but it is this concentration on the hands that is most calculated to make it appear so.

It has, too, another inestimable advantage, in that it provides a check on swinging too quickly and 'snatching' at the top of the stroke. If you are thinking of your hips, or your feet, or of where you want the ball to go, or of the consequences if it goes out of bounds, you can make a lightning swing and still remain blissfully unaware of the fact. When your best friends tell you, you are aggravated and refuse to believe them. But if your mind is focused on your hands, *they* will tell you—and there is no disbelieving them!

CHAPTER VII : The Swing (*continued*)

SHIFTING THE WEIGHT

Gene Sarazen : 'Though the weight of the body comes heaviest on the right leg at the top of the swing, it should not be transferred to such an extent but that there should be a firm pressure on the ground with the left big toe . . .'

Only one quotation will be found at the top of this chapter, since at last we have discovered a subject on which the experts truly agree.

We talk of 'getting the weight well into the ball', but this highly desirable action cannot be performed until the weight has first been taken away from the ball. Much of it must be transferred to the right foot during the backswing; later almost all of it will be transferred to the left during the follow-through. A man weighing twelve stone should, in Compston's opinion, have at least ten stone of his weight on the *inside* of his right foot at the top of the swing—and about eleven stone on his left foot at the end of it. Whether these figures would prove mathematically correct, were we able to measure them scientifically, I do not profess to know; but I quote them without hesitation because they convey accurately the correct *conscious* impression.

I believe that some time ago—in the United States, of course, where nearly all such inventions seem to have their origin—a man invented a twin set of independent scales, one for each foot, on which could be measured the exact stress on either leg at any point during the swing. The results were said to be startling, to prove all sorts of things that the golfer was unaware that he was doing. The very fact, however, that he was not aware of them detracts, to my mind, from their importance. Compston's advice, on the other hand, whether his figures are correct or not, does convey the impression that should be in the golfer's mind.

Some people find this simple transference of the weight a matter of no little difficulty, and he tells a story of one of his pupils who was never able to master it at all. This man was an expert dancer and had, in addition, musically speaking, a fine sense of rhythm. 'But do you think', said Compston, 'he could get his weight on the right foot and then back on the left while he made a golf swing? No, sir! he could not!'

The explanation, I suspect, may be in the words 'on the inside of his right foot'.

'How often', says Alfred Padgham, 'will one not observe a powerful player getting no length into his drive, simply because he has started his backswing with a lateral shifting of weight on to the right foot which he has never been able to get back on to the ball'.

This inability to get the weight back once it has been transferred to the right foot is due almost always to the fact that it has been transferred to the wrong part of that foot—in other words, to the outside or even to the middle—instead of to the inside. If the weight is concentrated on the inside, it is still within the control of the player—a slight thrust will send it back towards the left. But once it has passed the middle, all control over it has gone, and a frantic heave of body, arms, head and legs is the only means of getting it back to the ball.

The left heel can be made to act as a powerful check on this action. So many people make the mistake of letting it rise four or five inches in the air and probably turn at the same time. 'The Little Man', as Sarazen puts it, 'has the idea that he should be on his left toe at the top of the swing, as though he were dancing. You cannot move the hands properly, it is true, without shifting the weight, but there is no need for the heel to do anything more than just leave the ground, or even for the foot to bend on its inside edge.' I have myself seen Henry Cotton play a complete round during which, I am prepared to swear, his left heel was never more than half an inch from the ground.

The mistake arises in most people's minds, I am inclined to suspect, from the notion that the two halves of the swing are exactly symmetrical—that, in other words, the position at the top of the swing is an exact reverse of the position at the end of the follow-through. In the latter, it is true that the player's right foot has turned and come up on to its toe 'as if he were dancing', and so it is mistakenly assumed that the left foot should take a corresponding position on the backswing.

Most of the experts would be able with very little effort to lift their right foot completely from the ground when they have finished the shot; but it is very, very far from the truth to suggest that they could similarly lift their left foot when they have reached the top of the backswing. By making sure that the left heel does not come up too far, and that the left knee, as it bends, points outwards towards the ball, and does not, as it were, droop inwards towards the right leg, it should become a matter of no great difficulty to see that the weight is transferred to the right foot, not only in the proper proportion, but in the proper place.

There is also, it should be observed, a kind of four-cornered transference of the weight. At the beginning of the swing we may assume it to be fairly evenly disposed, though actually it will do no harm to have rather more on the left foot than on the right. During the swing itself, however, the weight is shifted, not only to the right and to the left, but also backwards and forwards —that is, towards and away from the ball. As the hips turn, it is concentrated on the right heel and the left toe; then, as the body comes back again in the natural course of the stroke, it swivels round and finishes on the left heel and the right toe.

Without this swivelling movement it is impossible to generate and deliver the necessary power and at the same time retain a perfect balance.

CHAPTER VIII: The Swing (*continued*)

BODY TURN

Bobby Jones: 'I have come to regard a free body turn as the most important factor in my own method'.

Tommy Armour: 'Ninety-nine out of a hundred average amateur golfers . . . lack the confidence to turn the body, and through that emanates 80 per cent. of their major faults'.

The weight that we were busy transferring in the last chapter comes from the body. And the question as to what happens to the body during the stroke brings us at once to the Pivot—an elementary movement that remains shrouded, for some reason, with a veil of mystery that the Average Golfer often fails to penetrate to the end of his days.

The first step in exposing the pivot for what it really is will be to abolish its name. Let us call it instead

Body Turn. Jones refers to it as a body turn, and what is good enough for him will be good enough for us.

Jones is the master of the body turn *par excellence*. It pervades all his writings, and is made to serve alone as the justification of his excessively narrow stance.

The greatest possible turn can be achieved, whatever the physique of the performer may happen to be, by standing with the feet together: with the feet straddled wide apart it is reduced to a minimum. I refer to Jones's stance as 'excessively' close, because if the average golfer tried to play with his feet so near together he would undoubtedly lose his balance and topple over. An inborn sense of balance enables Jones to make use of a method which would spell disaster to most of his fellow-men.

There is no mystery about the body turn that need frighten the golfer. It is really a perfectly simple procedure. Make any elementary movement with either arm—it may be picking up the telephone, swatting a fly, reaching for a book, or hitting a golf ball—and you will find that one detail common to all is a sympathetic turning of the body in time with the arm.

Imagine yourself, again, playing golf standing between a miniature set of those parallel bars that one sees in a gymnasium, with the bars parallel with the line of flight, one close in front of your hips and the other close behind. The hopelessly constricted position in which you would be, with the hips thus locked, emphasizes at its true value the importance of being able to turn the body in order to get 'wound up' for delivering the blow.

Body turn consists of a movement of the hips and shoulders. Envisage, if you like, a couple of giant hands descending, one on each shoulder, twisting the

ALMOST A CARICATURE—

but a caricature of everything right. Densmore Shute, British open champion in 1933, is one of the most lissom players in first-class golf. Years of training would not enable the average week-end player to reach the position shown here, but there are many lessons that he may learn from it, in particular that of the correct turn of the body. The hips should make a half turn, the shoulders a complete turn—though Shute is so supple that his shoulders have gone even farther.

Notice, too, that he is thrusting the weight onto the *inside* of the right foot and that, although his left arm is as straight as a poker and his wrists cocked to the full, he still has a firm grip with the last two fingers of the left hand.

Rotofotos

'Sports Illustrated and The American Golfer'

depends largely on the physique of the player. Some people cannot keep the arm straight without such strain as is liable either to upset the rhythm of the stroke or to force them to release the grip with the left hand. Neither is a price worth paying for an academic virtue. Densmore Shute keeps it straight because he finds no difficulty in doing so.

body round to the right while the feet remain clamped on the ground. The movement is not unlike that with which we clasp the end of a wet bathing-suit with one hand and then with the other twist it round in order to wring out the water!

Some people are more lissom, of course, than others, but there is no need for the stoutest man to give up body turn as a bad job. The ideal amount of turn on the backswing is probably about 45 degrees with the hips and twice as much—that is to say the complete right angle—with the shoulders, which naturally have a greater range of movement. Thus the left shoulder at the top of the swing should be pointing, as near as no matter, at the ball. If Nature prevents your revolving yourself to that extent, go as far as you can without undue strain.

Both power and direction spring to a great extent from the body turn. You have only to attempt to play a shot with your hips parallel from beginning to end with the line of flight, to see how utterly helpless you are without this ability to turn the body during the shot. As for direction, I am prepared to wager (reassured by the certainty that these things can never be proved) that a good 40 per cent. of all the slices in the world come from a failure to make an adequate body turn on the backswing. The point is this. In order to make a blow with any force in a forward direction, the hips *must* rotate to the left—unless, that is, one is prepared to stop the blow immediately at the moment of impact. Now if the hips remain parallel with the line of flight on the backswing, their left-handed turning movement during the stroke must by all the laws of Nature cause the club to draw across the ball. It is only by 'winding them up' on the backswing that one can allow them to turn leftwards during the stroke, and yet at the same time can retain the ability to hit out and through the ball. We hear a great deal about 'getting the left hip out of the way' as the club comes through the ball. To my mind, it is every bit as important to get the right hip out of the way as the club goes back.

CHAPTER IX: The Swing (*continued*)

THE STRAIGHT LEFT ARM

Harry Vardon: 'I am firmly convinced there is no such thing as a straight left arm at the position where so many golfers have been informed there is. A straight left arm at the top of the backward swing is impossible in anything approaching a correct movement. This fact must be apparent to any one who gives it a moment's thought.'

Alfred Padgham: 'Neither at the address, nor at the top of the swing, is my left arm without a slight curve, not so pronounced as Vardon's perhaps, but certainly not stiff'.

Bobby Jones: 'I play a straight left arm in all full shots from the time the club has started back until after the ball has gone. There is no easing of the elbow at the top of the swing.'

Gene Sarazen: 'Without the straight left arm it is well nigh impossible to ever become a consistently good golfer, for there is too much leeway for error'.

It is a curious but undeniable fact that some of the soundest features of the golf swing have from time to time been the most thoroughly misunderstood through having been carried to excess. Some people seem constitutionally unable to do things in moderation. Tell them to turn the body, and they become a human corkscrew; to take a firm grip of the club, and the ferocious pressure they exert sends all the blood from their knuckles; to keep their right elbow in, and they glue it to their sides until neither arm can move.

Some years ago the golfing firmament was swept by a vogue for the straight left arm. Nothing would do but that this arm, whatever the physique of the player might be, must remain stiff as a ramrod from one end of the shot to the other. I suppose the number of people whose game was temporarily ruined by this fetish must have run into thousands.

And yet, within reasonable limits, the straight left arm represents one of the soundest doctrines in the game. Taking the extreme case, I should say that if one were able to lay hand on that *rarissima avis*, the Perfect Golfer—the man, that is to say, whose physique, temperament, and technique were to be a model to the world—the straight left arm would be found to form part of his equipment.

But we are none of us Perfect Golfers, and my duty in this volume, as I see it, is to offer practical suggestions as to how we, with our limitations, can approximate most nearly to that ideal.

Let us examine first of all the theoretical advantages of keeping the left arm straight. From there we can proceed to find out what sacrifices, if any, it is worth while making on its account.

The first advantage is concerned with the fact that in making a golf stroke we are describing, as nearly as makes no difference, a circle; at any rate the curve described by the clubhead is an *even*, as opposed to a wavy, curve.

The club itself cannot miraculously change its length during the course of the swing, and so, as long as the left arm remains straight, the radius of the circle will remain constant, and no instinctive adjustment by the player will be required to see that the club comes back to the position whence it started, *i.e.* directly behind the ball.

Secondly, it is admitted on all sides, I think, that width in the swing is a desirable end. The club must not, as it were, creep up round the body. It must be swept away in as wide and generous an arc as possible. If the left arm bends overmuch, it stands to reason that the swing must be cramped.

It is admitted, again, that it must be straight at the moment of impact. The less it bends on the backswing, therefore, the less adjustment will be necessary to straighten it out to the hitting position on the way down.

Anyone could, with a special effort, reach the top of the backswing with his left arm still stiff and straight; but in many a case the sacrifices entailed would destroy the value of the operation. Such is the strain of the unnatural attitude that some other part of the body must yield in order to make it possible. Perhaps it is the head that moves away from the ball; maybe the grip has relaxed with the left hand; but whatever it is, the odds are that the sacrifice has not been worth while.

Some people, Bobby Jones included, are so gifted by nature that they can retain a straight left arm without unbalancing any other department of their body. Jones, it may be added, is so supple, despite his somewhat stocky physique, that he can not only keep his left arm straight on the backswing, but also—what is to my mind infinitely more difficult—keep his right arm straight throughout the follow-through.

To anybody who can boast these natural gifts I have not the slightest hesitation in recommending the straight left arm from the moment they address the ball until as long as possible after it has been struck. It is advice, I may say, that is tinged with envy.

For myself I am not so constructed by nature that I can keep my left arm straight throughout the swing. It has to bend, or at any rate 'give', a little at the top of the swing, otherwise the last two fingers of the left hand inevitably begin to lose their grip. Nevertheless, nothing would induce me to abandon the *impression* of having the left arm straight: I know it bends, but I continue to think of it as being straight. That, simple as it is, is my solution of this vital problem.

Every golfer, I feel perfectly certain, will be more likely to keep his club on its proper course if he concentrates on keeping his left arm straight as long as he possibly can—that is, until the natural strain forces it to yield. The more rotund the player, the more careful he should be to get as full a body turn as his 'corporation' will allow, in order to make way for his left arm.

It may be that, in order to prevent too noticeable a bend at the left elbow, he may have to curtail slightly the swing that he is normally in the habit of taking. A loosening of the grip with the left hand is not a worth-while sacrifice, but this shortening of the swing, I think, may well be.

CHAPTER X: THE SWING (*continued*)

A 'LEFT-HANDED' GAME

ARCHIE COMPSTON: 'Ninety-nine out of a hundred golfers have a bad left—a dummy left arm'.

TOMMY ARMOUR: 'How well you play golf all depends on how well you control that left hand of yours. It is the left hand that always lets golfers down.'

SOME years ago I conducted a kind of census of opinion in the columns of the *Evening Standard* concerning one of golf's age-old controversies—namely, which was the master hand, the left or the right. I sought the views of about a dozen of England's leading professionals. Some said the left, and were quite certain about it; others said the left, and were not so sure; others again, acting presumably on the old principle *in medio tutissimus ibis*, replied, 'Both hands'. A few were in favour of the right.

Once again it may be largely a question of personal impression. If a man, for instance, who has not been in the habit of making a great deal of use of his left hand, suddenly begins to concentrate on making that hand play a bigger part, his immediate impression will be that he is playing almost exclusively left-handed; that, in fact, his right has almost ceased to function. It is a sensation that I have experienced myself.

One trouble is that, owing to its superior leverage power, the right hand can exert its influence upon the club so much more easily than the left hand: to put it another way, if you want to exert a given pressure on the club, a great deal more force must be used by the left hand to obtain it than is necessary from the right. Once again, therefore, I suspect that if we had our patent pressure-recorder, it would show a different state of affairs, as between the two hands, from that which we imagine actually obtains.

The right is so much the master hand in everyday life that it is difficult to prevent its playing a disproportionate part in the golf swing. I have related how Archie Compston's immediate reply to the question 'Why does the Average Golfer Remain Average?' was the words quoted at the head of this chapter. 'The weakness of the Average Golfer', he went on, 'is that his strongest side—his right—is always in control. It ought to be the other way round. The trouble with my pupils is to eliminate the right side. Golf is a left-handed game played right-handed. . . .'

If you asked the Average Golfer which, in his opinion, were the two most important fingers in the golf swing, I am sure that in nine cases out of ten he would reply, 'The first two fingers of the right hand'. In those two fingers is centred most of the feeling of power, together with any delicacy of touch that he may possess. But his answer would be just about as wide of the mark as possible. In fact, he could not be more wrong.

The two important fingers in the golf swing are not the first two of the right, but *the last two of the left hand*—the two, in fact, to which the Average Golfer pays the least attention. He never exerts with these two fingers a grip worthy of the name, even in the address, and when he gets to the top of the swing they have probably relaxed themselves into what Cotton picturesquely calls the 'piccolo' grip. 'There are thousands of what I call "piccolo players",' he says, 'struggling around the world's golf courses ignorant of the fact that it is necessary to hang on to the club all the time the swing is being made'.

When I was in the United States, watching the Walker Cup team of 1936, I was interested to listen to Albert ('Scotty') Campbell's theories of the game. They were ranking him level with Johnny Goodman as America's leading amateur at the time. He said, among other things, that he regarded the whole foundation of his game as being based upon these two little fingers of the left hand. He had concentrated on training them and strengthening them until he had reached the state when, directly he placed them on the club, they became, as it were, part of the club itself. However far he swung the club, however hard he hit the ball, these two fingers remained inseparably joined to the club from beginning to end. How many average golfers, I wonder, can truthfully tell themselves at the end of the shot that they did not relax their grip with the left hand?

In case you should think that this concentration on the importance of the left hand is a personal whim of my own, let me refer you to the opinion of yet another of the masters, Alfred Padgham. 'Any laxity with the left hand', he writes, 'is bound sooner or later to lead to trouble. Hold firmly and consistently with the left hand, and let the right hand, right palm to left thumb, not vary in its relationship to the left. . . . It is the left hand that is the master hand throughout.'

And here I would add some constructive advice. Firstly, go and buy yourself, at a cost of not more than half-a-crown, a glove for your left hand. Your professional will sell a special fingerless variety that will not seem unduly strange if you have not been in the habit of wearing a glove before. The sense of strength and

THE 'PICCOLO' GRIP

'Never mind taking the club back as far as the horizontal just because it looks nice. Only go as far as your wrists will permit, still hanging on to the club with the left hand,' says Henry Cotton.

The sacrifice made in the lower picture, in order to obtain a slightly fuller swing, is not worth while. The left hand has relaxed its grip: somewhere between this point and the moment of mpact it must take hold of the club again. The clutching movement as it does so will probably throw the swing from its true arc and upset the rhythm of the stroke.

Bertram Eary

Bertram Eary

POINTING THE CLUB

This is not, by itself, responsible for the direction taken by the ball, but it is a very good indication of what is to come. Not many people, for instance, could produce anything but an 'outside-to-in' movement—and with it a slice—from the position on the left.

Correspondingly the right-hand position, with the club pointing away to the right of the green, must lead, other things being equal, to a hook. As may be seen from the height of the left arm, it is a flatter swing than the other two.

The centre position, which has a more free body turn than the 'slice' position on the left, is an attempt to strike the happy medium between the other two, with the club pointing straight at the hole. If you must err, let it be towards the attitude on the right.

importance that it will add to your left hand will astonish you.

Secondly, I do most earnestly advise you to have the grip of all your clubs, except the putter, padded out under the left hand. The cost will be trifling and the reward enormous.

To say that the part played by the right hand is negligible is, of course, nonsense. It plays a tremendous part. Its rôle, however, is reserved for a comparatively late moment in the swing. In the backswing, for instance, it should take an almost imperceptible part in helping to lift the club, while any action on its part at the beginning of the downswing is generally fatal to the stroke. It is not until the clubhead has reached a point roughly speaking level with the hips on its downward journey that the right hand comes in to deliver that last-minute flick that goes generally by the name of 'delayed wrist action'. Here the right hand is all-important, and from this flick of the wrist, in which, owing to its great leverage power, the right hand plays the larger part, most of the length of the shot is derived.

If the right hand is to deliver successfully this delayed power, it must have something to hit against; and just as the two hands together need a firm left side to hit against, so the right hand in its more humble way needs a firm left hand.

If resistance collapses on the part of the left hand, not only does the potential power of the right waste its sweetness on the desert air, but also something worse befalls. The club comes across the ball from right to left—and we all know what happens then. Here, indeed, is one of the principal causes of the slice.

Once again the experiment of deliberately doing the

wrong thing may be worth while. Take any club you like and make a swing with it, hanging on like grim death with the thumb and all four fingers of the left hand, and letting the right hand hang limply in its normal position on the club. The swing, with any luck, will bear a fairly good resemblance to the proper stroke, the only real point of difference being that it will lack that vital snap, just as the club approaches the ball, that gives life to the shot.

Now try it the other way round. Grip violently with the right hand and leave the left hand limp and lifeless. The club will come up with an upright jerk on the backswing, the right elbow will probably be pointing to the sky, and at the moment of impact all the power in the shot will vanish into thin air as the left hand gives way under the strain.

CHAPTER XI: The Swing (*continued*)

HOW FAR BACK?

George Duncan: 'Personally I am rather in favour of the shorter swing. . . . Nobody can hit the ball any farther with a swing that goes beyond the horizontal than it can be hit with a shorter swing.'

James Adams: 'I take a very long swing myself because I find that I can keep the club *swinging* that way. If I try to curtail it, I feel that I am swinging in two pieces. But I think the Average Golfer would be better off with a shorter swing than mine.'

Henry Cotton: 'I do not fix the length of the backswing for anybody. I leave it to their natural tendencies.'

One of the outstanding changes of fashion in the golf swing since the earlier days of the game has concerned the length of the backswing. Many can recall the time

—and those who cannot may judge from the photographs of the period—when the golfer's ideal was a long, sweeping flourish of the club, that continued until at the top of the swing he was able to see the clubhead again out of the corner of his left eye. That has all changed, and the modern spectator is accustomed to seeing the ball despatched 300 yards with nothing more than a three-quarter or even half swing.

Cotton, Padgham, and Abe Mitchell are among those players of the 1930's who possess renowned names and curtailed backswings. Their example is being followed by a whole host of younger imitators.

The reason for this gradual change, I am inclined to think, lies with the rubber-cored ball. The old guttie demanded, if I am not mistaken, a rather more sweeping motion: at least, I have always found myself, when I have played with one, to be taking a longer and, as I like to think, smoother swing. Whether there is any truth in this theory I am not prepared to argue, for the point is immaterial. What matters is that the present-day experts take a substantially shorter swing than did their predecessors.

For some people the swing is restricted by nature. Provided that they neither bend the left arm double nor release their grip with the last two fingers of the left hand, they are unable to take the club back past the horizontal, if indeed they can reach the horizontal at all. For them—and they represent, I imagine, a goodly percentage of the total number of golfers over 35 years of age—I would quote the words of Henry Cotton: 'Never mind taking the club back as far as the horizontal just because it looks nice. Only go as far as your wrists will permit, still hanging on to the club with the left hand.' For all of these people the length of swing is easily determined by the old principle of going on until the strain reaches a point where it becomes liable to upset the rhythm and smoothness of the stroke.

There are a good many people, however, to whom these words will not apply. I remember arguing the subject one day with Eric Martin Smith, the amateur champion of 1931, who has a particularly full and generous swing. Something had 'gone wrong with the works', and I suggested that he could not possibly retain a firm grip and control of the club if he swung it so far round his neck. It was a theory that proved to be entirely wrong, since such was the suppleness of his wrists that he could take the club back with his left arm straight, and then by cocking the wrists send it back far below the horizontal without in the least degree releasing his hold.

James Adams, as you will see from his picture, is another who favours a long backswing. The fact that the photograph was taken immediately before the Open Championship of 1936, in which he failed by a hair's breadth to tie with Alfred Padgham, shows that this is a style which can certainly prove effective. Adams is a burly fellow, but his robust physique is deceptive. He can stand with both feet flat on the ground, bend back and lay the palms of his hands flat on the ground behind him. That does not mean, however, that his method is to be recommended to the man in the street who may happen to be gifted with an equally pliable physique. It seems to me that it is a style to be adopted only by those who, first of all, are sufficiently acquainted with the technique of the game to know exactly what they are doing and, secondly, have sufficient leisure to keep their swing well greased, as it were, and in good working order.

A REMARKABLE SIMILARITY

The experts have their idiosyncrasies, but these two pictures show how closely they conform in many respects, even down to their trousers and shoes. Had Bert Gadd, on the right, been using a driver, his back-swing must surely have reached a position exactly identical with that of Compston. Note, in each of them, the weight firmly on the inside of the right foot, slightly towards the heel ; the half turn with the hips and full turn with the shoulders ; the firm grasp with the last two fingers of the left hand ; the left arm straight as possible without strain and the right elbow well in to the side, and—eye riveted on the ball. A position worth practising in front of a mirror.

Sport and General

Fox

Brownlow Wilson

Keystone

HOW FAR BACK?

Here are two more of the masters caught at the top of the back-swing. James Adams (left), the longest swinger in first-class golf, is more lissom than his burly physique would suggest and takes this length of backswing without effort. If he tries to curtail it, he says, he feels as if he were swinging in two pieces. The average golfer could only take the club back as far as this by bending his left arm and relaxing the grip with the left hand

On the right is Johnny Fischer, amateur champion of the United States in 1936–7 He has a flatter swing than is usual in first-class golfers on this side of the water—but note the rock-like support of the right leg, the half turn with the hips and full turn with the shoulders. A wonderfully 'wound-up' position.

I cannot believe that the extra foot or two which the clubhead can be made to travel after the horizontal can really make any difference to the length of the stroke; that is to say, I believe that either Adams or Martin Smith could hit the ball just as far if they took the club back no farther than the horizontal. I am not suggesting, mind you, that either of them would necessarily be more accurate with a shorter swing.

On the other hand, it does seem to me that there are grounds for saying that the longer-handicap player who uses an equally full backswing might very well gain accuracy from shortening it. Nothing is more valuable in the course of the golf swing than a really sensitive perception of the exact position of the clubhead throughout the whole course of the stroke. Indeed, it occurs to me that the whole definition of the word 'touch' is contained in those terms.

Except to a man with a very delicate touch this sense of relationship with the clubhead is liable to diminish with every inch that it travels after the horizontal.

The number of people who are sufficiently lissom by nature and have enough leisure to keep in constant practice to make the ultra-long backswing worth while must be extremely small. My own conclusion is that for all the rest the horizontal should be the absolute limit of the backswing. I am talking, of course, though I do not recall having said so before, of a full swing with a driver.

As a case in point, it may be noted that Miss Pamela Barton, when she was already champion of Great Britain and the United States, announced that she had made a substantial improvement in her game by shortening her backswing.

Once again I think that the trouble may be that people

are inclined to regard the golf swing as two symmetrical halves. A far sounder mental conception of it is of the backswing being one-third and the follow-through two-thirds. The mathematicians could undoubtedly prove these figures inaccurate, but they stand very well for what Compston terms the ' mind presentation ' of the swing.

After all, to put it at its very lowest, the less far you go back the less chance you have of going wrong.

Pointing the Club

And now for what I regard personally as one of the major secrets of golf. It is a subject upon which little appears to have been written, and which is rarely a topic of discussion among the theorists of the game, judging at least by the fact that I had been playing golf for fifteen years before anybody happened to emphasize its importance in my presence. I refer *to the direction in which the club is pointing at the top of the swing.*

The direction of the club at this point may not be actually responsible for the direction that the ball takes on its flight, but it seems to be a very good indication of what is to come. If the club, for instance, is pointing to the right of the hole, it seems to me that the plane in which it will come down will, other things being equal, be an ' inside-to-out ' plane—with the shot, that is, developing into a hook or ' draw '. On the other hand, if it is pointing away to the left, it must surely come down in an ' outside-to-in ' plane, thus developing a slice or fade—or at least it would appear to require an almost acrobatic feat in order to make the club strike the ball from ' inside out '. Similarly, it appears that if the club is pointing straight at the flag, the face will come straight through the ball at impact.

No allowance is made at the moment, of course, for any inadvertent opening and shutting of the clubface, either of which would naturally influence the stroke in its own way.

I feel sure that every golfer would benefit from making a few experiments upon this theory. If you are the victim of the occasional or habitual slice—and you probably are—try the one with the club pointing out to the right, and see if you can produce a deliberate hook. Keep the right elbow well down (this is particularly important), hold up the left hip a little longer than usual, and hit well out to the right of the green. If you exaggerate the motions—and it is a good plan to do so at first—a very quick hook should result. That will do you no harm, however, for you know very well whence it came, but it will add something to your store of general golfing knowledge. After this, play a few with the club pointed at the top of the swing deliberately to the left of the green, and watch the resultant slice.

Then, with some of the feelings perhaps which the shipbuilder launches his vessel and watches to see whether it floats, try one with the club pointing straight at the flag. . . .

CHAPTER XII: The Swing (*continued*)

STARTING THE DOWNWARD SWING

Archie Compston: 'The majority of people can gather up the power alright in the backswing, but they do not know how to apply it. They *will* start the movement in the wrong place. You ought to learn this by heart . . . the correct order of the downswing is left hip, left shoulder, left hand and then the clubhead.'

Henry Cotton is one of the closest and keenest students of golf that the game has ever known. Since his earliest days he has analysed the swing, taken it to pieces like a small boy dissecting a watch, put it together again, taken it to pieces. . . . While some of his rivals have been content to go along in a somewhat lackadaisical manner, working on odd theories from time to time and practising when it suited them, he has been busy trying to discover the why and the wherefore of every little movement that takes place during the swing. Some say that he has overdone this form of keenness, that it has caused him to waste too much of his energy on the unessentials of the game. That may be true, though I must say that it does not represent my own view. I think that this passion for knowledge for its own sake has been largely responsible for his success.

A splendid example of his intimate acquaintance with the golf swing appeared during a course of lectures which he gave at an exhibition in London in 1935. When he had finished his discourse he invited questions from the assembled company, and one man said, ' Will you please show us exactly the correct position at the top of the swing ? '. Without a moment's hesitation he replied, ' There is no such thing as the top of the swing '. Everyone in the room was somewhat taken aback, and was inclined to think for a moment that he was trying to be a little too clever, but a short demonstration sufficed to remove so unworthy a thought from their minds. The golf swing, he explained, is a continuous movement. It is not composed of two halves, the backswing—stop—and then the downswing ; not so much the gathering up of power and then, after a suitable pause, the delivery of that power, but a continuous *flow*.

His demonstration went on to show that if you want to talk of the top of the swing, you must confine yourself specifically to one part of the body at a time. He showed beyond question, for instance, that *at the moment when his hands were about to finish their upward journey, his hips were already beginning to turn to the left—that is to say, beginning their downswing.*

The top of the swing, for the average mortal, is one of the chief danger points of the stroke, and 'snatching' is one of his cardinal sins. The desire to 'hit from the top' is an irresistible temptation, especially when the situation is tense and the mind is strained. Every moment of the backswing seems an age when one is anxious to get on with the business in hand. The hands are dragged convulsively down before the wrists have had time to 'cock', the clubhead is left stranded in the air, as if uncertain whether to try to finish its own backswing or to come scuttling back in order to keep up with the hands, and the whole rhythm of the stroke is lost. The clubhead is always fighting a losing battle, the hands win the race by a foot or eighteen inches, and away goes the ball to the right.

It is to combat this fatal tendency that so many people make the mistake of going to the opposite extreme, and making a conscious stationary pause before beginning the downswing. As a fault it is not in the same class as that which it is designed to prevent—but fault it is. It, too, destroys the essential rhythm of the stroke.

Compston's rendering of the correct order of the downswing, that heads this chapter, is undoubtedly right; the motion-pictures do, in fact, show that the left hip is the first part of the body to begin to unwind. Whether it is the part that should take the principal place in the consciousness of the player is another matter. I believe that he would do better to be *aware* that his left hip may begin to unwind before his hands have finished their part of the backswing, but at the same time to concentrate his actual attention on his hands—or perhaps I should say his left hand.

I have often seen it written that the first motion of the downswing should be a downward pull with the left hand. I believe, though, that the authors of this advice have missed out a vital step. The left hand does start the downward swing—so far as, at any rate, the hands and arms are concerned—and it does during the course of it exercise a downward pull. But the first pull that it should exercise should be, to my mind, outwards—that is to say, along the shaft of the club directly away from the clubhead.

The advantage of making a conscious pull in this outward direction is that, if the left arm has bent—and in the vast majority of cases it will have bent a little—it will be straightened out with the least possible delay: and, of course, the sooner it is thus straightened the greater will be the width achieved in the swing and the truer the circle described by the clubhead. If the initial pull is vertically downwards, the hands may creep down the side of the body and a lot of the power available for the stroke may be dissipated.

It is my impression that a player's length is governed to a large extent by the amount by which he can 'break' his wrists at the top of the swing without releasing his hold of the club. It is absolutely vital, therefore, that the wrists should be given ample time to do their best at the top of the swing, and not be snatched downwards before they have had time to store up their maximum power.

The importance of consciously starting down with the

NO 'BEGINNER'S LOOP' HERE

Compston says that the correct order of the first downward movement is 'left hip, left shoulder, left hand and then the club-head'. Lawson Little is here seen putting the maxim into practice. Despite the fact that the ball is about to be propelled upwards of 300 yards, the right hand has not yet come into the shot. Note the similarity, especially in the position of the arms and elbows, between Little here and Cotton overleaf—allowing for essential differences due to the fact that Little is using a far more powerful club.

'Sports Illustrated and The American Golfer'

British Steel Golf Shafts

A WONDERFUL ACTION PICTURE

of Henry Cotton coming down to the ball with a No. 5 iron. There has been no appreciable shifting of the weight in a stroke of this length. Both heels are already planted firmly on the ground and he is relying on his hands and forearms to supply the necessary power. The wrists are still cocked, as at the top of the backswing, and will remain so until the hands are almost opposite the right leg—merely a few inches behind the ball. Then the right hand, which has until this point played no active part in the downward swing, will flash the club across with a speed that almost defeats the moving camera. The reason why the average player should be at pains to strengthen his left hand is in order that it may be able to provide a suitable resistance to the right hand at this moment.

The average player, however, who has not, like Cotton, nursed his left hand and forearm for many years, will not be able to delay the wrist action quite so long.

left hand and leaving the right hand out of the picture is that in no circumstances must this stored energy in the wrists be delivered at the ball until the last possible moment. Any influence by the right hand at this point will almost certainly make for an unwinding of the wrists and a premature release of their power. All of which brings us naturally to the vexed question of delayed wrist action.

CHAPTER XIII: The Swing (*continued*)

DELAYING THE WRIST ACTION

Henry Cotton: '. . . this flick of the wrist occurs as my hands are a few inches behind the ball, but because it is an unconscious effort I cannot tell you where it should be applied . . .'.

Bobby Jones: 'In my stroke the hitting area seems to begin when the club is about parallel with the ground and the hands opposite the right leg'.

It is the delivery of the power stored up in the wrists that gives length to a golf shot; delayed wrist action, in other words, is the life blood of the stroke. It is responsible, as Compston puts it, for the *devil* in the golf swing. Nevertheless, to those who are unaware of its true nature and purpose, it is extremely difficult to define. Nobody quite knows where it begins, where it ends, and what is the best method deliberately of applying it to the best advantage.

Watch the experts play, with their smooth and lazy rhythm, and you will see their wrists break at the top of the swing, you will see their hands begin the downward journey in the same relative position, and you will see them finish with their wrists turned over and 'broken' in the opposite direction. But what goes on in the meantime will defeat your eye. So quick is the movement, indeed, that it almost defeats the moving camera.

It is generally agreed that the distance that a golf ball can be propelled depends directly on the speed with which the clubhead is applied to it. And the speed with which you apply the clubhead in turn depends directly upon how long you are able to delay this last-minute flick of the wrists.

Bobby Jones is particularly strong in the wrist and fore-arm. I remember comparing my own wrist with that of a friend's, and finding that his was very nearly twice as big as my own: yet he assured me that it appeared positively wizened beside that of Jones.

He, with his enormous strength, can withhold this last-minute action until his hands are opposite his right leg and the club has already travelled over enough of its downward journey to be parallel with the ground. For the rest of us it may not be possible to delay the vital thrust for as long as this, but I am convinced of one thing—namely, that it is better to aim at delaying it too long than expending it too soon.

This delayed action of the wrist takes place in the space of a split second, and for that reason it seems to me that it must be catalogued, important though it is, as one of the *subconscious* movements in the golf swing. One may be conscious of having brought it off, but not conscious of the actual performing of it.

The truth is probably that, having ' broken ' the wrists in the approved manner at the top of the swing, one may trust to instinct alone to make them play their part when the time comes. Judging by personal experience, I should say that it is infinitely more difficult to hold the wrist action in check long enough than to make sure that it comes in in time.

Nobody has yet been able to formulate a complete and satisfactory definition of that elusive quality known as timing. There are innumerable features of the golf swing, any one of which can prevent the shot being perfect. It may be a turn of the hips, a lifting of the head, a wrong distribution of the weight, or, indeed, any of the hundred and one things that are popularly supposed to be liable to go wrong.

Conversely, it requires a successful combination of a good many separate actions to produce the perfect stroke; but if I were asked to name any single item that took precedence over the rest, I think I should vote without hesitation in favour of this delayed action of the wrists. I believe it is the application, at the critical moment, of the energy stored up in them that goes, more than any other single feature, to produce perfection of striking.

CHAPTER XIV: The Swing (*continued*)

THE FOLLOW-THROUGH

Archie Compston: 'It is a wise policy to visualize the proper finish before you play a shot and then, at the end, try to keep that finish for a split second'.

One's individual valuation of the relative importance of various features of the golf swing changes as rapidly as fashions in the swing in general. One day the secret of golf is the straight left arm; the next it is a proper transferring of the weight from one foot to the other;

the day after that it may have shifted to the position of the little finger of the right hand halfway down the downward swing—or something equally trivial. It all depends on one's personal reactions of the moment.

The follow-through is a department of the swing that is particularly liable to such fluctuations of favour. To-day it is all-important, to-morrow one may be convinced that, since the ball has already gone, the follow-through can have no possible influence on the stroke. Of the two extremes, I favour the former as being nearer the truth.

The follow-through is not an end in itself—but it *is* a reflection of what has gone before. *Get a correct finish, and the movements that led up to it are likely to have been correct.*

It seems to me that a great many golfers are not only careless about what actually happens to themselves and the club after the ball is struck, but also have failed to include a complete follow-through in their preliminary mental impression of the shot. Like everyone else, they have formed some picture in their mind of the stroke that they are hoping to play, but this picture is incomplete. They see themselves on the backswing, they see themselves on the downswing, they hear the click of the ball as it leaves the club, and they see it soaring away into the distance. If they are in good form and on top of the world, they see it sailing down the middle; if they are nervous or out of sorts, they see it fading out of bounds.

Their imaginings, however, have omitted one vital feature: they have not seen themselves *finishing* the shot. The picture is incomplete and is cut off at what is, if they only knew it, a critical stage.

Although the experts vary so widely in their style of

action that there would be no mistaking them at a distance even if they were dressed in uniform clothes, each of their swings is governed by the same basic fundamentals. And so it is with the follow-through. Jones, for instance, finishes with his hands high above his head and his right arm straight, at any rate for that split second at the end of the swing before the whole body relaxes. It is a posture that I find myself physically incapable of imitating, much less imitating with that air of natural relaxation that characterizes every picture of Jones at the end of his swing.

Cotton, on the other hand, finishes with a rather greater turn of the body, with his hands well away to the left and scarcely higher than the level of his head. Others, again, vary from these two, each according to his individual light.

That does not matter. What matters is the points they share in common, not the differences between them. And the greatest of these common assets is *balance*.

It is strange, but undeniable, that whatever clothes he may wear, whatever clubs he may carry, one can always tell an amateur golfer from a professional: even if the amateur drives down the middle, and the professional tops the ball into the heather beneath his nose, there is no possible mistake as to which is which. I think that perhaps this sense of balance is the outstanding point of difference between the two. The professional seems, as it were, to 'find his feet' directly he takes up his stance at the ball—and, having once found them, never loses them. He finishes poised and steady at the end of the shot, and one has the impression that if one gave him a shove he could resist it with ease. The amateur, on the other hand, makes a great deal more fuss with his feet, and at the end of the stroke may well find that one, or even both of them, have moved. The slightest touch from any direction would send him toppling.

That is because he has not taken the trouble to visualize the proper finish of the shot before he has played it. The week-end golfer cannot expect to achieve, either permanently or from time to time, the graceful follow-through of the first-class professional, but he *can* hope to evolve some more humble finish of his own that will serve the purpose equally well. His arms, having both been straight at the moment of impact, should remain straight as long as is possible without undue strain, as they continue their journey upwards and round his body to the left. Above all things he should be perched firmly and securely on his left leg. If the shot can be performed without his left foot turning towards the hole, so much the better; if it cannot, no active harm is done. What matters is that having finished the shot he should be in perfect equilibrium.

No one quite knows what to think about during the course of the swing. There are said to be a hundred and one things that we must not forget, but that does not mean that we can be consciously mindful of them all as we swing the club. On the other hand we can scarcely be expected to think of nothing at all. One of the many differences between the first-class player and the rabbit has been defined by Compston as follows—the rabbit thinks simply of making a blow at the ball, whereas the first-class player concentrates his attention on a particular point in the swing.

It seems to me that unless you are conscious of some point that is troubling you, and have therefore to devote

THE LONG AND SHORT OF IT

The follow-through is largely a matter of individual choice. Abe Mitchell (left) uses the old-fashioned 'two-fisted' grip and gives the impression of a man giving the ball a tremendous rap with his right forearm. His club never follows through farther than is shown here

Cyril Tolley, on the other hand, despite his more bulky physique carries the club on without effort right round his neck.

What matters to the handicap golfer is not a stylish appearance, but an attitude of *equilibrium*. In other words, he should concentrate on *finishing* the shot.

L.N.A.

Sport and General

Photos by Sport and General

THE END OF TWO PERFECT SHOTS

Bobby Jones in action during a Walker Cup match at St. Andrews. The follow-through, it may be repeated, is not an end in itself, but it *is* an indication of what has gone before. It is easy to see that no heaves or jerks or sways could have preceded Jones's arrival at this attitude of balance and poise.

your attention to it, you cannot do better than to focus your concentration not only, as I have previously suggested, on your hands, but also, in particular, on your hands leading the rest of your body smoothly to a balanced follow-through which you can hold at the end of the swing. If you have in mind during the stroke the sense of balance that comes from a good follow-through, you will tend automatically to retain your balance at each one of the preliminary stages of the swing. 'If you start falling over now', your mind seems to say as you shift the club, 'you will never get your balance back. You'll never reach that follow-through that we have been thinking about.'

Beauty in the follow-through means nothing to anyone but the first-class stylist; balance, on the other hand, means everything to everyone. *Finish the shot* is a maxim that anyone who is off his game might find it worth while to recall; for in straightening out his finish he may well find that he has straightened out the rest of his swing on the way.

The best finisher of a golf shot that I know is John Langley, who at the age of seventeen reached the final of the English Championship. This ability to stand perfectly poised at the end of every stroke, be it a drive or a putt, is perhaps the most noticeable of his many admirable golfing qualities.

Every man has a follow-through of a kind, some posture in which, if he *had* to be photographed at golf, he would prefer to be found. Provided that it conforms to a few basic principles—provided, that is, that his hands are well away from his body, that his shoulders are facing the hole, and that he is firmly poised in a position of equilibrium with nearly all the weight on the left foot, it does not matter whether the resultant effect is that of a Greek statue or of a man who has just flung a stone for his dog. The fact remains that, if he is balanced and in control now, he has probably been balanced and in control throughout the previous course of the swing.

If, on the other hand, his right foot has moved round and he is standing square to the hole, pulling his hands up and down in front of him like a bell-ringer, or if he has pitched forward and has had to use his club in the manner of a walking-stick to save himself from falling over, or if his weight is back on his right foot like that of a cricketer defending himself from an attack of bodyline, then it is a thousand to one that these faults were developed *before* the club reached the ball.

CHAPTER XV

WOODEN CLUBS

The essential principles of the swing that we have been busy dissecting in the past few chapters hold good for every shot in the game except putting and the short approaches. There are differences in technique, of course, in playing the wooden clubs and the irons, the heavy irons and the light irons, the 'forceful' irons and what we may call the 'delicate' ones, with which are played the vital strokes within 80 yards of the flag. These differences are concerned with modifications of the stance, the length of swing, and sometimes the grip; but in no case do they violate the fundamentals of the golf swing as a whole.

The swing to which we have been devoting our attention has been tacitly assumed to be that used with a driver; the swing, in other words, calculated to produce the longest shot in the game. One or two points peculiar to the driver must, however, be noted, although the swing itself has been dealt with in full.

If I took a serious interest in competitive golf and were permitted to carry as many clubs as I like, I should have not the least hesitation in carrying five wooden clubs. As it is, I may say, I carry three, sometimes four—but that is neither here nor there. Two of these clubs would be drivers, one with a very deep face and the other with a definitely shallow face. Neither of them would have, to all intents and purposes, any loft.

A golf shot demands not only correct direction but correct height, in order to give it a perfect shape—and height is a thing which the average golfer finds almost as difficult to control as direction.

His chief difficulty is in keeping the ball down—though I can imagine a good many people who read this saying to themselves with devastating sarcasm, 'My goodness, he should watch me. *I* can keep it down alright!'. I do not, of course, mean half topping the ball and making it fly at the height of a man's head: I mean hitting it fairly and squarely in the middle without giving it a kind of 'rocketing' trajectory.

The trouble is that the average man, who as a rule fails to get sufficient width in the swing, comes on to the ball with a blow that is descending too steeply—and one of the great paradoxes of this fantastic game is that hitting *down* on a ball sends it *up*. This downward blow, if it does not entirely smother the ball, sends it limply skywards, where it soon loses its momentum and is at the mercy of the winds of heaven and the spins imparted by man. In a head wind or a left-to-right wind this is a particularly fatal tendency—it is in fact the principal cause of so many people admitting with resignation that they ' can't play golf in a wind '.

This is where the deep- and straight-faced driver comes in. If you will tee the ball up at least an inch in the air (in other words, so that you can pass an upright halfpenny between the ground and the bottom of the ball), you will find that with your deep-faced weapon, although you do not actually top or smother the ball you can obtain a low, running trajectory, even against the strongest head wind. Correspondingly in the side winds you will find that the momentum thus imparted to the ball will minimize the effect of any spin that you may have unwillingly put on it.

With the deep-faced club the ball returns to earth sooner and runs a great deal farther than if the shot is played in the normal manner with a shallow-faced club.

A number of people habitually tee the ball very low, often on the grounds that there is otherwise too much difference between shots with the driver and the brassie. This to my mind is either an affectation or a misapprehension, or both. I believe that the drive and the brassie shot, although they are closely akin, should in fact be regarded as two different strokes ; if you do not so regard them, the only logical conclusion must be that you should use no tee at all and play both shots with the same club. If you are going to tee it up, why, tee it up !

It is difficult to say that any particular height of tee is ' correct ': but if you hold the tee between the first two fingers of your hand and thus press it into the ground, I think that when the top of the tee begins to press on your fingers it means that you have probably reached the right height. On the other hand, if you are one of those people who find it difficult to get under the ball, let no one deter you from teeing it as high as you like.

The Brassie

The third of the five wooden clubs that I should carry would be the brassie. The difference in technique between the drive and strokes with the other wooden clubs is concerned solely with the fact that getting the ball into the air is a primary, vital consideration with the brassie and the spoon. On the tee you can start with the ball at any height you please—you can even put it on top of a beer-bottle, if you like, as a famous golfer used to do some years ago: for the rest of the time you must take it as you find it.

A good many golfers seem constitutionally incapable of getting the ball in the air with a brassie except when they find it sitting up on a tuft of grass, in which case they might just as well take their driver. Inability to play the stroke from a moderate lie can be traced not only to a lack of knowledge of the mechanical principles involved, but also to the fact that, in nine cases out of ten, they are equipped with a club that makes the shot extremely difficult even to the expert.

I hold strong views on the ideal shape and construction of the brassie. I believe that it should have a very shallow face and an extremely narrow head. I had such a club constructed in my earlier days to combat the close lies at Mildenhall. It has proved to be a great success, has served its purpose admirably, and has been copied by a large number of people who have from time to time played shots with it. The face is no more than 1¼ inches deep, and the total length of the hitting surface at its longest point measures only 2½ inches. It has, practically speaking, no loft at all, for the simple reason that its other characteristics make loft unnecessary. The measurement of the average brassie head comes to something like 1½ inches by 3 inches.

The shallower the face the more easily will a club raise the ball in the air, as anyone who has discarded an old-fashioned jigger in favour of the modern rather deeper-faced irons will readily admit. In a close lie the principal difficulty is to get the club down to the centre of gravity of the ball without at the same time digging into the ground, and for this purpose a shallow face is quite indispensable.

The *length* of face seems to be a subject that has been sadly neglected by club-makers in general. Some margin of error is obviously necessary—we could not, for instance, expect to hit the ball consistently well with a clubface no bigger than a penny—but that is not to say that we need an inch to spare on either side of the centre, where we hope to hit the ball.

With a driver this point is comparatively unimportant, except that anything calculated to increase the wind resistance must obviously be deplored: with a brassie, however, it is of considerable consequence. If a club has a long, flat sole, it can only be applied to the ball successfully if there is enough room to accommodate it without interference on either side of the ball—in other words, if the ball is lying perfectly. If it is in any way 'cupped', either the heel or the toe of the club must come into direct contact with the ground, and thereby dissipate much of the force behind the blow. A narrow head will, as it were, fit the 'cup' in which the ball is lying, and thus be able to supply its entire strength to the ball. Diagram 4, below, which is of course slightly exaggerated to fit the case, illustrates this point.

On a club such as I have described there is no need for a great deal of loft. The shallow face will itself see that the ball rises sufficiently, but at the same time will ensure that it does not have the high and rather shorter trajectory that one wishes to achieve with the spoon. I am sure that it is as easy to get the ball into the air with a completely straight face that is shallow, as with a more lofted face that is comparatively deep.

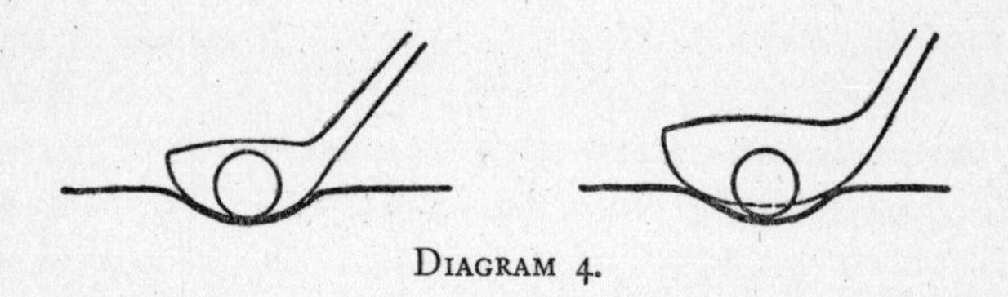

Diagram 4.

With regard to the technique of the brassie shot, the differences between this and the drive seems to be fairly straightforward. Generally speaking, the flatter the swing the lower will be the trajectory of the shot. A flat swing is liable to keep the ball down—to impart a draw; an upright swing is liable to send the ball into the air—to impart, if anything, a fade. Thus when there is any question of getting the ball up, as there is in the brassie shot, it is obvious that an upright swing is more calculated to do the trick.

Bobby Jones, who tee-ed the ball well up and used a fairly deep-faced driver, found that his tendency from the tee is to hook. With the brassie and spoon, on the other hand, his shots, on the rare occasions when they did go wrong, generally drifted away to the right.

For the average man this slight fade with a brassie and spoon is by no means to be condemned. A fade is more easy to play, more controllable, and less liable to disastrous consequences than a draw. The fact that people do not more often play it deliberately is due probably to its obvious relationship with its ugly brother, the nvoluntary slice.

The best tip I ever had with regard to brassie play was given me many, many years ago by Jack Seager, now professional at Rothley Park, near Leicester. It impressed me so much at the time by its effective simplicity that I have never forgotten it. He said that the secret of successful brassie play was to imagine yourself slapping the flat sole of the club on the ground immediately behind the ball—hitting the ground quite hard, that is, but not taking a divot. It is rather a question of bumping or bouncing the underneath part of the club on the ground instead of hitting the face of the club *into* the ground and through the ball, as one does with an iron. The shot is really akin to that played with the very broad-soled niblick, usually known as the blaster. If you carry out these simple instructions, making sure not to shut the face of the club, you need have no further worries about topping the ball.

Topping, of course, is the principal fault in brassie play, a fault that is as much psychological as physical. It comes not so much from an inability to swing the club with sufficient accuracy as from a natural and inherent desire, on seeing the ball lying rather close to the turf, to hit in an upward direction instead of allowing the club itself to do the lifting. Height in a golf shot, it cannot be too often recalled, comes not from the action of the man, but the action of his club.

One last thing is worth remembering—namely, that a partly topped brassie shot is by no means to be despised. If the lie is not good enough to put a perfect trajectory within the bounds of reasonable possibility, length can still be obtained by taking the brassie and being content not to get quite under the ball, provided you can be sure of not topping it completely. I am not suggesting that it is a particularly graceful stroke, but it is one, nevertheless, that will not only run for miles, but will also defy both wind and slopes in their effort to change its direction. And, after all, it's the result that counts!

Finally, I must not be guilty of omitting the traditional advice to the inexpert player—'When in doubt take the spoon'. It is advice that most of us neglect to our dying day, but my conscience demands that, for all that, it shall find a place in these pages. 'I should never have taken a brassie—I knew I should miss it,' tells a mournful, unnecessary, but oft-told tale. If the lie is not good enough for a brassie and you do not feel yourself capable of playing the mongrel stroke described in the last paragraph, cut your losses and take a spoon. Half a miss with a spoon goes twice as far as a whole miss with a brassie.

The Spoon

I believe—and so, I fancy, do the vast majority of golfers—that the spoon is the most useful club in the bag. Of the five wooden clubs that I have mentioned, two would be spoons. For myself, I carry only one, a perfectly orthodox and normal weapon, though of course it conforms to the principles already laid down for the construction of the brassie, and therefore has a short and comparatively shallow face. The other would be a type of club that you do not often see these days, but which is, all the same, extraordinarily useful. It is really a kind of spoon in miniature, with an ultra-shallow face and a tiny head. No great length can be expected from it, but it will get the ball into the air from anything but a hopeless lie, and is liable to prove a wonderful stroke-saver in the rough.

A further type of spoon that seems recently to have dropped from favour was one which bore a variety of names, each of which contained in some form or other the word ' pug '. Pug-faced or pug-nosed it used to be called, I remember, and sometimes the ' bull-dog '. It had a small, squat head with a great deal of loft and its sole was so completely rounded that the club had no set ' lie ' at all. You could address the ball with your hands low or high, you could stand near to it or far away, but still the club seemed to sit naturally on the ground. I had one myself for some years, and a very good friend it proved to be. In the end I only threw it out because I did not like to have too many clubs in the bag.

The spoon as a whole seems to combine a good many of the merits of both wooden and iron clubs. It does not demand a good lie, but, on the other hand, will hit the ball a fair distance and keep it straight with reasonable ease. Once again I think an open stance is advisable, since the cut-up stroke is even more natural to the spoon than to the brassie. The spoon is essentially a high dropping shot that should stop fairly soon after it pitches. A stance somewhat closer to the ball seems to be indicated, with the elbows just close enough not to touch the body. As for the ball itself, I am inclined to think that a position midway between the left heel and the point opposite the middle of the space between the feet is indicated. No great harm will come to anybody who plays every shot with any wooden club in identically the same manner. All the same, these slight adaptations in the style for the brassie and the spoon will probably prove worth while to anyone who becomes genuinely familiar with them.

The average golfer is inclined to make too little of the opportunities offered him by the spoon at longish short holes. One of the easiest shots in the game is that with the spoon played from a tee; one of the most difficult that with the No. 1 or No. 2 iron, whether it be played from a tee or not. Except in a strong wind, it seems to me to be madness to play any shot with an iron when you could equally well play it with a spoon.

CHAPTER XVI

IRONS

The difference between iron and wooden club play is sometimes exaggerated. A beginner is taught to play with his driver and then, having 'mastered' that according to his lights, is often led to believe that having learnt one game he may now embark upon another. At any rate, he may be forgiven for suspecting that playing golf with wooden clubs is one thing and playing with iron clubs another.

I number among my acquaintances a good many men who play to handicaps of, say, twelve and upwards, and a great many of them play their wooden shots and iron shots in identically the same manner—for no better reason than that they have been led to believe that the difference between the two, according to the textbooks, is so great that it is now no longer worth their while to attempt the change.

That is all wrong. I should be the last to deny that there is a difference between the two types of shot, but the first to assert that that difference can be mastered by the handicap player. The stance and swing that are calculated to produce the best results with a driver will not, unless modified in various directions, produce the best results with an iron: but these modifications are so straightforward that I believe it is worth everyone's while to investigate them.

The general difference between the two swings is that the one is shorter, more compact, more concise than the other. One is a sweep, while the other is more of a punch—and a punch, it must be remembered, can possess rhythm just as well as a sweeping movement.

On some aspects of the iron shot the experts disagree in a most engaging manner. They are, however, in complete accord, so far as I can see, on the ideal length of the backswing. They all agree that in no circumstances should it equal that taken with a driver—should never, in fact, exceed what is generally termed the three-quarter swing. I think, therefore, that we may take it for granted that 'three quarters' shall be the absolute limit of the backswing with the bigger irons, adding the proviso that of course it shall be progressively reduced as the grade of the club becomes smaller.

On the question of the stance, disagreement is at its height. Tommy Armour, whose iron shots are a delight to the eye—he is often called the best iron-player in the world—says that the stance should be square. The school of thought represented by W. J. Cox, to which I have referred before, prefers to shut the stance and the face of the club and everything else, and to rely upon strong forearms and a hearty follow-through to produce the goods. Gene Sarazen, on the other hand, as neat and effective a player as has ever wielded a golf club, strongly favours the open stance. If you want length with iron clubs, he says, the most natural thing in the world is to get the right foot behind the left, if only because you feel that you can hit so much harder that way. But he thinks, all the same, that it is a snare and delusion, the chief difficulty being to get the clubhead through correctly after the ball. An open stance, he holds, not only makes the follow-through a great deal more easy, but also holds the right side well up to the ball.

With the shorter, crisper movement of the iron shot, it should be noted, there is not the same necessity for a full and flowing turn of the body. Thus almost every expert is agreed in placing the right foot square to the hole, or even in a pigeon-toed manner, turning the foot in to point slightly towards it. That is the posture adopted, incidentally, by Abe Mitchell for all his shots. Bearing in mind the fact that this book is not addressed primarily to scratch players, I throw in my lot with Sarazen, and recommend with confidence the slightly open stance for all iron shots.

As to the position of the ball, it must unquestionably be a little farther back than usual; directly opposite the middle of the space between the feet is perhaps the safest position. In the drive the club should meet the ball either at the bottom of its downward curve or later as it begins the upward curve: under no conditions must it meet the ball while it is still coming downwards, however slightly.

In an iron shot, however, the ball *must* be hit a downward blow. The ball first and the turf afterwards—that is the rule. So many average golfers for some unaccountable reason find it perfectly easy to ram the ball down against the turf with a wooden club, but quite impossible to do the same thing with their irons: in other words, they cannot play an iron shot with their irons, but they can play it with their woods.

It is to assist in making this movement correctly that one stands rather more in front of the ball with an iron club, so that the lowest part of the swing's curve comes naturally at a point an inch or two in front of the ball.

The grip with the hands need scarcely be modified, except that I think most people will find it perfectly natural to turn both hands very slightly in a clockwise direction—that is, to place the left hand rather more on top of the shaft and the right rather more under it. That this is not an artificial movement can be proved by the simple experiment of taking the two extremes, and putting the ball first of all right behind the right foot and then right away outside the left foot. In the first case, you will find that the natural instinct—indeed, almost the only course—is to turn the left hand all the way over on top of the shaft, and in the second to turn it completely round in the other direction.

The immediate trouble of the man who is not used to this principle of hitting downwards and through the ball is that he finds himself inclined to 'smudge' the shot, or to push it away rather limply to the right. Both these faults, once you know their origin, should be cured without undue difficulty.

The ball and the ground together set up a far greater resistance than does the ball alone in a shot like the drive, and the force of the impact takes the inexpert player by surprise. He is not used to it, he does not make sufficient

THE BEGINNING AND THE END

Perfect iron play by Cambridge University. On the left a copybook position by John Langley. Note the weight shifted to the *inside* of the right foot—three quarter backswing—straight left arm—firm grip with the last two fingers of the left hand—elbows close together—and eye glued to the ball. The player gives the impression that no amount of shoving would knock him off his balance.

On the right the left-handed P. B. Lucas finishes the shot. The weight has gone wholly through to the forward foot and the position is one of complete control and equilibrium.

Fox

Sport and General

Sport and General

THE INTERMEDIATE STAGES

The 'middle' of the perfect iron shot by Gene Sarazen. This was a full iron, yet notice the absence of visible effort. The left hip gets out of the way to let the hands come freely through. Note that the head, outlined against the fence in the background, has not moved a fraction of an inch, despite the releasing of power sufficient to send the ball nearly 200 yards.

allowance for it, and the result is that it knocks the club out of his hands—knocks it, at any rate, out of his left hand. The force of impact is at its strongest in the long iron shot, and, although the last-minute power is supplied by the right hand, nearly all the brunt of the blow is borne by the left hand, particularly by its last two fingers.

Hit your club hard on the ground in front of you, and you will find that these two fingers are the first to 'give': in fact, unless you have specially trained them for their task, only a stout effort of concentration will keep them up to their work.

In a long iron shot the left hand, I am convinced, should do almost all the work on the backswing, and absolutely all the work on the first part of the downswing, until the hands have come down again level with the hips and the wrists are ready to make their combined flick which is to send the clubhead three or four feet while they themselves move merely a few inches.

Having successfully carried out its work so far, the left hand is liable to quit at the critical moment. The right takes charge, and then, as the club strikes the ground, the left fades away, thus entirely destroying the good work of the right by leaving it nothing to hit against—leaving it, as it were, stranded in mid-air. The cure, therefore, for this half-hit 'smudge' is a firm grip with the left hand, not only on the upward and downward swings, but also *at* and *through* the ball.

With regard to the slice—well, this can, of course, be caused by any of the 'orthodox' causes that will produce a slice in any kind of shot. They are dealt with later. What concerns us at the moment is that particular tendency to slice which descends upon people who are trying to hit the ball down with an iron club for the first time. In the drive, after the clubhead has travelled back perhaps 18 inches, lagging slightly behind the hands, it begins to open—that is to say, turn outwards—until at the top of the swing the face is pointing away from the player in the direction of the ball. As it comes down it automatically closes, and should become dead straight as it meets the ball. At any point before this it is liable to be open, the angle varying according to its position.

The natural tendency, therefore, when you stand a little in front of the ball, and the bottom of the arc of the swing has not yet been reached at the moment when the ball is struck, is for the clubface to be very slightly open. Hence your slice. There is no special trick by which this fault can be cured—it is simply a question of seeing that the face of the club is *not* open, seeing that it closes in time.

One might also point out, of course, that the deliberate desire to punch the ball crisply is often liable to make you hit too soon from the top of the swing, or lean forward unduly far in order to get just one precious extra ounce into the blow, where no extra ounce is needed. In either case the result is liable to be a slice—but slices of that order, as I say, belong to a later chapter.

Short Holes

Before we leave the subject of the irons, let me offer some advice about playing the short holes. In the first place, never take an iron club simply because the card tells you the bogey of the hole is three. I have played with so many long-handicap players (my father was one) who on reaching a short hole automatically demanded an iron club—regardless of the fact that the hole measured, say, 180 yards and their best iron shot in thirty years never passed the 160 mark. Remember, too, that except in a high wind the spoon is a much safer club than a long iron, especially when played from a tee. The long iron represents one of the most difficult shots in the game, the spoon the easiest.

Which brings me to a second point—namely, that it is easier, with any club in the bag, to hit the ball from a tee than from the ground-level. I believe that that applies to the experts: I *know* it applies to the average golfer. This game is difficult enough without scorning anything calculated to make it easier, and to neglect the opportunity of teeing your ball at a short hole is a childish form of pride.

I do not suggest that one should tee it as high for an iron club as one normally tees it with a driver. I mean simply that it should be clear of the ground, high enough to rule out any difficulty of getting it into the air. Do not compromise by knocking the turf up, as a rugby footballer about to take a place kick: make no bones about it, and put the ball on a peg-tee. The idea that you may top the next shot with that club because the ball is no longer teed up is, I can assure you, nonsense.

CHAPTER XVII

THE PITCH

I AM taking this out of its turn because it represents the opposite extreme to the run-up, and it will be of material assistance in describing the pitch-and-run to be able to say that it lies midway between the two.

The pitch, as its name implies, is nearly all 'carry', its length of run ranging from 'minus something' when it is made to bounce backwards on a wet green, to a few yards when it pitches on the same green in midsummer. The shot is played almost exclusively with a mashie-niblick or niblick.

This stroke has a combination of backspin and side-spin—all of which sounds very complicated, but is, in fact, quite simple. The only way to impart true backspin is, as we have seen, to hit straight downwards through the ball, and not across. It is an action which requires a certain amount of force to make it effective—and force is a highly undesirable feature of the short game.

A certain amount of backspin is essential, but it can be achieved without any serious loss of touch if deliberately combined with a left-to-right spin. The result is that the ball, on pitching, screws away to the right.

A high cut-up shot with a niblick that carries the intervening hazard and drops lifeless on the green is one that will always bring gasps of admiration from the gallery. It is, however, though it seems a shame to reveal the fact, one of the easiest and most natural shots in the game. Of the millions of persons in this world who now play golf, a slicing movement must come naturally to 98 out of every 100: drawing the hands inwards across the body is their instinctive action. Here at last they may give free rein to their natural tendencies and slice away with a will.

The pitch is a shot that should be played with an open stance—a wide-open stance: indeed, it is possible to play the shot perfectly well with the body facing almost directly towards the hole. But here is a trap into which a great many people unwittingly fall, even when they have mastered the correct stance. They forget that the face of the club must face the hole—which is another way of saying that the clubhead must be laid open. What it comes to is this. You stand, roughly speaking, as if you were going to play an orthodox straightforward shot with a square stance right away to the left of the

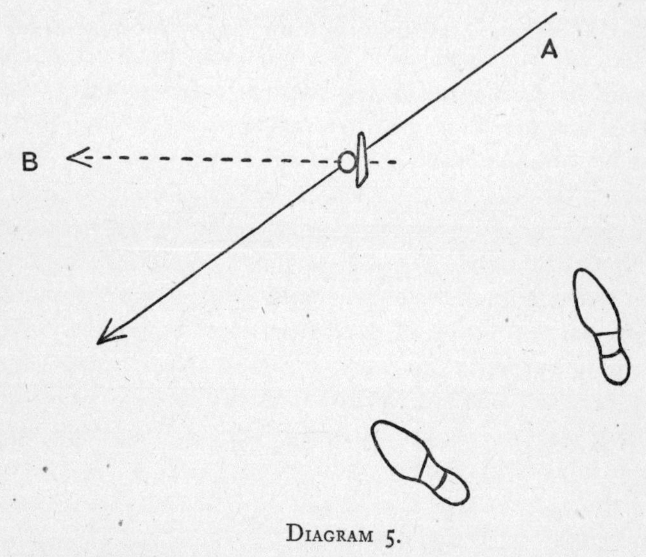

DIAGRAM 5.

This is the stroke R. A. Whitcombe is playing opposite page 193. The line to the hole is B. The stance and position of the ball are those for a perfectly orthodox pitch-and-run to the left of the green. So is the swing. The difference is that the clubface is *open*, *i.e.* pointing towards the hole. The club should be a mashie-niblick or niblick, whose loft will automatically ensure elevation of the shot.

green. You have the ball about midway between your feet. You then make the perfectly orthodox swing that you would have made had you really been playing the stroke in this left-handed direction. But since the face of the club is wide open and pointing in fact towards the hole, the shot becomes, *relative to the direction of the hole*, a cut-up slice.

Here is a vital warning with regard to the grip. It is through ignorance of the point, I think, that so many people find this shot difficult instead of supremely easy. Do not take up your grip with the club pointing squarely to the left and then deliberately turn over your hands in a clockwise direction, in order to open the face of the club and make it point towards the hole. By doing this you will get the left wrist well over on top of the shaft, and give yourself automatically that grip which is most calculated to produce the very opposite of what you are trying to achieve—namely, a hook. The thing to do is to take up the normal grip with the club facing squarely to the left and to keep your hands in the same position relative to the body, sliding the club round in your fingers, if you like, so as to open the face, and then taking hold of it again. That is to say, your grip is the orthodox one for playing a shot to the left, and the fact that the clubface is open is merely incidental: it is not that you have started with it square and then by a turning over of your wrists have opened it.

This impression of playing an orthodox shot to the left and leaving the open face to take care that the ball will actually be directed towards the hole, is a valuable asset, for the chief difficulty of the shot lies in the fact that people are so often tempted to make some thoroughly unusual and unnecessary deliberate movement to get the ball into the air and impart the required cut. Sometimes they dig into the ground in order to make sure of cutting underneath it, sometimes they top it, through an ill-considered effort to hit upwards. It is not until they understand the conception of playing a simple and straightforward shot in a left-handed direction, allowing the face of the club to take care of both the loft and the line, that they understand how easily it really can be done.

The ball should be addressed, incidentally, with the heel of the club, for its action during the time of impact will be to slide across the clubface. That, of course, is where the sidespin comes from. And the more of the clubface that the ball can slide across, the greater will be the spin that is imparted.

Trying to lift the ball of one's own accord without allowing the loft of the club to do the work is the cardinal sin in short pitches and, for this reason, it is perhaps well to emphasize that both in mental impression and actual execution the early follow-through should be low along the ground. The nearer the clubhead can be kept to the ground after striking the ball, the more easily it will be enabled to skid underneath it and cock it up in the air.

It is easy to see how much *finer* a stroke this is than the run-up and what a much smaller margin for error it offers. The perfect run-up is an artistic production and a thing of joy to watch, but an ill played run-up is still effective. With a high pitch, on the other hand, there is no such margin for error. It is an 'all-or-nothing' shot, and should be duly respected as such. For this reason, unless it happens to be a particular favourite of yours and you find that confidence and a laid-back niblick go hand in hand, never play a pitch where a run-up or a pitch-and-run will do. It is asking for trouble.

The Pitch-and-run

As I suggested a page or two ago, I can save us all a lot of trouble by describing the pitch-and-run as something of a cross between the other two. It is the maid-of-all-work of the short game. When in doubt—pitch and run. Broadly speaking, it can be played with any club that has a fair amount of loft and a straight sole. Anything with a rounded sole is barred, as being almost sure to put on a certain degree of backspin.

For myself, I favour a weapon designed by Ben Sayers and known as the 'Benny', which corresponds roughly to a No. 7 but has not the cumbersome depth of face that is a feature of that club in most of the modern matched sets.

The pitch-and-run is golf's dullest and most ordinary shot. The stance is square and close to the ball, the ball itself centrally placed between the two feet. A little wrist action—but not too much; a little body turn—but not too much. The clubface should open a little on the backswing, but there is not the same exaggerated roll of the wrists to impart the topspin characteristic of the run-up.

The one vital requirement of this shot is an assured knowledge of the exact nature of the ground on which it is going to pitch. Thick grass or a damp patch in front of the green can kill a shot stone dead, can give it, in fact, the same result as a pitch—the only difference being that it pitches in the wrong place. It is a lack of consideration of the ground in front of the green that leads one to be consistently short with one's approaches throughout the winter. A ball that pitches a foot past the edge of the green may run up to the hole, while another that pitches a foot short may stop dead in its tracks, three putts away.

Still, these are questions that every man must decide for himself in the light of bitter experience. It is as profitless for the author of a book to set them all down in detail, as it is for the reader to try to glean them all from his pages.

One final word of advice, however, I should like to offer, and that is—don't expect too much of yourself. Walter Hagen goes down to history as the greatest exponent of the dramatic art of turning three shots into two. Don't forget that each of these two shots played its part. He did not always lay the first of them stock, stone dead: he laid it within anything from a foot to 5 yards—and then holed the putt.

To put the ball within a few inches of the hole from 50 yards or more offers an exquisite satisfaction, but the man is not born who may hope to reach such a state of perfection that he can do it every time. My advice is to allow yourself a circle round the hole, within which you will be satisfied to see the ball stop. Some approaches are easy, others are difficult; the radius of your circle will vary accordingly. 'If I don't get this within four feet, I ought to be shot' you may feel on one occasion. 'Anything within five yards and I shall be happy' may be your legitimate thought on another. If you will only set yourself a reasonable standard and give yourself a fair latitude, you will arrive at the ensuing putt in a far more tranquil and contented state of mind than if you insist on regarding as a failure any shot that does not finish within a foot of the flag. And the more peaceful your attitude of mind the more likely you are to hole the putt.

The high pitch to the green is an unobtrusive but extremely important shot. By a high pitch I mean anything from 140 yards down to the range where the shot can reasonably be classified as a short approach. It may be played with an ordinary mashie, a spade mashie, a mashie-niblick, or even a niblick—or in modern parlance anything from a No. 6 to a No. 9. For most people it is a negative kind of shot, in the sense that they have much to lose and little to gain: they expect to put it on the green, but they do not play it with any deliberate intention, or even a great deal of hope, of putting it within the range of one putt.

Compston considers the straightforward mashie-niblick pitch to represent the easiest movement in the game, and finds it a matter of surprise that as a rule the average golfer is unable to play it successfully. Bobby Jones, on the other hand, always found it the weakest point in his armour. The No. 4 iron and the slightly bigger mashie-iron were his favourite clubs, and he preferred a full-blooded iron shot of 160 to 180 yards to a pitch of 100 or 120 yards. That is the reason, according to his own estimate, why he was always liable to perform better on a long course. During his two historic rounds of 68 and 66 at Sunningdale in 1926 it is significant that he had only to play three mashie shots in 36 holes.

The championship itself was held that year at St. Anne's, and here he was forced to play a mashie-niblick at the eighth and ninth holes. The ninth is a short hole of about 160 yards—and nearly cost him the championship. There was a strong following wind all through the week, and he was forced to take his mashie-niblick in every round in order to get the necessary stop on the ball. He found the green only once—and then took three putts! At the eighth, where the green is high up on a plateau, he evaded the issue each time by taking his mashie and playing a sort of scrambling pitch-and-run against the front slope of the plateau, happy enough to get fours where many of his rivals where snatching an occasional three.

All the same, I am inclined to fancy that Jones' inability to play this simple shot was highly exceptional. Most of the experts seem to find it supremely easy; perhaps the best exponent of all time being Walter Hagen. He was a great putter, it is true, but in praising his holing out, people were inclined to forget that the preceding shot had finished substantially nearer the flag than most of the others would have put it.

I believe at any rate that if the average golfer would only take the trouble to look into the matter, he would find that, although he might never be justified in terming any shot easy, this at least would become the easiest in the bag.

The pitch is a simple stroke because it cuts out a great deal of the body turn and the transference of the weight from one foot to the other that are so vital to the longer strokes. Almost every one of the experts, in writing of the shot, mentions the fact that the left heel can, and should, be kept almost on the ground from one end of the stroke to the other. The weight will probably shift a little, but it should never shift enough for there to be any danger of its getting out of control.

The club itself being shorter, the stance is correspondingly nearer the ball. Incidentally a good many people make insufficient allowance for this and are inclined to have to 'reach for it' with a mashie or mashie-niblick. Frankly I believe that it is almost impossible to stand too near the ball with these clubs.

At any rate, the natural result of a closer stance is that the swing becomes more upright, and therefore there is less necessity for the body to turn either at the hips or the shoulders.

The swing itself is a great deal shorter. Just as the movement with the bigger irons was shorter than the long, sweeping action with the driver, so is the swing with the mashie-niblick a miniature edition of the swing with the bigger irons. When properly played, it will lack many of the sensations experienced in the full shot with the wooden club. It adheres to the same fundamentals, but to the player gives the impression of being infinitely shorter, stronger, neater, and more crisp.

Very few people can gauge the exact length of their swing. They will show you where they think the club stops at the top, but make them play a shot, and they will find that in actual practice it goes a great deal farther. The mental impression of the correct length of the backswing for a pitch that is to travel, say, 120 to 140 yards is that the club should not pass a vertical position. In practice the ideal swing reaches a point about midway between vertical and horizontal. The thing to remember is that if you aim at this correct position, your club will almost certainly travel on as far as the horizontal —and that is much too far.

This shortness of swing has two advantages, each of which operates towards making the shot so much more simple. The first is that there is now no excuse for the most portly business-man golfer not to keep his left arm straight. It should be straight in the address and remain straight on the whole of the backswing, the whole of the downswing, and then for as long as possible after the ball is struck. The hands, as we have seen, move roughly speaking in a circle during the swing, and if the radius of that circle can be kept constant by means of a left arm whose 'length' does not change, the accuracy of the stroke must clearly be increased.

Secondly, there need be no danger, in this length of swing, of the club being taken so far back as to tempt you to release the grip with the last two fingers of the left hand. The thing is essentially a left-handed stroke—and for once the average golfer has no excuse for playing it as anything else.

The stance should undoubtedly be open, as well as nearer the ball, in order to make the follow-through more easy. This, like the backswing, is considerably curtailed—but none the less important for that. For myself, I find the follow-through almost to govern the direction of the shot. A preliminary imagining of it will also help you, I think, to set yourself up in a comfortable stance. If you will ask yourself at the beginning of the shot, 'Now can I, standing like this, follow through dead straight towards that hole?', you will find very often that the answer is, 'I am not so sure that I can'. You must then adjust the stance until the answer is a confident 'Yes'.

This is a shot that must essentially be played with backspin—and backspin, mark you, does not mean side-spin. Anyone can, voluntarily or otherwise, draw across the ball and give it a left-to-right spin. When done deliberately it is not to be despised as an aid towards imparting stop to the ball—at least it is to be preferred to its opposite number, the right-to-left spin, which, generally speaking, makes the ball run.

Plain straightforward backspin is imparted, speaking purely mechanically, by causing the face of the club to come into contact with the ball when moving in a downward direction. That is fairly plain sailing, but the snag is that the club must not also be moving in a sideways direction. Straight downwards is the rule, not downwards and across.

Thus it is more than ever essential to hit the ball first and the ground afterwards. No man can defy the laws of nature by hitting the ball a downward blow when his clubhead has already reached the bottom of its arc. Owing to the round-soled nature of the mashie-niblick and the resilience of the modern ball, most people find it necessary to take a healthy divot with this shot. It may look ungainly, but it is the right thing to do, so do not be perturbed by it. Take a look at the pictures of Lister Hartley playing this shot opposite page 128.

The divot, as a matter of fact, will serve another purpose besides ensuring that you hit down on the ball: it will tell you whether you are hitting straight through towards the hole. A club laid down on the ground pointing along the mark of the divot will often tell you a surprising tale.

One warning is necessary with regard to this stroke. It concerns the right elbow. Owing to the more directly upright nature of the swing, there is a great temptation to let the elbow stray away from the body and start pointing outwards or even upwards. The ideal position for this elbow is pointing directly downwards. If you experience any trouble in this direction, it is not a bad idea to put a handkerchief under your right arm and see that it remains there throughout the shot. Ultimately it should do so without any conscious pressing down

PERFECTION

as exhibited by Lister Hartley. He is standing well in front of the ball, so as to be able to strike it a downward blow without any adjustment during the swing. The left arm is straight and will remain so during the stroke. The club and the two arms are roughly in the same position as at the moment of impact.

AFTER IMPACT—

Both arms are still stretched and taut, the right hand just beginning to turn over the left. The weight is well on the left foot and the head has not moved. The whole position is one of power combined with balance and stability. A 'copybook' stroke.

Fox

Photos by Sport and General

THE HIGH PITCH

as executed by Bobby Jones (left) and Henry Cotton. Jones found it the weakest point in his armour. Compston, on the other hand, maintains that it represents the easiest movement in the game.

Note that Cotton, who is playing a slightly longer shot, keeps the face open from impact onwards, whereas the more orthodox Jones tends to close it.

Behind Cotton is the observation hut from which the author broadcast the first running commentary on golf.

of the right arm. Any straying of this elbow can lead to the most disastrous consequences, including, as I believe, the iniquitous 'socket' or 'shank'—though my own and the general ignorance of the subject is being reserved for a later chapter.

CHAPTER XVIII

THE SHORT GAME

As I see it, there are three basic shots in the short game, and three only. They may vary slightly within themselves—thus a cut-up shot with a mashie-niblick or niblick may simply be played with a definite shade of cut, or it may be played with sufficient to send the ball spinning at right angles when it pitches—but every shot still falls definitely into one of the three categories.

These are:—

The Run-up pure and simple, where the ball keeps close to the ground in flight and where its carry forms a comparatively small proportion of its total length.

The Pitch-and-run, where the carry is rather longer but the ball still bounces and runs forward on pitching.

The Pitch, which implies a more lofted trajectory in which practically all of the shot is carry, the ball coming to rest almost as soon as it drops.

The short game exemplifies the infinite variety of golf. One may go for days, perhaps even weeks, without playing two approaches that could truthfully be termed identical. The contours of the ground, the state of the turf, the size of the green, the position of the various hazards, and the actual lie of the ball all play their part in making one shot different, however slightly, from the next. But whatever the combination of circumstances, somehow or other with some club in the bag there is a

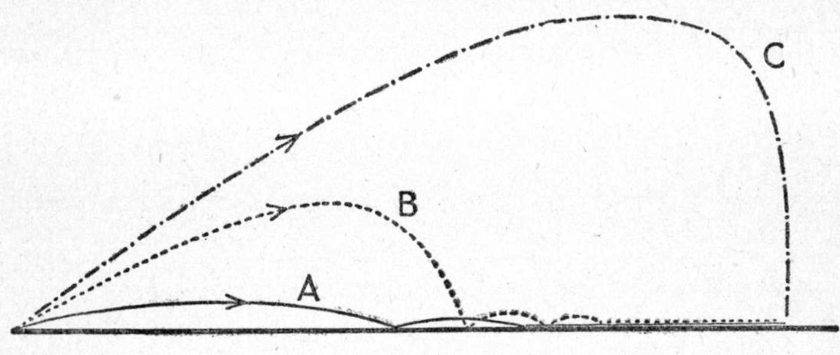

DIAGRAM 6.

Here are the three basic shots of the short game.

A is the run-up, where less than half of the shot is 'carry': the ball never rises more than 2 or 3 feet from the ground.

B is the straightforward pitch-and-run, roughly half of which is 'carry'.

C is the pitch. The ball comes to rest almost immediately upon reaching the ground, the amount of run depending on the surface of the green and the spin imparted to the ball.

means of getting the ball deliberately and legitimately close to the hole.

The first thing to be decided is 'Which of the three types of shot is going to give me the best chance of leaving this ball near the flag?'. Sometimes any one of the three will do; sometimes either of two; sometimes only one. When there is a doubt, your own particular preference may assist in guiding you to make your choice. You may find that one of these three strokes comes more easily and naturally to you than the other two, in which case you will be justified in playing it when another kind would have been a safer and more suitable alternative to other people.

The one that comes most easily to the average player is the compromise between the two extremes—the pitch-and-run. A straightforward orthodox kind of shot, it is, so to speak, a long iron in miniature.

Perhaps before we go into details of the execution of the three varieties of chip shots, it may be better to look into some of the principles that govern the playing of all of them.

The position of the feet varies with each, but is uniform in the sense that the two feet are much closer together than for longer and more powerful shots. The stance is at its widest for the drive and at its narrowest for the short chip at the other end of the scale. On the green it may become narrower still, but that, as we shall see, is a matter of individual preference. Some people have their feet as wide apart on the green as on the tee.

Secondly, one should, I am sure, stand a great deal closer to the ball. Development of power, which comes from a healthy body-turn and a broad sweeping swing, is not a matter for the least consideration in the short game: what is required is accuracy and a sense of touch. Standing well over the ball gives you a fine sense of control, that disappears directly you have any sensation of having to reach for it. You feel that, having 'got it where you want it', you can now begin to play tricks with it. On a good day you may even experience that exquisite feeling of having it on a string.

A close stance, moreover, leads naturally to an upright, as opposed to a flat, swing. In the little backswing that is necessary the club scarcely has time to leave its original plane of movement, a plane that leads it to and fro along the line pointing towards the hole.

Apart from these elementary considerations, the truth of which will probably be admitted unanimously by the experts, I have evolved, and advance with due humility, four golden rules for playing the short game. Most of them concern the mind as much as the body. They are as follows :—

I. Let the focal point of your concentration in every shot be your *hands and fingers.* You may argue that power comes from one thing, and direction comes from another; that a slice comes from this and a hook from that: but you cannot deny that all your sense of *touch* lies in your fingers. And in the short game this sense of touch is of paramount importance. That is not to say that your body remains fixed and rigid, or that it plays no part in the stroke. What I mean is that it must play no *constructive* part. It must play second fiddle to the hands and follow obediently and without resistance wherever they may lead it. In any case, they will not lead it far.

That advice sounds simple enough, yet it is sometimes terribly difficult to follow. Some people, I honestly believe, have gone through their entire golfing career without ever letting their hands take complete charge of a stroke, however small. Try an experiment and you may see what I am driving at. Take the club in your fingers delicately, as if it were a precious musical instrument, and consciously *feel* every inch of the grip where it comes into contact with your fingers. Moving it slowly and deliberately, careful to avoid any jerking movement strong enough to alter the pressure of any part of your grip, place the club behind the ball. Having done so, relax firstly the muscles in the small of your back and then the muscles in the back of your legs just above the knee (it will not be until you come to relax them that you will realize just how taut these muscles were). The action will give you a drooping sensation, but that does not matter in the least, for at the same time it will throw a pronounced emphasis on the feeling in your fingers and hands, a feeling which you may never perhaps have experienced before.

Swing the club gently, guiding and governing its whole action with your hands. Make sure that no part of the body offers the least resistance to anything that your hands may wish to do. The hips may wish to turn a little, the left heel to come up perhaps half an inch: if so, let them. But don't let them, in doing so, obtrude upon your consciousness. Keep your mind focused steadfastly on your fingers.

Now, as a further experiment, tighten up those muscles again and try a shot with your body taut and stiff. The result may enlighten you.

II. Swing the clubhead *really slowly*.

By this I don't mean simply 'Do not hurry the swing'—though that is a piece of advice that holds good for every shot in the game. An unusual slowness of delivery is valuable for two reasons. Firstly it aids this all-important sense of touch. If you will only move the club slowly enough, both going up and coming down, you will find that you will be able to sense the exact position of the clubhead at any point in the swing; you will feel almost as if there were no shaft separating your fingers and the face of the club.

Secondly, you will cause the ball to remain for a fraction of a second longer on the face of the club—and in these days that fraction of a second is going to save you more strokes than you know. The modern ball is so resilient that anything in the nature of a sharp blow sends it skidding away from the clubhead almost before the two have come into contact, certainly before the clubhead has time to transfer accurately to the ball the exact power and direction that you are trying to impart.

Anyone who has played with the old and far from resilient guttie will realize how much more accurate one can be with that type of ball. Being comparatively lifeless, it seems to hang on to the face of the clubhead long enough for one to hold it for a split second and literally fling it in the desired direction.

This illustrates a problem with which the manufacturers of golf balls are constantly faced. The public's estimation of the merits of a golf ball being based solely on the distance it can be hit, the manufacturers have wound the elastic tighter and tighter and made the cover thinner and thinner in their efforts to achieve length from the tee, the inevitable result being that the ball is now so lively that it is almost beyond the powers of mortal man to distinguish the minute difference in shots of, say, 20 and 22 yards. Those 6 feet may mean a difference of a stroke, and that stroke to a professional may be worth hundreds of pounds per foot. A fortune awaits the man who can make a ball travel another twenty yards from the tee without at the same time being so unduly responsive as to be uncontrollable in the short shots.

III. *Leave the club to do the work.* This applies

A STRAIGHTFORWARD PITCH-AND-RUN

The shot will have plenty of loft, but no backspin to prevent its running forwards on pitching. Both E. F. Storey (left) and A. J. Lacey have taken the orthodox close stance, with the left foot slightly behind the right. Notice, too, that each has taken a very short grip of the club, a method that helps to combine firmness with delicacy of touch in a shot where no great physical power is needed. There is very little body movement and both players give the impression of having played the shot with their *hands*

Fox

Sport and General

'Evening Standard'

ALL ALONG THE GROUND

Archie Compston shows the beginning and the end of the run-up shot. The clubface opens on the way back and is then completely closed by an exaggerated roll of the wrist, having met the ball with the face square at impact. An essential stroke for the seaside all the year round, and for inland courses when the ground is hard and there is not too much grass. A particularly safe shot in a wind.

particularly to the question of loft. Do not try to hit the ball deliberately along the ground or deliberately into the air: the control of its trajectory comes more from a choice of the appropriate club than by any specific movement of your own—though that is not to say, of course, that the swings used for all types of approach shots are the same.

Similarly, you will find it more satisfactory to regulate the length of the shot rather by the length of your backswing than by the strength of the blow. We are not concerned here, of course, with full shots with any club. In the short approaches that are the subject of the present discussion length is much more difficult to judge than direction. It is comparatively easy, for instance, from 40 yards to hit the ball within 6 feet of one side of the hole or the other: it is not half so easy to judge the distance of the stroke with the same accuracy.

Let me illustrate it this way. The ball can be hit the necessary 40 yards with a backswing of as little as 18 inches, provided you give it a sharp and energetic blow. Alternatively, you can take a full swing, as with a driver, and by keeping the action slow enough and limp enough, also manage to send the ball 40 yards. Somewhere between these two lies the ideal. Most people, perhaps in a desire to get the stroke over quickly, verge towards the former extreme. In other words, they try to do some of the work themselves, instead of leaving it to the club, which is perfectly able and prepared to do all of it. Personally, my own test in the matter is to see that the backswing is long enough to enable one to get the distance *without changing the pressure on one's fingers.*

Anything in the nature of a jerk, you will find, results

in a greater pressure on the right hand, particularly at the first movement of the downswing. And I am convinced that any such change of pressure deprives you of some of that sense of touch upon which the success of the shot depends.

IV. Be sure of having in advance a clear mental image of the *shape* of the stroke you want.

This implies deciding upon the exact spot on which you wish the ball to pitch. Don't just push the ball along towards the hole and hope that you have hit it with the requisite strength to make it stop somewhere near. It won't. It never does. Luck plays a decreasing part in golf as the length of the shot diminishes and the margin for error grows finer and finer—until, in putting, it is narrowed down to perhaps one inch on either side of the exact centre of the hole. The shorter the shot the more deliberate and carefully thought out your efforts must be.

Once you have decided on the shape of the shot—that is to say, to which of the three categories it is to belong—you will know in advance what will happen to it when it pitches; whether it may be expected to run or to pull up in a few feet. It seems to me advisable, therefore, to concentrate not on the hole, but on the spot where you wish the ball to pitch. It is easier, for instance, in a run-up shot of 40 yards, to visualize the stroke as a single low pitch of 15 or 20 yards than to visualize the whole stroke consisting of this pitch followed by a series of short bounces and a final movement all along the ground. Once the ball has pitched, there is nothing more that you can do to influence its course, so you may as well narrow down the issue by concentrating simply on its initial flight, which is the part you *can* control.

The first University match in which I played was held at Princes, Sandwich, where the greens are surrounded by all manner of minor undulations. Having duly missed the green with one's second, the third shot, as often as not, was a delicate approach over the little humps and hollows that lay between the ball and the flag. For the whole of one day, though I had but a vague impression of what I was doing, I scarcely failed to lay one dead. My caddie, taking complete charge of the situation, would walk forward, having handed out the requisite club, and indicate the exact spot on which the ball should pitch. Very often it was nowhere near the spot where I should have tried to pitch it had I been left to my own devices, but the man had not been carrying clubs at Sandwich for thirty years for nothing. I pitched the ball on the required spot—which, you will find, is a matter of surprising simplicity—and Nature and the caddie's good judgment took care of the rest.

Clubs for the Short Game

Steel shafts have been a great blessing to most of us. Frankly, if I take up a hickory-shafted driver, brassie, or spoon, I cannot hit my hat. The same remark applies to iron clubs down to the mashie—or, in modern parlance, the No. 5: but below that it is no longer true. I suspect that what we have gained from steel shafts in the long game we have unwittingly thrown away in the short.

Steel shafts are not alone to blame: the designers of clubheads and the material used are partly responsible. To the clubs with which the delicate work has to be done they fit heads the size and shape of frying-pans, made of hardened steel—great, cumbersome, glistening things that would make Hagen himself look ham-handed.

The modern ball, whose liveliness militates against accuracy in the short game, cannot apparently be changed, but our clubs still remain a matter of individual choice. With a large soup-plate head of hardened steel and a steel shaft, the ball leaps away at impact like a startled rabbit. All sense of touch comes via the fingers—and it is difficult with an implement of this kind to feel in the fingers any difference between a shot of, say, 25 yards and another of 28 yards. Indeed, it is difficult to feel anything at all. Yet success in the short game lies in the ability to detect the difference between these two little shots.

While I am the first to admit the benefits to be derived from a well-matched set of irons, I cannot believe that those benefits extend to the short game. I feel sure that every golfer would be well advised to equip himself with a mashie, mashie-niblick, niblick, and putter with hickory shafts and small compact heads. Having done so, I should advise him to go one step farther, and let them all go rusty.

The Run-up

The low run-up can be played equally well with a variety of clubs, though some people carry a special club for the purpose. A simple way of ensuring that the ball does not rise is to play the shot with a No. 2 iron, but this, to my mind, has two drawbacks: firstly that the shaft of the club is so long that if you stand, as you should stand, close up over the ball, the end of it will catch in your clothing. Secondly, it is extremely difficult to judge distance with so big and powerful a club: indeed, the difference in the impression conveyed to your fingers by shots of 30 yards and 40 yards is almost indistinguishable.

A number of people, among them Fred Robson, advise playing the shot with a No. 4 iron, but for myself I always find that this suffers the same disadvantages, though not, of course, in the same degree. The ordinary mashie, or No. 5, is perhaps the most generally satisfactory club.

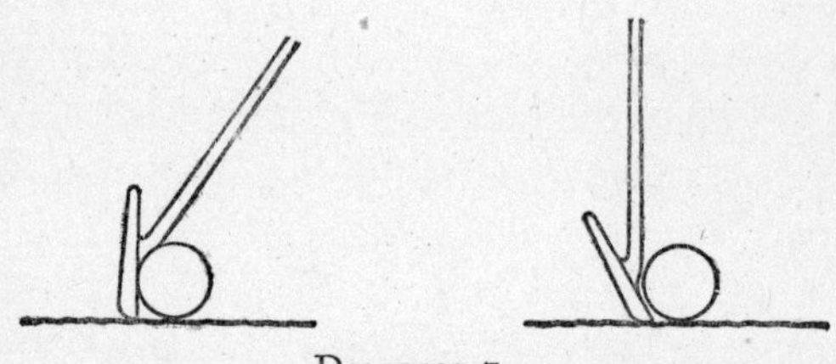

DIAGRAM 7.

Here is the same club—say, a mashie—held to the ball in two different ways. In the normal manner, on the right, it will impart normal loft. On the left it is shown 'turned over' on the ball for keeping it low in a run-up shot. The player must, of course, stand farther in front of the ball for this stroke.

Whatever club you may favour, the point to remember is that you must stand to the ball in such a manner as to counteract any loft the club may have. Thus by playing the ball from a position behind the right foot and keeping the hands right in front, you could cause a niblick to act as if it had the loft only of a No. 2. The fact is that the shot can be accomplished equally well with several clubs, and it is up to you, by experimenting, to discover with which one you find it easiest.

The backswing, as I have said, should be long enough to enable the clubhead to do most of the work. It should also be low as opposed to upright, since anything in the nature of a downward jab is liable to cock the ball up in the air with backspin, which is exactly the reverse of what you are trying to do.

What contributes more than anything else towards imparting the topspin that will send the ball scuttling along like a startled rabbit immediately after it pitches, is a good roll of the right wrist, starting just before the moment of impact.

On the whole, I think that everyone will find it wiser to play this shot without taking any turf at all. The ideal stroke is a perfectly clean blow with the sole of the club just grazing the grass, but if one is to err on one side or the other, it is better to top it than to dig for it. Contact with the turf, especially if unexpected, may lead to a complete fluff: a top, on the other hand, though the execution of the shot may leave much to be desired, will at least send the ball three-quarters of the way to the hole—and straight.

CHAPTER XIX

PUTTING

PUTTING may be a matter of inspiration, but at least it has its material aspects. The first to come under our notice is the putter itself. I suppose that since the early days of golf more than a thousand varieties of putter have been designed and 'perfected' by their proud inventors. Among all this hybrid collection only one was an outstanding success—the Schenectady, which carried Mr. Walter Travis to victory in the British

BOBBY JONES. A close, upright stance and an obviously right-handed action. Reverse overlap grip. The angle between forearms and the shaft of the club is unusual among great putters.

GENE SARAZEN. A smooth firm, decisive putter with no sign of body sway. Ordinary overlapping grip. The ball was opposite the left heel. Compare the follow-through with that of Hagen.

JOHNNY REVOLTA. Reputedly 'dead' from 15 feet. A close stance with the left foot well behind the right. He takes a very short backswing, even for long putts, and has a peculiar grip that is gaining favour in the United States. Note the right thumb pressing on the shaft.

EUSTACE STOREY. Freely quoted at one time as 'one of the world's six best putters'. A style of his own evolved after months of trial and error. The putter is short and extremely light. The eye, like Revolta's, is *outside* the line of the putt.

1, 2, and 4, *Bertram Eary* ; 3, '*Planet News*'

1, '*Sports Illustrated and The American Golfer*'; 2, *Sport and General*; 3 and 4, *Bertram Eary*

WALTER HAGEN. An incomparable holer-out. A wide, open stance with the weight well forward and the ball just inside the left heel. Note particularly the low follow-through, the club still almost grazing the ground and the face square to the hole.

ALFRED PADGHAM. This style won a fortune in 1936. An ordinary overlapping grip with the back of the left hand presented squarely to the hole. The hands and arms are well away from the body and the stroke resembles a short chip in miniature.

LAWSON LITTLE. A delicate touch despite his tremendous strength. His eye is directly over the ball and his forearms and club are in the same plane, in contrast to Jones. The grip is right-handed and closely resembles that of Revolta.

ARCHIE COMPSTON. Another giant with a delicate touch. Overlapping grip and a stance like that of Jones. His eye is directly over the ball and his movement, with the club keeping square to the hole and close to the ground, is notable for its smooth, unhurried rhythm.

amateur championship of 1904. So successful indeed was it that it has been banned in Great Britain ever since.

The Schenectady has the shaft coming down into the middle of the blade, thus giving the head of the club a heel and toe of almost equal proportions. In 1936 a variety of this club was having a great vogue in the United States, and I recall that one of my first impressions on arriving to watch the qualifying rounds of their amateur championship at Winged Foot was that almost a quarter of the competitors were using a club of this pattern. Gene Sarazen too, who has a superbly delicate touch on the green, brought one over for the British Open of that year, only to find that it was barred. It may be added, not only as a matter of interest but also to show that putting depends on the man and not the club, that he borrowed a forty-year-old brass-headed putter from Alan Graham and suffered no loss of skill. He had some metal attached between the shaft and the protruding heel of his original club to bring it within the regulations, but said it had lost its balance. The club is in my possession now, and I can certainly confirm the fact.

The Putter

It is abundantly clear that the putter which suits one man may not suit another, even though they may use substantially the same method. A certain amount of trial and error will have to be undergone before a man can choose the club which in the light of experience is going to prove best suited to his needs. Here are some of the questions that you must decide for yourself. It is impossible to lay down the law, so I content myself with offering a few pointers which may assist you in making your choice.

Steel or Aluminium? You will observe from the photographs that every one of the eight players who are shown happens to use a steel putter. That, however, is only a coincidence. It does not represent a fair proportion between advocates of the two types of club. Aluminium, by reason of its greater driving power, is useful on slow and heavy greens but, on the whole, experience and weight of numbers incline one to suggest that a surer touch and better all-round results can be obtained from steel.

Light or Heavy? It is a truism worth repeating that a light putter is useful for the fast and fiery greens of summer, whereas a heavy instrument will assist you to get up to the hole on inland and less-favoured courses in winter.

I have experimented in my time both with very heavy and very light putters, but, like the poet, ever more came out by the same door as in I went—in other words, returned to the conventional club of medium weight. Light putters I discarded because they encourage a quick, sharp swing which to me is one of the three cardinal sins of putting. The ultra-heavy type I abandoned because, although they are good for direction, they impair one's sense of judgment in regard to distance, especially on fast greens.

Short or Long? Again, I have experimented with both extremes, and am inclined to believe that the average putter is, if anything, too long. I do not suggest that one should crouch over the ball like a broody hen, but I do suggest that one should get as far down over it as is possible without cramping the movement. It should not be forgotten, however, that to take an inch or two inches off the shaft of the club reduces, in effect, the weight of the head.[1] A heavier head, for instance, is required to produce any given effect on a 30-inch shaft than on a 32-inch shaft. A short putter certainly gives a greater sense of control in short putts, but loses its advantage in the longer ones, which have to be hit substantially harder.

Steel or Hickory? Here the experts seem to be fairly evenly divided. For myself, I can only say that I have never yet found a steel-shafted putter that gave the same sense of touch as a club fitted with hickory. It is a fact that while the master players almost without exception use matched sets of steel-shafted irons, their putters are nearly always a club apart. Very often they are the only hickory-shafted club in the bag.

General. The *lie* of a putter is of vital importance. Putting is a matter of such precision in comparison with the rest of the game that it is essential for the sole of the club to be resting firmly and squarely on the ground, when you have taken up what you decide to be the easiest and most effective position. It seems to me to be vital that the eyes should be *directly over the intended line of run*—that is, in such a position that a coin dropped from the bridge of the nose would fall directly on the ball. That is a principle common to every stance, method, and grip in putting. This position demands a definitely *upright* lie.

The head of the club should, to my mind, be on the small side. One sees a great many clubs made these days with heads as long as a banana, and very elegant they look, with their glittering polished steel and their

[1] See Diagram relating to 'Grip' on page 28.

coloured shafts; but they flatter to deceive. They make you think that you have a greater margin of error from the centre before you begin hitting the ball with the heel or the toe, but in point of fact that is not true. Only the centre will do, however long the face may be.

Finally, I would recommend you to have practically no loft on the club. A number of people still use what is generally called a putting cleek, which has about as much loft as a No. 1 iron. That may help the confirmed stabber of putts, who is liable to hit the ball a downward blow and thus make it start its run with a small hop; but the way to stop stabbing is to straighten out the swing, not to buy a club that allows for it.

The Grip

Two grips are popular in putting: the ordinary overlapping and the reverse overlapping. The latter is not to be confused with the interlocking grip: it simply means that the club is clasped with all four fingers of the right hand and that the forefinger of the left hand rests on top of the little finger of the right hand, instead of *vice versa*. The reverse overlap is rather more popular in the United States, where it has had a tremendous vogue, than in this country. Bobby Jones uses it, and so does Macdonald Smith; Revolta, reputedly the world's best putter, uses a peculiar grip of his own invention, which appears, as you can see, to have something of the overlapping, reverse overlap, and interlocking combined. Padgham and Compston, on the other hand, are among the many celebrated players who see no advantage in making any substantial change of grip—and both of them have been as effective on the putting-green as anyone that Britain has produced since the war. So once again it seems to be a question of paying your money and taking your choice.

Nearly all the experts do agree, however, on one point—that the putt is largely a right-handed stroke. 'The only stroke in golf, bar the run-up, that is right-handed,' Compston calls it. The reverse overlap throws a tremendous emphasis, as soon as the club is grasped, upon the part that the right hand is going to play. My own experience of this grip is as follows. For some time I was an enthusiastic convert to it, but I have since abandoned it and returned to the ordinary overlapping method. The reason was that I developed a tendency for the right wrist to overtake the left completely, instead of hitting against it. The result was that the clubhead, immediately on hitting the ball, either remained square to the hole and followed a steeply upward curve, or, more often, turned sharply over to the left and hooked the ball away from the hole. One was as undesirable as the other.

On the other hand, the Americans are the best putters in the history of the game, and if they use the reverse overlap there must be something in it. The difference between the two methods is not so great that a temporary change from one to the other will do any harm to one's game, and since most people find one of the two, in their own case, definitely superior to the other, I suggest that no one should make up his mind until he has given each a fair trial.

A point which cannot be over-emphasized is that the position of the left hand is materially different from that which it takes in the longer shots in the rest of the game. For the longer shots two or even three knuckles of the left hand should be visible on the top of the club. In the putt there should be absolutely none. *Twist the left hand over to the left until the thumb is pointing down the shaft.* As a matter of fact, you will probably find this to be the limit of its natural turn and so, with any luck, you will have gone far towards ruling out the possibility of turning the clubface over to the left—the most fruitful source of the pulled putt. See Hagen, Sarazen, and Padgham.

You will find, too, I think, that it improves your sense of touch to point the right thumb directly down the shaft, instead of diagonally across it, as in the rest of the game. See Compston, Sarazen, Storey, and Revolta.

Stance

Here a glance at the photographs will save a great deal of verbal explanation. In this gallery of stars are the world's finest putters, yet how little they have in common! Some stand with their feet parallel and close together (Jones, Compston, and Revolta), one with his heels together and his toes sticking out (Padgham), one with one foot behind the other (Storey), others with their feet definitely apart (Lawson Little, Sarazen and Hagen). This much, however, you will notice—that none of them has the left foot in front of the right. In other words, they stand square or open—but never closed.

Another somewhat negative observation is that while some have the weight noticeably on the left foot and others appear to have it about equally divided, none (except the unorthodox Storey) has it on the right.

As a general rule, then, we may say that it does not matter a great deal how you stand, but that unless you have good reason to do otherwise, you would be well advised to stand with the feet fairly well apart, the right slightly in front of the left, and to throw the major portion of the weight on to the left.

Style and Method

Putters may be divided roughly into those who use their wrists and those who do not. The stiff-wristed

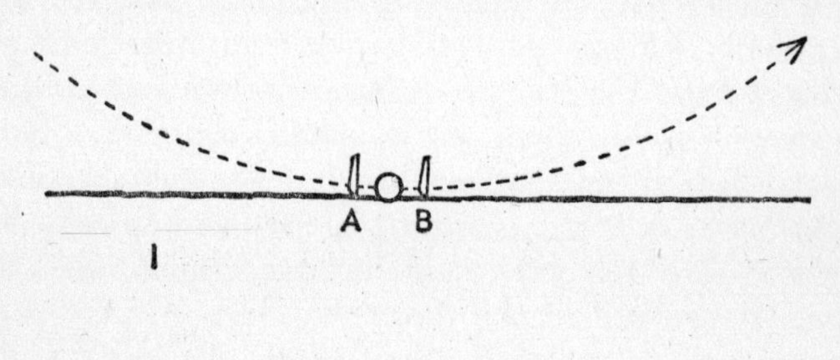

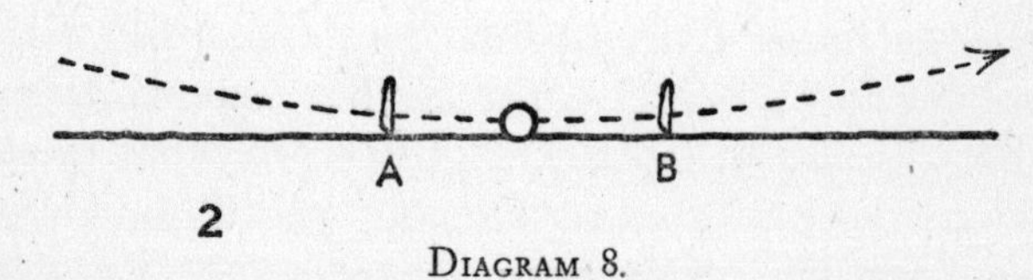

Diagram 8.

The fallacy of the 'Pendulum Theory'. If the path taken by the club is that of part of a circle, as described by a pendulum, the hitting area in which the clubface may come squarely to the ball (A to B) becomes very small—theoretically infinitesimal (1).

If the backswing and follow-through are extended low along the ground, this area is much increased and the margin available for error becomes accordingly greater (2). A clean, square blow will result if the ball is struck anywhere between A and B. Latitude is thus allowed for a sway of the body or an incorrect movement of the hands which may shift the whole arc of the swing bodily to left or right.

method is not popular among the experts, but for the average golfer it has one insuperable advantage—it encourages him to keep the blade of the club low along the ground.

We hear from time to time a lot of nonsense about the 'Pendulum Theory'. I have done my best not to be dogmatic in these pages, but I take the risk of dismissing this theory as nonsense, because I am so perfectly sure that it is. The pendulum of a clock makes an arc of a circle about a fixed centre—and I defy any man to do that with a putter. If the centre of the circle—*i.e.* the top of the shaft—is fixed, the head of the club must come up and away from the ball on the backswing, and up and away from the ball again on the follow-through. And no man has yet made movements like that and remained a good putter. I do not say that it is impossible to hit a hundred-per-cent. perfect putt in this manner, but I do say that it cannot be done time after time. If the path described by the clubhead is part of a circle, the margin for error in striking the ball becomes infinitesimal. At the other extreme, if the clubhead could be made to travel without leaving the ground at all, the margin for error would be infinite—in other words, the face of the club would stay vertical and square to the ball, in the ideal hitting position, at every point during the swing. Diagram 8 will show what I mean.

The only man, so far as I know, who has truly exploited the pendulum theory is Leo Diegel. He secured the 'fixed centre' by having a long club and anchoring the top of the shaft to his waistcoat—hence his peculiar stance. Compston relates how in desperation when he was suffering a particularly bad patch of putting at Lakeland, Florida, he borrowed the assistant's putter and, more for fun than anything else, adopted Diegel's method—and won the tournament. For the rest of us, I think we may render to Diegel that which was essentially Diegel's.

In the face of the overwhelming majority of the experts who use their wrists in putting, one cannot logically recommend the entirely stiff-wristed method: but I believe, all the same, that for those whose aspirations do not run unduly high, it *is* a very sound method. If it does not lead to perfection, at least it does not produce the desperate results that come from a wrist method that has fallen out of gear. A fine sense of direction can be had from keeping the wrists and arms locked and pushing the ball along, as it were, with the shoulders. It may not give you a sense of delicate artistry, but at least it produces the goods. Keep it in reserve and one day, when you have thoroughly lost touch with your putter, give it a trial.

A good many people find that it aids their sense of direction if they point their left elbow towards the hole: it seems to help them to keep the club running on a straight line. There is no need to have a pronounced bend at the elbow. The thing is more of a mental impression of pointing at the hole than a physical fact. Too pronounced a bend is liable, in my experience, to lock the left wrist: it allows the club to go back, but stops it on the follow-through almost immediately after impact with the ball. An exaggerated thrust with this elbow is worth remembering, however, as an antidote to hooking.

Personally, I am a supporter of the theory that, no matter what is your putting attitude, *the forearms and the shaft of the club should be in the same plane*; in other words, should appear, to a person standing at the hole and watching the player putt towards him, to be in one straight line. The picture of Little exemplifies this theory. If you were standing at the hole-side, his left arm would entirely obscure his right from your view and would form a continuous straight line with the shaft of his club. The fact that his elbow has a pronounced bend, it will be noticed, makes no difference to the question.

The angle between the plane of the forearms and that of the shaft is at its maximum with the driver, and gradually decreases as the club becomes shorter and the ball nearer to the player. With the putter, I fancy, it should disappear altogether. It is a theory to which a great many famous players, perhaps unconsciously, conform; but it is fair to add on the other side that Bobby Jones, who has a pronounced angle between the forearms and the club, seems to have got along perfectly well without it.

Some people like to anchor the left forearm to the left thigh, or alternatively the right forearm to the right thigh. It sounds good in theory, and certainly makes a rock-like foundation for the shot, which is missing when the arms are allowed to move freely to and fro—but it has its drawbacks. For a short putt that demands no great length of backswing, it may perhaps improve one's sense of direction, but with a backswing of more than a few inches, if either forearm is to remain completely stationary, there can be only one result—the head of the club must rise.

If only one could elongate one's forearms like elastic, so that the clubhead would go back and at the same time keep near to the ground, and yet the top of the forearms remain securely anchored in their original position, all would be well; but, being neither contortionists nor magicians, we have to submit to the laws of Nature.

Either we can keep the forearms still and take an almost vertical backswing, or we can keep the club low along the ground by allowing the hands and forearms to move.

In the ideal backswing the right arm can, as a matter of fact, remain almost stationary, provided that you will allow the left hand to move not only backwards but *downwards*. A lot of people have a peculiar horror of this movement, yet if they will watch the experts closely they will find that nearly all of them make it. The fact is that you cannot keep the clubhead low unless you do. Similarly, on the forward stroke, when your right hand and forearm begin to move, you will find that unless you allow the hand to move in what feels to be a downward direction as well as forwards, the head of the club will be cocked in the air.

Padgham, whose putting won him upwards of £2000 in 1936, holds his hands and arms deliberately well away from the body, but in this respect he is an exception to the rule. Most people like to use the body as a kind of guide-rail along which to groove the putt. Without in any sense anchoring either forearm, they like to retain contact by just brushing the hands or forearms along the trouser leg.

Three Universal Principles

In the long game no two men swing the club in precisely the same manner, but there are certain fundamental principles to which they all conform. So it is with putting. Here the differences in their individual methods are more striking, but the underlying principles rather less easy to detect. Personally, I divide them into three.

1. *Stand Still.* That sounds a trite and somewhat

obvious piece of advice. The reader is not, after all, likely to try to hit the ball on the run. But the fact remains that very few people understand what it means to stand absolutely motionless while they putt. They fail to realize that, although their feet may remain still, their bodies may sway like a reed in the wind.

Putting is a precise art. In a fairway that is 60 yards wide there is a 30 yards' margin for error on either side of the centre: the true margin for error, one might say, is even greater, for the worst of drives, unless it be out of bounds or the ball be lost, does not necessarily entail the loss of a stroke. A bad drive is a failure in itself, but need not imply failure for the hole.

The margin for error in a putt, on the other hand, is extremely small—not more than one inch on either side of the dead centre. Furthermore, when a putt is missed, the stroke has been lost for ever: the failure is definite and final. Nothing that follows can retrieve what has gone.

On a long approach putt a slight forward sway of the body is forgivable, but in a holing-out putt it signifies failure in ninety-nine cases out of a hundred. Sway—and you will look up too soon to see where the ball has gone. Stand still—and you will probably keep your eye on the ball. Nor is that the only virtue of standing still. All that matters in putting is that the middle of the ball should be struck squarely with the middle of the club—and if you sway, you will lose that vital precision of striking. The club will hit the ball slightly on its downward arc, or with the heel, or with the toe, or with the face slightly open or slightly shut. The whole thing will be thrown, scarcely noticeably, out of its groove.

It often happens, as anyone knows who has watched

a major golf tournament, that the spectator, craning his neck or peering beneath the legs of his fellow-watchers, is able to catch a vision of the player, but not of the hole at which he is aiming. On these occasions it is amusing to watch the man's left side. If in his anxiety he moves it, be it ever so slightly, towards the hole, in a moment a groan will arise and the untutored will cry 'Bad luck'; if he stands steady as a rock applause is a foregone conclusion.

Putting may well be compared with the act of firing a rifle. Every influence that man can exert upon the shot must be exerted at 'this' end: once the bullet has left the rifle no human power can influence its course. All that we are permitted to do is to give it a fair start in life, to dispatch it fairly on its errand: we must trust to the forces of nature to do the rest.

The reason why shooting is easier than putting (or so I have always found) is that in putting one can see the 'bullet', in shooting one cannot. Very often one cannot even see the target clearly enough to note the result of the shot. Thus there is less temptation towards that premature lifting of the head that is the bane of all putters, good and bad. *We are not so much trying to hit the bull's eye as trying to fire the rifle accurately:* all our thoughts are concentrated on *this* end. If only on the putting green we could confine our ambitions to making a correct movement with the head of the putter, realizing that this represents the maximum human contribution towards placing the ball in the hole, how much better off we should be!

2. *Swing Slowly.* Like the rest of the short game, successful putting depends entirely on a sense of touch

—and a sense of touch cannot operate in a quick swing. If you move the club slowly and gently, you have time to feel any possible errors, sometimes even to correct them while the club is on its way. You will find that you can make every inch of the swing a deliberate, conscious movement. As a putt increases in length, instead of hitting it harder take a slightly longer backswing and hit it as slowly and gently as before. In this way you will find that, so far as feeling in your fingers is concerned (and that is where your sense of touch comes from), you will have the impression that you are hitting every putt, long or short, with the same strength. You will in fact be able to standardize your putting stroke.

One of the best putters day in and day out in Britain is Archie Compston, who swings the club with a slowness of rhythm that is wholly delightful. His deliberate, unhurried action leaves one with the impression that he is aware to within an eighth of an inch of the exact position of the clubhead all the way through the stroke.

I shall always remember his exhibition in the final of the 1935 Roehampton Tournament. The greens are large and the holes were cut in a series of somewhat unlikely places, with the result that he had to negotiate a number of extraordinarily long and difficult approach putts. Every one of them found its way, after what seemed a lifetime of gentle rolling, to the side of the hole; but with such leisurely smoothness were they struck that it seemed to the spectators impossible that they should ever reach their destination. There arose each time a confused murmuring of voices saying, 'O-o-oh, he's short', but each time it gave way to an astonished applause as the ball, propelled as if by some invisible force, continued on its way to the cup. The uninitiated, lacking Compston's precision and timing of the ball, would have had to strike it twice as hard.

3. *Follow Through.* A protracted follow-through is an essential corollary of a slow putting swing. Indeed, it seems to me vital, in a movement in which accuracy of direction is of such overwhelming importance, that the follow-through should be longer than the back-swing. If you swing very slowly, and then make sure that the clubhead, having struck the ball, follows right along the line to the hole, you will not only reduce errors in direction to a minimum, but you will also experience the exquisite sensation, which may perhaps be new to you, of the ball seeming to hang for an appreciable time on the face of the putter. Then try the same method, deliberately checking the follow-through: I am sure that the difference will astonish you.

In connection with this exhortation to follow through perhaps I may mention a small tip that may assist the confirmed 'stabber'. When this first appeared in print, a gentleman to whom I was introduced, on learning that I was responsible, called at once for the waiter and presented me with a bottle of champagne. With tears of gratitude in his eyes he assured me that I had saved his life and his reason. Here, for what it is worth, is the magic formula.

Take a couple of peg-tees and set them up on the green about a foot apart; then retire to a distance of, say, four or five yards. From here, given a reasonably flat green, you will probably back yourself to run the ball between the two tees five times out of six—if not every time. As you perform this feat, you will notice that your one desire is to push the head of the putter right through towards your object, this being the perfectly natural manner of ensuring good direction. Your efforts will almost certainly be successful, and you will notice, furthermore, that you are never short—so long as your mind is directed towards running the ball between the tees, and not upon making it stop near them.

Having got into the habit of running it between the tees, place the tees three or four inches on each side of the hole and *without changing your mental attitude* continue as before, taking care to concentrate on the tees, and not on the hole. As a result you will find that your putts, if they do not actually drop, will touch the hole in passing; or, if they do not touch it in passing, will miss by a mere two inches. And that, from five yards, represents a very high standard of putting. For shorter distances the same rules apply: you simply place the tees correspondingly nearer together.

If you fancy yourself to be blessed with a strong command over your imagination, you may care to prolong the experiment to a further, slightly dangerous stage and, casting from the mind the original notion of running the ball *past* the object, to concentrate once again on the idea of *making it stop somewhere near*. You will be astonished that the rhythmical, flowing motion to which you were becoming accustomed could give place so suddenly to such an ill-timed, tentative prod.

CHAPTER XX

THE STYMIE

A QUESTION that might be entitled the Journalists' Hardy Annual is that of the stymie. On and on it goes, year after year, spurred into a new liveliness from time to time by tales of rebellion by golfing Associations in the United States.

That luck could not, indeed should not, be completely ruled out of the game, nobody denies. But the stymie has always seemed, even to its staunchest supporters, to represent a different species of luck from that which ordains that on one day our ball shall kick to the left on to the green and on another leap merrily to the right and lie unplayable in the heather. The stymie is a soulless, unexciting form of luck, the sort of luck that is accepted with a sullen impotent fury.

'The stymie must go!' represents an annual agitation—yet in Britain it is safe to forecast that the stymie never will go. It is all a question of that little Rule 6—'The ball shall be played wherever it lies . . .'—guiding the minds of our golfing legislators. The basic principle of the game is at stake, and despite all the revolutions that may take place on the other side of the Atlantic, St. Andrews will probably stand firm.

Logically the stymie should go. Golf is so essentially an individual game, and no small part of its charm lies in its being the only game where one is not directly influenced by the play of one's adversary. The stymie alone violates this rule.

Total abolition may never come in this country, but it should be mentioned that a kind of half-way stage may well be reached whereby, if the player's opponent lay him a stymie, the intervening ball may be moved, since the obstruction is no fault of the player; but if the player shall lay it himself, then he shall take the consequences of his own carelessness and play the balls as they lie. That is a solution that at least merits attention.

The supporters of the stymie are liable to allege that it is really a perfectly simple shot, just as easy as a putt, provided the player does not allow himself to be frightened by it, and that golfers, instead of grumbling, should go out and learn to play it as an orthodox shot.

That is a view with which I cannot concur. Lofting a stymie is essentially a difficult stroke, demanding a finer precision of striking and a more rigid control of nerve and muscle than any in the game, unless it be a delicate approach taken clean from loose sand in a bunker.

At any rate, whether we like it or not, we may as well become resigned to the presence of the stymie in our midst and learn to tackle it with what skill we may.

I imagine it to be literally true that out of a hundred failures to 'negotiate' a stymie, eighty at least are due to a mental rather than physical inability to make the shot. And as to the mental aspect of golf, a writer can only point out the pitfalls: he cannot effect a cure.

From the physical aspect the stymie is an extremely interesting little shot, the manner of playing it depending, of course, on the distance of the two balls from each other and from the hole.

If the intervening ball is more than, say, 5 yards from the hole, dismiss all question either of pitching over it or chipping round the side. You will not hole it once in two hundred times—and every now and again will take the equivalent of three putts. Take the putter, aim to miss the other ball by 6 inches (unless it is very close to your own, in which case you will command sufficient accuracy to miss it by less), and be satisfied to lay your ball dead, on the right or left of the hole. Two putts are what you would probably have taken in any case.

For shorter ranges—one cannot be arbitrary about such matters, but let us say from 5 to 15 feet—a 'screw' shot is often practicable instead of the more dangerous procedure of attempting to pitch over the other ball. It is a shot that should always be played with a left-to-right spin, for a slice is inherent to the golfer, and the motion of cutting across the ball, alas, comes as second nature to him.

The stroke is best played with the most lofted *straight-soled* club in the bag—probably a deep-faced mashie or some such weapon. If a shallow mashie with plenty of loft is available, so much the better. To take a niblick or mashie-niblick, with its rounded sole, is a snare and a delusion: they are dangerous clubs, both of them, and will 'fluff' before you can say Jack Robinson.

Play the shot as a tiny pitch-and-run, the only differences being that the backswing is noticeably outwards (to give the stroke a slicing movement) and that the ball is pinched or squeezed from the turf in order to impart the maximum screw.

And now for what we generally have in mind when we talk of the stymie—the putt that was regarded as almost dead before the other ball was found to be in the way. Here is the real poignancy, the true frustration, of the stymie. Here lies the real art of stymie play.

Before we go any farther, however, it is as well to record that a great many so-called stymies are not stymies at all, in that it is still possible to trickle the ball into the edge of the hole on one side or the other with an accurate and delicately judged putt. Where this is remotely possible, I believe that it will bring a greater measure of success than attempts to pitch over the intervening ball. Points to be remembered in playing such putts are: firstly that they demand a finer judgment of *distance*, since the ball must topple in, as it were, at its last gasp; and secondly that although only one inch of the hole may be available as a target, one need not always aim at this microscopic objective. More accurate results will come from aiming at the space immediately on one side of the other ball.

For the pitch shot itself some prefer a mashie-niblick, others a niblick. Mr. John Ball could doubtless have brought it off with a cleek. For the ordinary mortal immediate elevation is the keyword: get the ball up and get it up quickly. Personally, I recommend the niblick on account of its greater loft—it being equally easy to fluff with either club—or better still, if you have a well-balanced, not-too-heavy specimen, the blaster. With this, if you make sure of bumping the back edge of the sole on the ground behind the ball, it is virtually impossible to fluff.

The essence of success at this stroke with the niblick is *simplicity*—or cutting out the frills. And the best way to learn the ideal simple stroke is, as it happens, to practise an illegal one. It is generally agreed that the surest method of lofting a stymie is to play a kind of left-handed, back-handed scoop, standing by the hole-side and drawing the club sharply towards one's self.

Diagram 9 will save any further complicated explanation of this thoroughly illegitimate stroke. The face of the club never leaves the turf, the ball is bound to leap sharply into the air, and a fluff is actually impossible.

This shot reveals in a moment all the essentials of the desired legitimate stroke. Of these perhaps the most important is the low arc on which the clubhead travels: indeed, in the illegal stroke it is not an arc of a circle at all, but a straight line—namely, all along the

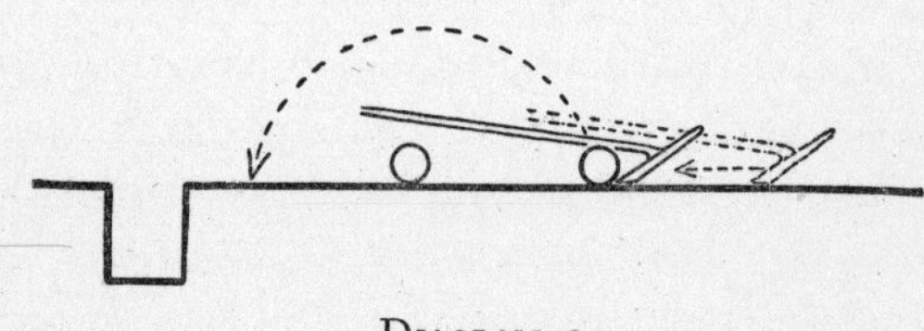

DIAGRAM 9.

The illegitimate, almost foolproof, stymie stroke. The player stands by the hole side and ' scoops ' the ball towards him, the club never leaving the ground. This method illustrates the ideal at which to aim in the legitimate stroke.

ground. In the proper two-handed shot this straight line is scarcely a practicable proposition, but it should be the player's aim to approach it as nearly as possible.

The diagrams on page 152, connected with putting, have a direct bearing on the stymie stroke. They show the extraordinary precision with which the ball must be hit if the wrists are allowed to cock the club up on the backswing and again on the follow-through, as compared with the liberal margin for error allowed when the head of the club travels parallel with the ground.

If the follow-through runs parallel with the ground, the loft of the club will produce its maximum result. The constant temptation, however, is to give the club a little help: to try, as it were, to scoop the ball up and throw it over the obstruction. The clubhead comes slightly up, the ball is hit with the sharp edge, and of course fails to rise sufficiently, if indeed it rises at all. When you hear a man complaining that he 'knocked the other fellow in', you may be sure that this is how it happened.

I think it will be found on experiment that the easiest way to ensure this low path for the clubhead is by cutting out the use of the wrists altogether. A stiff-wristed stroke is the thing, with the hands starting slightly in front of the ball and themselves also running parallel with the ground.

One word of warning is necessary before we finish with the stymie, and this concerns the mental side of the shot. It has always been my experience that *delay is fatal*. One or two practice swings are obviously called for, if only by the unusual nature of the stroke: these produce a sudden, but extremely transitory, access of confidence. While it lasts, step up to the ball—one, two, three, bang, and off she goes. Three or four seconds of brooding over the ball is alone sufficient to bring to mind the extreme difficulty of the stroke, the fact that you may knock the other ball in, that you may fluff, that you may 'top', that if you had only been up to the hole with your first putt this unfortunate situation would not have arisen, and that stymies in any case ought to be abolished for the general good of the game.

CHAPTER XXI

SOME FAULTS—AND THEIR POSSIBLE CURE

'To slice is human, to pull is divine,' the old saying goes. And how right that is! The slice is the average golfer's besetting sin: for every man who habitually hooks, there must be fifty who habitually slice. If the words that follow do anything to rescue those wanderers in the wilderness, the whole volume will have been worth while.

'How do you cure a slice?' people often ask. There is only one reply—'What sort of slice?', for there is no universal cure applicable to every shot that finishes on the right.

This much, however, we may safely say—and just as people in their anxiety to exploit the latest magic theory of golf sometimes forget the essential business of striking the ball, so do slicers in the agony of the moment forget this—that it is impossible to make any of the multitudinous forms of slice without drawing the club across the ball. That, at least, is common to all of them. The answer to 'Why did I slice?' is definitely and irrevocably, 'Because your clubface came across the ball'.

The manner in which the club is drawn across the ball determines the kind of slice; or, if you like, the kind of slice indicates the manner in which the club has been drawn across the ball. Glance at the Slice Diagram (10) on page 169, and I am sure you will see what I mean. In each case, you will notice the firm line travels to the left of the dotted line. Now, the firm line represents the actual path taken by the club; the dotted line shows the way the face of the club was pointing. So that, even

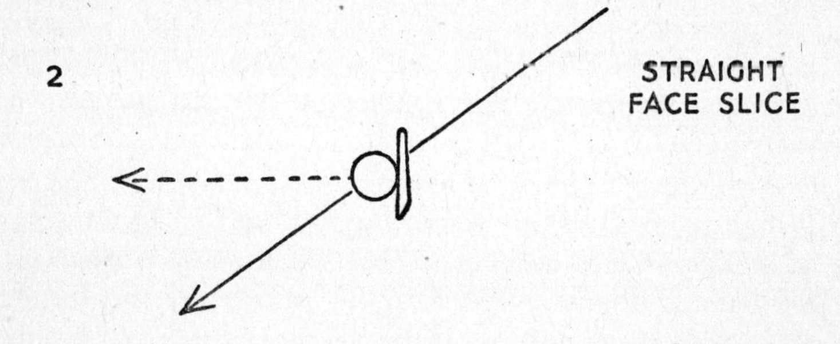

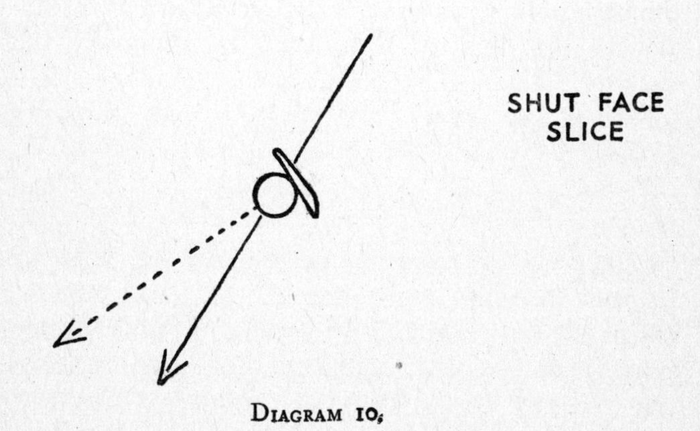

Diagram 10

though the club may, as in Figure 1, have travelled straight towards the hole, it has, *relative to the way the face was pointing*, been drawn across. Similarly, although in Figure 3 the face is already pointing to the left of the hole, the line actually taken by the clubhead is even more to the left, thus once again drawing across the ball.

Now, notice that the ball will always *start* its flight as near as no difference at right angles to the face of the club—*i.e.* in these pictures, along the dotted line. Then it fades away in a curve to the right, as the spin imparted by the drawing-across movement begins to operate. Directly you realize this, you will be able to narrow down your own variety of slice and eventually trace its origin.

If it starts to the right and then fades farther to the right, you *must* have had the face of the club open. (We are not nearly home yet, for there are many ways of opening the face of the club, but at least we have made a start.) Correspondingly, if the ball starts to the left, as most slices do, and then whistles off to the right, you must have come on to it with a shut face.

Here are some of the principal causes of the various types of slice :—

A. The Open-face Slice

This is rendered the more mysterious by the fact that you may all the time be conscious of hitting straight through towards the hole, or even hitting slightly from inside out; the point being that *relative to the way the clubface is pointing* this may still be equivalent to drawing across the ball. If you made the same set of movements with the face of the club exactly square at the moment of impact, all would be well. Slice Diagram (10), Figure 1.

The face of the club may have remained open for any of at least four reasons :—

1. In a correct stroke the face of the club starts square to the ball at the address and then by a natural movement gradually opens during the back-swing. Normally it is closed again by an instinctive roll of the wrists as the club speeds down towards the ball. Sometimes this rolling movement is not quite completed in time, with the result that the face is still slightly open at the moment of impact. The simplest cure is to make the roll of the wrists temporarily a conscious instead of instinctive action.
2. You may be making a perfectly good swing but be standing slightly too much in front of the ball. Thus at the moment of impact the club-face is still slightly open—for the simple reason that it has not yet reached the bottom of its arc, where it would have had time to become properly squared up to the ball again. Cure—obvious.
3. You may be committing one of the cardinal faults of golf—*snatching* at the top of the swing. This is what is meant by ' not giving the clubhead time ' ; what the professional means when he tells you to ' wait for it '. It is a movement that unfortunately comes naturally to almost every golfer and is extremely difficult to detect for oneself. The result of this premature snatching of the club from the top of the swing is that the hands remain in front of the clubhead and the latter never has time to catch them up. Thus at the moment of impact the face is still open, and it

does not become square to the line of flight until a foot or even 18 inches past the ball. The cure is to make sure of plenty of width in the swing and, as the professionals say, 'Wait for it'.

If you happen to possess a spare driver with a very whippy shaft—or limbershaft, as it is often called—a few rounds with this will work wonders in slowing down your swing and preventing your making a jerk at the top. The whippiness of the shaft so exaggerates any tendency for the hands to be too much in front at the moment of impact, as to make the whole swing ridiculous unless one 'waits for it' properly at the top.

4. Faulty grip. You may have a strained grip with the left hand too much under the shaft and the right hand too much over it. The true natural position would be reached by twisting both hands slightly to the right—in other words, opening the face of the club. While they are able to hold up the artificial position during the address, when the club is stationary, they tend to take up their more natural position when the club is in motion and delivering the blow—in other words, at the critical moment the face is open.

B. The Beginner's Loop

Who was responsible for styling this particular movement the 'beginner's loop' I do not know, but it is a splendid description of a series of actions that is carried out almost automatically by the beginner and frequently by the more experienced golfer. The trouble starts at the top of the swing. 'Most people can gather up the power alright in the backswing', as Compston puts it, 'but they don't know how to apply it. They *will* start the movement in the wrong place. Instead of starting with the left hip, which puts the weight where it should be—on the heel of the left foot—they start with the right hand and make a complete reverse movement with the weight falling forward on to the ball of the left foot.'

One of the chief canons of successful golf, we are rightly told, is 'hitting against the left side'. The trouble with the beginner's loop is that it leaves no left side to hit against. The body, having turned towards the right in the backswing, must naturally revolve in the opposite direction if it is to be facing the hole at the end of the stroke. The temptation is to let it start turning back to the left at the *top* of the swing, instead of doing so during the later stages of the stroke. Having stored up the power, one expends it recklessly in one fell swoop by this turning movement at the top of the swing. It is a not unnatural tendency, and comes, I think, largely from the fact that the average man's right hand is stronger than his left. He starts the downward movement with his right hand and right side, instead of with his left hand and left side, which would have brought him into the correct hitting position. Slice Diagram (10), Figures 2 and 3.

The cure is to hold the left hip up to the ball consciously for a longer period. Ensure that the club at the top of the swing is pointing towards the flag, or even towards the right of the green, and then make absolutely certain of bringing it down in the same plane of movement.

C. Aiming to the Right

Here is another subconscious tendency to which a great many golfers succumb. A shut stance somehow gives an impression of greater power than an open stance. But a shut stance is easily confused with what is really a normal stance aiming to the right. Personally I have to confess that no sooner do I begin to play well than I find myself gradually aiming farther and farther to the right. It is a tendency that can only be detected

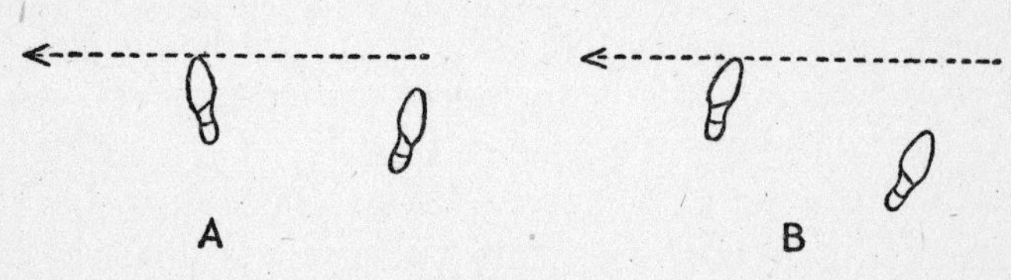

Diagram 11.

Here are two easily confused stances. A is the orthodox shut stance, B is one which often conveys the same mental impression, but is in fact nothing more or less than an orthodox stance aimed incorrectly to the right. If, in stance B, the clubhead travels directly towards the hole, the movement, *relative to the stance*, is that of a slice.

either by causing someone to stand directly behind you and see where you are aiming, or by having them take up your own stance and then standing behind them to see which way *they* are aiming. The result is often surprising in the extreme.

The trouble is that while one *aims*, perhaps unconsciously, to the right, one *hits* instinctively towards the hole. The correct shot from a stance that is facing towards the right is a straight ball finishing on the right of the objective: to move the club directly towards the hole is equivalent to drawing across the ball, relative to the correct line of flight. The shot is exemplified by Slice Diagram (10), Figure 1.

The cure, again, is obvious.

D. Standing Too Far from the Ball

If you stand too far from the ball, you may be able to do so with moderate comfort in a state of rest, but in a state of motion you will swing yourself off your balance. The momentum of the clubhead as it travels away from the body on the downward swing will tend to throw you forwards and off your balance. If you were content to fall flat on your face at the conclusion of the stroke, you could still get the centre of the club to the ball. In order to preserve your balance, however, you make an instinctive movement to shift the centre of gravity inwards—*i.e.* from the ball towards the body—and thus draw the clubface smartly across the ball. Figure 2.

E. No Body Turn

If any power is to be imparted in the stroke, the forward movement of the arms and the club must be accompanied by a turning movement of the hips. That sounds a little complicated and artificial, but it holds good for every game, and a moment's experiment will show it to be true. Imagine yourself, for instance, trying to hit the ball with the hips locked between two bars parallel with the line to the hole—that is to say, free to shift laterally to the right and left, but

MANY A FAULT

comes from a failure to ensure that the clubface is square to the hole at impact. Too late or too early a roll of the wrists will cause it to be open or shut. On the left is W. J. Cox, the clubface still open and the wrists just about to begin their turn. On the right Henry Cotton has completed the turn. Despite the tremendous power exerted in the delayed action of the right hand, his straight left arm has stood up to the strain and he still has a firm grip with the last two fingers of the left hand.

Fox

Bertram Eary

Sport and General

WHAT *HAVE* I DONE?

The handicap man takes a malicious satisfaction in finding the masters at fault. Here is Arthur Lacey caught in the act of perpetrating a stroke that every great golfer has made in his time. Note the firm grip, secure stance and smooth follow-through. It is fair to add, however, that Lacey won the 1937 Dunlop–Metropolitan tournament by a display of putting that remained consistently brilliant for 72 holes.

N

not free to rotate. It would prevent both the storing up and the delivery of power. Failure to turn the body on the backswing (and a free body turn, let us repeat, is described by Bobby Jones as the most important factor in his own golf) is a common fault among beginners. They rotate the hips to the left as they come down, this being, as we have seen, a natural movement in the application of power; but they have forgotten to turn them to the right as they go up. The result is a chronic slice and a hopeless lack of distance.

The obvious cure may be assisted, once again, by emphasizing the part played by the left hand and arm.

F. The 'Anxiety' Slice

Fear and over-eagerness are the principal ingredients of this one. It is not so much the habitual slice that lasts for a day or a week or a lifetime, but the slice that reserves its appearance for the moment when it is least desired—for the eighteenth tee in the monthly medal or the last few holes of the open championship, according to the calibre of the player.

It comes, as its name implies, from a desperate anxiety to know one's fate. Its physical components are a leaning forward of the body to steer the ball down the middle to safety and a premature lifting of the head to see where it has gone, each of which tends to draw the left side away from the scene of action and prevent a vigorous, full-blooded follow-through. The most difficult of all slices to cure, its remedy lies more in the mind than the body. An exaggerated turn on the backswing may help, and, once more, a determination to 'wait for it'. Easier to write than to perform.

Shanking

In his memorable address to the electors of Oxford in 1935 Mr. A. P. Herbert included the words:—

"*Agriculture.* I know nothing of agriculture." And that is about the extent of my knowledge of shanking.

I am not ashamed of such a confession. Indeed, I take a certain pride in my ignorance—not for its own sake, but in having had the courage to admit it. For this is more than some of the experts have done—and their ignorance is assuredly as profound as my own.

No one has yet been able to offer an intelligible, practical, and certain cure for golf's most ignominious shot, the socket. That it is caused by hitting the ball with the neck of the club we all know: but what makes us hit it with the neck of thc club?

Some people are born to a lifetime of shanking: others suffer only from occasional bouts. One friend of mine will not have the word mentioned in his presence; another was once faced with the alternative of abandoning the game or losing his reason. A lifelong victim of the socket, he found himself one day a few yards short of the eighteenth green, with four shots in hand to win the medal. He knew that he was doomed—and, surely enough, his course from that point onwards resembled the jagged edge of a cogwheel. He never finished the hole.

A curious quality of the socket is that it nearly always gives warning of its approach. Powerless as the day we were born, we stand there knowing that no amount of shuffling of the stance, no amount of changing of the swing will enable us to escape our fate. We know that in a moment or two, despite all our efforts to propel it forwards, the ball is going to fly, at the height of a man's knee, at right angles to the right. Sometimes we even contemplate aiming at the rough on the left and allowing for it.

Two causes of shanking are obvious and can be dismissed forthwith. You can shank from standing either too near the ball or too far from it. If you stand too near, you may make a perfectly orthodox, copybook shot which would have finished on the green had the ball been in its correct position an inch farther away from you. As it is, the neck of the club comes into contact with the ball, and the inevitable result is a shank. If you stand too far away, you may subconsciously overreach for it and once again hit it with the neck. The same fault with the bigger iron clubs is more liable to produce a slice than a shank, because the bigger momentum of the clubhead will throw you completely off your feet unless at the critical moment you draw in your hands to correct the balance.

Those are comparatively simple points; but the second is often overlooked by victims of the shank who say, logically enough, that the way to avoid hitting the ball with that part of the club which is nearest you is obviously to stand farther away.

Bobby Jones describes the cause of shanking as 'a failure to keep the left elbow close into the body when the ball is being struck'. This, he says, is in turn caused either by bending the arm too much at the top of the swing or by making the hitting stroke too much of a right-handed affair from start to finish—a view that is borne out by Compston when he says, 'I have never yet seen a shank that did not come from the right hand'. The remedy suggested by Jones is to try to brush the left trouser-leg with the left hand when you hit the ball.

Compston elaborates his statement that all shanks come from the right hand by saying that they are 'nearly always caused by a sort of outward movement by the right hand, just at the critical moment; that is to say, half-way down the downswing'. His cure is to eliminate the right hand and keep the action moving with the left, but he adds that it must be a *conscious* movement.

Though I am perfectly prepared to believe that this simple action may be the means of curing certain types of shank, I know from bitter experience that it does not cure them all. I remember teeing up seven balls in a row one day at Dunstable Downs and shanking six of them at right angles into a chalk-pit. With the aid of the local professional I discovered the cause to be too flat a swing—what the Americans describe as a 'round house' movement. But I was conscious at the time, I recall, of playing the shot almost entirely with the left hand.

George Duncan offers the theory that the shank generally comes from having the left wrist locked. 'The player gets this wrist bent', he says, 'and will not carry it boldly enough and far enough back. He gets his left wrist and also the clubface too much into the position which they should occupy in putting.' His cure is to 'shove the club from the left shoulder and get the blade of the club open'. A shank may also come, he adds, from the player having got his left heel off the ground and failing to bring it back to the ground by the time he hits the ball.

Harry Vardon, on the other hand, subscribes to Bobby Jones's theories with regard to the cure, if not the cause, of the shank. He suggests that players often imagine themselves farther away from the ball than is actually the case. 'The idea seizes them at the top of the swing, they reach forward directly they start to come down in order to make sure of getting to the ball, and the whole operation is ruined.' He thinks, with Jones, that the best cure is to determine that the left arm shall graze the coat both going up and coming down. If the left arm can be induced to caress the jacket all the way, the right arm cannot stray, and the action is correct.

There, for what they are worth, are the views of some of the experts. They may all be right or they may all be wrong. As I have admitted, I do not know. Perhaps, after all, the simplest cure for shanking is to address the ball in a normal manner with the exact centre of the club, take an orthodox swing—and *keep the weight on the heels*. Having paid your money, you are at liberty to take your choice.

Hooking

I am tempted, for the sake both of simplicity and the saving of trouble, to dismiss the reasons for the hook with the statement that they are the opposite to those for the slice. But I am afraid that, while those words are in principle true, there is rather more to it than that.

The comparison with the slice is worth carrying at least this far. Just as the answer to 'Why did I slice ?' was 'Because your clubface came across the ball', so the answer to 'Why did I hook ?' is 'Because somehow or other your clubface was pushed outwards across the ball'.

All the movements that cause a slice would, if reversed, cause a hook—but that is not to say that golfers habitually reverse them in actual play. It is a fact that nearly every golfing beginner can slice, but very few can hook. The movements leading to the slice come instinctively to most people, and they have in their early days to take special pains to guard against them. The hook, on the other hand, is not instinctive, but artificial, caused by movements made deliberately but wrongly.

Here are some of the main causes of hooking :—

A. The Shut-face Hook

Here we may repeat what was said of the Open-face Slice—that it is rendered the more mysterious by the fact that one may be conscious of hitting straight through towards the hole. Yet although the clubhead follows a true and direct line, the ball, because the face of the club has been shut, curves away to the left. Once again you may have made the correct set of movements: if only the clubface had been exactly square at the moment of impact, all would have been well. Diagram 12, Figure 6. (The 'Hook' Diagram on page 184 is the opposite to the Slice Diagram on page 169. In each case the firm line shows the path taken by the clubhead; the dotted line shows the way the clubface was pointing.)

The face of the club may have been shut for any of at least three reasons :—

1. You may have overdone the roll of the wrists as the club speeds down towards the ball (this is the precise opposite of the first reason for the Open-face Slice given on page 171). The easiest way to stop it is to cut down the action of the right hand and concentrate more on the left.

2. Faulty grip. This is the exact opposite of the

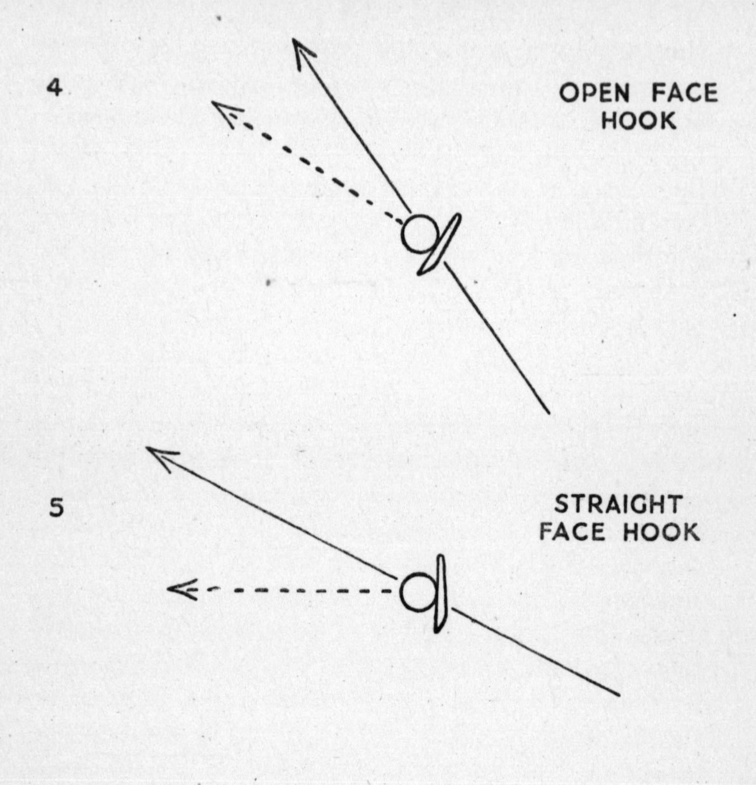

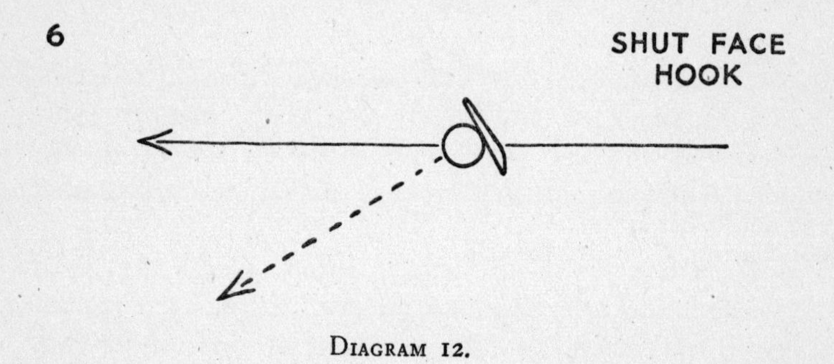

DIAGRAM 12.

slicer's grip mentioned on page 172. This time the left hand is turned over on top of the shaft, with three or even four knuckles visible, and the right hand is under it with the palm facing the sky. Once again the hands, if allowed to resume their natural, most comfortable position, would twist over to the left, thus shutting the face of the club. This natural position is the one to which they instinctively return as they deliver the blow.

3. Right elbow. Letting the right elbow stray away from the body and point horizontally behind you at the top of the swing is one of the commonest faults in golf—and it leads either to a hook or a slice. I include it here because in my experience it leads in four cases out of five to a hook. If you will take a club back with the right elbow held well in to the side, and then at the top of the swing shift the elbow upwards and outwards, you will see that it automatically shuts the face. That disposes of any possibility of a straight shot. Whether it develops into a slice or a hook depends simply on the direction taken by the clubhead—and this again depends largely on how much you have turned your body and whether or not you succumb to the Beginner's Loop at the top of the swing. If you hit straight through towards the hole, the shot will be a quick hook, conforming to Diagram 12, Figure 6; if you hit inwards from 'outside-to-in,' you will produce either a violent hook or a shut-face slice (Diagram 10, Figure 3), according to whether the path taken by the clubhead is outside or inside the line on which the face is pointing.

The most effective cure for this complaint, once you have detected it, is to put your handkerchief under your right arm before you address the ball and to complete the whole swing without dropping it. A feeling of keeping the two elbows always close together will also help.

B. Overdoing the 'Inside-Out' Theory

This conception of hitting from inside-out, which has been highly fashionable for many years and, like most other transient fashions in the golf-swing, came from the United States, has been a splendid corrective for the average man's inherent slice, but a good many people, having discovered the patent remedy for their ills, have taken an overdose. They have become so obsessed with the dread of drawing across the ball that they have ruined their game by going to the other extreme and pushing outwards across it instead. This shot is exemplified by Diagram 12, Figures 4 and 5. This, I think, is the most important cause of hooking in general, but there is nothing more to say about it than simply to warn people of its existence.

C. Standing too Near the Ball

This is extremely difficult to detect in comparison with its opposite number, standing too far from the ball, which causes a slice. Whereas the latter will advertise its presence by throwing you off your balance in the course of the shot, standing too near the ball leaves you with a comfortable sense of stability and security.

The momentum of the clubhead as it travels down towards the ball carries it temporarily away from the body and automatically stretches and straightens the arms. If you started too near the ball, the clubhead will probably be going outwards and across it at the moment of impact.

Topping

Less ignominious only than the ' shank ', the ' top ' is one of golf's most futile and humiliating strokes. Of all the shots that are topped in this world, I suppose 80 per cent. come from not looking at the ball—or lifting the head. Some people like to say that you weren't looking at the ball because you lifted your head, others that you lifted your head because you weren't looking at the ball. Frankly, I think you can lift your head without taking your eye off the ball—but I do not think that, humanly speaking, you can take your eye off the ball without lifting your head. But it does not matter. The result is the same in either case.

Here are some of the causes of topping.

A. Eye Off the Ball

Judging from my own fairly extensive experience, there are two main reasons why one fails to look at the ball, or lifts the head—call it what you will.

1. Flinching. Shutting the eyes at the moment of impact seems a stupid thing to do. Yet the best of us do it at times.
2. Looking to see where the ball has gone before it has left the club. Anxiety, again, is the root cause of this very human failing, but this time it reveals itself in a different form. Instead of fearing to see where the ball has gone, one is anxious to know one's fate

before ever the shot has been made. The head and eyes turn leftwards, the body comes round and upwards in sympathy. The arc of the swing is raised, perhaps only by half an inch, and the ball is hit with the sole.

The cure for both these faults is to rivet on the ball the attention not only of the eyes but of the mind; not only to *look* at it but to *think* of it. A man I know thought he had discovered the secret the other day. On every tee he placed the ball with the manufacturer's name directly facing him, his idea being that during the shot he would concentrate on reading the name. The scheme failed, and soon he was topping them again. 'The trouble is', he explained, 'that I'm such a —— quick reader!'

No. There is no patent cure for this form of topping. The answer, as I may have remarked before, to 'What do I do to stop lifting my head?' is just '*Don't* lift your head'.

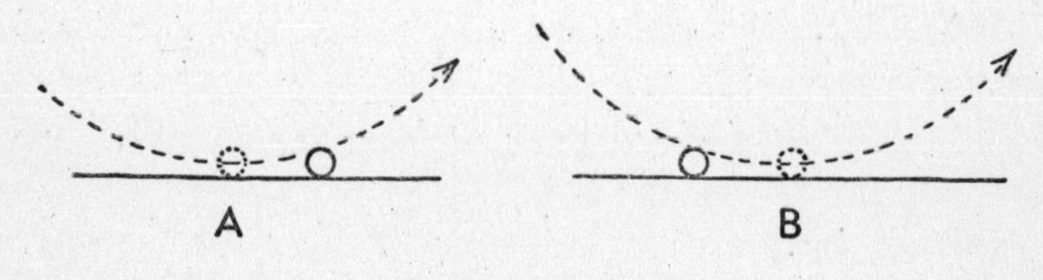

DIAGRAM 13.

B. SWAYING

Perhaps this is best explained by Diagram 13 above. If you get your weight too far back and fail to get it forward in time, you may complete the swing correctly in every other aspect but still top the ball, for the simple reason that you have shifted the lowest point in the swing's arc a few inches backwards. By the time it comes to the ball, the club is just in the upward curve. (Figure A.)

Alternatively, if you throw the weight too far forward, the club will strike the upper half of the ball before it has time to complete its downward journey. (Figure B.)

In the first case the ball will never leave the carpet; in the second it will probably, unless the ground is very soft, give a convulsive leap in the air and then scuttle away with tremendous topspin.

C. Trying to Loft the Ball

A frequent cause of a topped shot, especially into a cross hazard in front of one's face, is the mistaken notion that one must hit *upwards* in order to raise the ball. Hitting upwards merely means that the club strikes the ball as illustrated in Figure A. The way to make sure of getting it up is to take a more lofted club and hit *down and through*.

Digging

Not so frequent a fault as its opposite number—topping—but none the less aggravating for that. It comes generally from a determination to 'get under it at all costs', and I venture to suggest that its origin is inevitably the right hand and right shoulder. The rot sets in at the top of the backswing, which is started by the right hand and shoulder and follows a steep, almost vertical, course down to the ball.

A substantial divot is taken, and the resistance of the

ground, as the club bores into it, eventually overcomes the strength available in the hands and arms.

The way to cure this fault is to make sure of getting plenty of width in the swing on both the upward and downward journeys. Try to get the impression that, as you take the club back and again as you bring it down, you are trying to hit someone standing well away to your right. Then when the ball has been struck try to secure a similarly broad arc with the follow-through.

'EXAMINATION CHART'

Having run through perhaps 10 per cent. of the faults that can beset a golfer, I append, for what it may be worth, a kind of self-examination chart, which I hope you may find useful. It is designed not so much as a cure for specific golfing diseases like topping, socketing, or slicing, but as something to fall back upon when everything seems to go wrong at once.

It does not profess to cover the causes of every golfing ailment, though among the questions will be found an indirect cure for most of them. When your game reaches so low an ebb that it begins to get on your mind, you may find it useful to put yourself through this voluntary inquisition. Start at Question 1, and stop as soon as your conscience forbids your giving the correct answer. Failure to be able to answer any one of these nine points is alone sufficient to explain your troubles. If, for instance you cannot truthfully reply, 'Yes, I really was!' to Question 1, there is no object in proceeding to No. 2, for your game will show no improvement until honour is satisfied regarding Question 1.

1. Were you really looking at the ball at the *moment of impact*?

2. Did you *finish the shot—i.e.* were you in absolute equilibrium at the end of it? Or had you lost your balance and moved your feet from their original position?

3. Where were you aiming? (The safest way of finding out is to get somebody to stand behind you and see.)

4. In what position was the ball during the address? (Roughly speaking, it should have been opposite the left heel, and not so far away that you could not reach it comfortably with the centre of the club.)

5. Did you *snatch*? In other words, did you give the clubhead time to do its work, or did you snatch it down directly it reached the top of the swing?

6. Had you a firm grasp of the club with the last two fingers of the left hand at the top of the swing?

7. What were you thinking about during the stroke? Were you honestly giving your whole attention to the shot?

8. Was there any real *rhythm* in your swing?

9. When you started the club back, did you push it well away from the ball with your left hand, or did you jerk it upwards with your right?

CHAPTER XXII

RECOVERING FROM TROUBLE

So infinitely various are the hazards in which the errant golfer may place his ball that to offer advice as to the best

A QUICK RISE

by Alfred Padgham (left) and a not-so-quick rise by Fred Robson. Playing bunker shots is a matter largely of how far behind the ball to hit the sand. Padgham, in order to clear the steep little bank in front of him, has played a miniature 'blast', hitting well downwards and some distance behind the ball.

Robson, not requiring the same elevation, has cut a shallower trough through the sand, playing the shot more as a normal pitch-and-run. Note the calm and deliberate way in which he has played it.

Bertram Eary

Sport and General

Fox

AN ALMOST VERTICAL RECOVERY

by Reginald Whitcombe. Opening the face of the club, he has cut completely under the ball. The club has travelled along the line A but the clubface has all the time been pointing in the direction of B. Had he kept the face square, the ball would have hit the camera.

means of extracting it from each one of them would be a superhuman task. The solution in most cases must be left to the experience and intelligence of the player.

As a general principle one might offer the time-honoured maxim 'Don't attempt too much'—but what is the use of that? Golfers will always attempt too much: it is not in the human nature to do otherwise.

Nevertheless it is true that a great many of them attempt not only too much but even the impossible. They take their brassie where the acknowledged masters of the game would be content with a lofted iron, and their iron where the masters would be wielding a mashie-niblick. The trouble is, though, that the constitutionally foolhardy people who do these things are *ipso facto* unlikely to benefit by any advice they may read in this or any other book.

Some people can never distinguish the occasions when an element of risk is worth while. Supposing you are in the rough, lying moderately well: if a hundred-per-cent. shot with a brassie will reach the green, it is worth trying the brassie—provided you are assured that the club will, if the worst comes to the worst, at least get you far enough to be sure of reaching the green next time. But to take a brassie when even the perfect stroke will not reach the green is the action of an idiot (if a class of idiocy to which we all from time to time subscribe). Play safe with an iron—and save trouble, temper, and perhaps a couple of strokes.

Sometimes the position of the ball is so bad that the most blindly optimistic golfer has no alternative but to take his niblick—but here again his enthusiasm gets the better of him. He decides to 'play out safe', but instead of playing directly sideways on to the fairway, he takes a diagonal route—half forward, half sideways. The ball carries far enough to have reached the fairway had he taken the direct route, but not far enough to clear the few extra yards of rough which he has set himself the unnecessary task of carrying. It drops once again in the heather ; the next is a hot-headed 'top'—and the hole is lost.

Those are but a couple of what might be an inexhaustible supply of examples of a lack of strategy that can only be remedied by experience. We need not prolong the agony by going farther into the subject.

On the other hand, it may be instructive to offer a few practical hints for extricating the ball from long grass, heather, and such like.

Stand with the feet fairly close together—the natural impulse is to adopt a more straddling attitude, giving a sense of ferocious power. Take a sharply upright swing—the narrow stance will encourage this—and then bring the club back steeply downwards behind the ball. Don't try to loft it : let the loft of the club and the descending blow take care of that.

The upright swing, by the way, has a double purpose. Not only does it in the normal manner encourage the ball to rise, but it also enables the clubhead, both on the backswing and the return journey, to avoid too much contact with the heather, or whatever it may be.

Finally, a more than usually firm grip is called for at the moment of impact to withstand the increased resistance—but a violent grip throughout the stroke will destroy the power and rhythm of the blow and reduce the action of the wrists at the top of the swing (try this and see). A conscious change in the pressure of the grip during a shot is generally undesirable, but in this instance it seems to be worth while. My advice is to take a light grip of the club in the early stages so as to ensure plenty of freedom in your wrists, and then to tighten it consciously at the moment of impact.

As to the follow-through, it seems to me to be a wise plan to try to follow through, to be determined to follow through—but not to be in the least perturbed if in the end you don't. You cannot make a club pass through a gorse-bush—but the shot will be the better if your preliminary mental impression of it included its doing so.

Another observation that may be worth while is that the shallower the blade of the club and the smaller the head, the greater will be your chance of success. An ideal club for recovery shots is the old-fashioned jigger, whose shallow face enables it to squeeze under the ball where its modern counterpart, the No. 3 iron, might not loft it at all.

Bunker Shots

Here I must confess to being in something of a quandary. It is the object of both the writers and publishers that this series of volumes should have some lasting value; in fact, should not ' date '. No chapter on bunker play would be complete without a description of the nature and uses of that invaluable weapon known variously as the blaster, iron man, sand wedge, sand iron, and so forth. It is a a club that for the expert has brought bunker work to as fine and delicate an art as that of the normal short game, and for the handicap man can improve his general standard of skill by at least 100 per cent. But the blaster, at the moment of writing, lies under a cloud. Its enemies say that it destroys the essential artistry of the game, that it provides the golfer with the opportunity of buying a ready-made shot from the professional's shop. In either the near or distant future it might be banned and the reader find himself spending fruitless energy in reading of a non-existent club.

That is a risk that cannot be avoided now, but as a matter of fact an inquiry into those features of the blaster that were responsible for its sudden and universal popularity many bring with it a better understanding of the principles of bunker shots played in the old-fashioned manner with the orthodox niblick.

The difference between the two clubs may be appreci-

DIAGRAM 14.

ated by a glance at Diagram 14. The ordinary niblick rests on a sharp edge, ready to dig into the ground at the least opportunity. The blaster, on the other hand, has a broad, flat sole, of which it rests on the back edge, the front edge being perhaps a quarter of an inch in the air when the club is laid on a flat, smooth surface. The result is that although the front edge is low enough to nip underneath the ball and give effect to the maximum loft of the club, it is at the same time unable to dig deeply into the ground. It skids underneath the ball instead.

A short shot with the ordinary niblick either from grass or from sand demands an exact precision of striking—that is what makes the niblick the most dangerous club in the bag. Nothing but the best will do. Half an inch too high and the ball is topped: half an inch too low and the shot is a fluff. The blaster becomes an almost fool-proof club by reason of the fact that it eliminates one of these two extremes. You can top the ball perfectly easily with a blaster and very nearly cut it in half, though the extra weight in the head will mitigate against this—but it is very difficult indeed, if not impossible, to go too far underneath it, the reason being that the broad sole of the club and the absence of any sharp cutting edge simply refuse to permit it to dig into the ground. And while it requires a delicate touch to make sure at the same time both of not half-topping the ball and of not delving too far underneath it, it is a comparatively simple matter, even for the novice, to make sure of not doing *either one or the other*. The blaster gives no margin for error above the ball, but an almost infinite margin below it. In other words, make sure of not topping the ball and the thing is a certainty.

In almost every recovery shot from sand the same rules apply as for the short pitch—an open stance, an open clubface, and a slicing movement of the club. Look at the picture of Reginald Whitcombe opposite page 193, and you will see these three principles carried to the extreme. What complicates the situation is the variable resistance afforded by the sand, a resistance that one is prevented by the Rules from testing with the clubhead as one addresses the ball. Whereas the state of turf can easily be appreciated and remains fairly constant, the consistency of sand varies in wet weather and dry, between one course and another, often between different bunkers on the same course.

The difficulties of the golf game are physical and mental. In bunker play both are substantially increased. The sand on which the ball lies and the obstacle over which it is to be lofted constitute the physical factor; nervous apprehension and a sense of aggravation lingering on from the last shot provide the mental.

When a ball is lying cleanly on flat, firm sand and the intervening bank of the bunker is low, the shot can, and should, be played as a perfectly straightforward pitch-and-run. It is wise to take a club one grade more lofted than that which you would have taken from grass, but to avoid, if possible, anything with a rounded sole.

If the lie of the ball leads you to believe that a straight-soled club may not give you sufficient loft, then take the mashie-niblick, but hold the face up square to the hole and play the shot as a firm, deliberate jab.

Apart from this the shot can be played in identically the same manner as the pitch-and-run from grass, though you will probably find it advisable to pay a little extra attention towards ensuring a firm grip at the moment of impact. Any shot from sand is liable to be a nervous, half-hearted effort, due to a concentration more on the possible consequences of the stroke than on its actual execution. A firm grip and an aggressive determination to see the thing through will bring better results than any conscious change of technique.

Opportunities to play a recovery in this manner are comparatively rare. In most cases the circumstances will demand the niblick or, if you are still permitted, the blaster. Here I think we may simplify what could easily develop into a rather intricate and tortuous discussion by boiling the whole matter down to a single question. That question is 'How much sand is to be taken?'.

Distance is regulated not so much by the length of the swing or the strength of the blow, as by *the exact position at which the clubhead strikes the sand behind the ball.* To try to take the ball clean from the sand with a niblick is a foolhardy proceeding, and for every stroke it saves it will probably lose half a dozen. Generally speaking, the club should strike the sand anything from half an inch to six inches behind the ball. Archie Compston well describes the mental impression of the shot when he says, 'Hit down behind the ball with the heel of the left hand. Keep the face open, take a full swing, and explode everything into the sand behind the ball—one inch, two inches behind according to the texture of the sand.'

For this reason it is as well, I am sure, not to look at the ball, but to rivet your attention on the exact spot at which you intend the club to enter the sand. It reduces the difficulty of the stroke enormously if you can only envisage yourself not as hitting the ball, but as knocking a trough through the sand. Leave the ball to take care of itself—your clubface in any case will probably never come into actual contact with it—and concentrate on displacing the exact quantity of sand which you have decided to be necessary.

It would be a waste of time on both sides if we were to go into elaborate details of the exact amount of sand required for each and every class of shot—to try, as it were, to draw up a table of the distance and elevation to be expected in each kind of sand and from each position behind the ball at which the club can enter it. Those are matters which can only be decided by your own sense of judgment—and that sense of judgment can only be gained by experience. What matters is an acceptance and understanding of the principle of aiming at the sand and not the ball.

Broadly speaking, of course, the farther you hit behind

the ball and the steeper the blow, the sharper will be the elevation and the smaller the length of the shot.

When a ball lies right under the face of a bunker, a full-blooded ' blast ', with the club coming down as much as six inches behind the ball, is the only shot: at the other extreme when the ball lies in the back of the bunker but on sand that is not firm enough to permit an ordinary pitch-and-run, you may only need to take as little as half an inch of sand with a niblick.

One or two general observations come to mind. Firstly, I would stress the importance of the advice offered in connection with the short game: to take a slow and deliberate backswing, long enough to enable you to play the shot *without any change in the pressure on your fingers*. Loosening the grip at the moment of impact is certainly a major fault in bunker play, but the way to prevent it is not by a positive action in tightening the grip, but by a negative determination simply of not letting it slacken.

In the second place, anyone with any experience of the game will agree that bunker shots are largely a matter of confidence. One day they are easy and you find yourself hoping to get down in one putt; on another you are grateful to find yourself near enough to have a chance of getting down in two. Confidence, of course, is largely a state of mind: it cannot be summoned at will at a given moment. But you can at least increase it, give it a little encouragement, by forming a clear mental picture of the shot you intend to play before you descend into the bunker to play it. In other words, *do your thinking outside the bunker*. Every detail of the shot can be decided in advance except the question of how much sand you wish to take. That is all that need be decided when you are actually standing in the bunker.

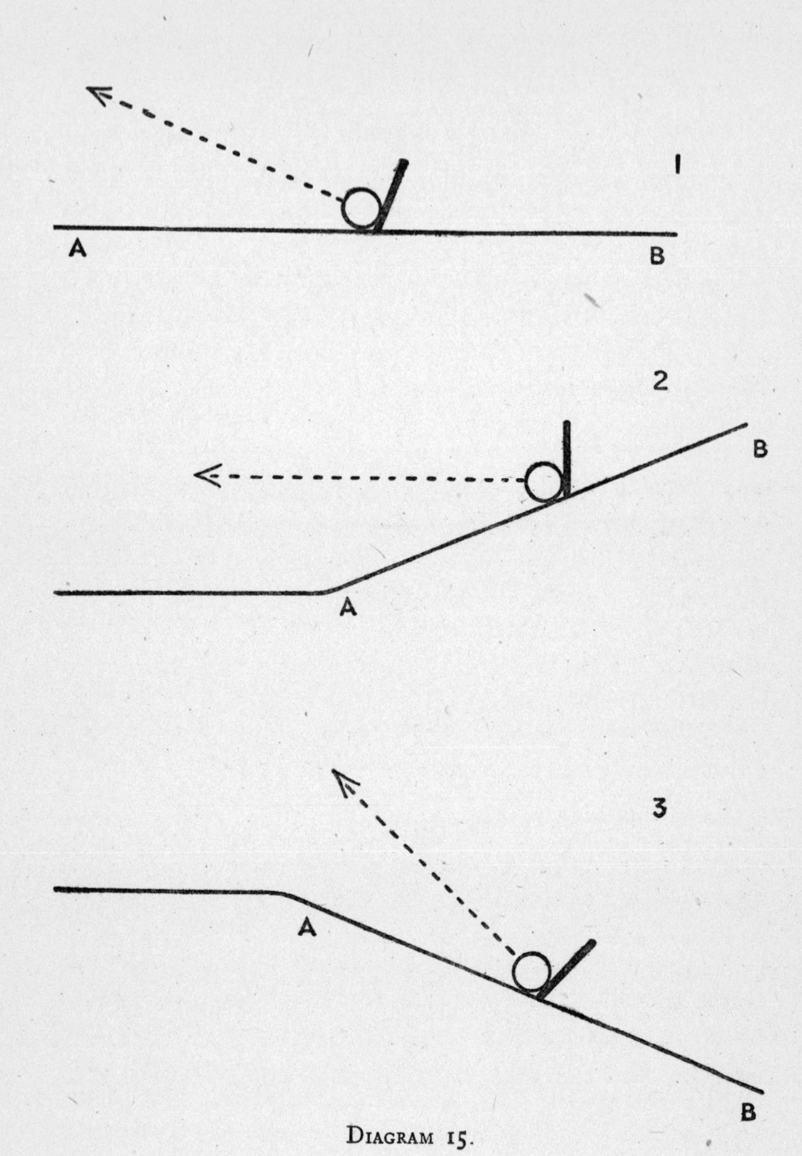

Diagram 15.

Sloping Stances

Uneven stances trouble the average golfer a great deal more than they need—principally because he does not bother to analyse the elementary mathematical principles involved. These are shown in Diagram 15. In each case the loft of the club, *relative to the ground on which the ball is lying*, is the same. The slopes are, of course, exaggerated.

If you find it difficult to raise the ball from a hanging lie, as shown in Diagram 15, Figure 2, bear in mind these two points. Firstly, you must take a club with greater loft than that of the one you would have taken for the same shot on a flat surface. The downhill slope, as the dotted line shows, may to a large extent nullify the loft of the normal club—may turn a No. 4 iron into what is, *relative to the horizontal*, a No. 2.

Secondly, having taken the more lofted club, you must line up the arc of your swing to the slope on which the ball is lying; not, as usual, to the horizontal. In other words, try to make your club perform its usual movements *relative to the actual ground.*

Just as in a flat stroke the clubhead moves, roughly speaking, along the line B to A, so on a slope it should follow this same line B to A.

This movement is fairly simple on the upward slope, but a special conscious effort must be made to make it work on a 'hanging' slope. In order to assume that the club may continue downwards—*i.e.* along the ground —after hitting the ball, it is as well to throw a lot of the weight forward on to the left foot and stand rather more in front of the ball.

With the other type of hanging lie—that is, with the

ball lower than the level of the two feet—the natural tendency is to slice, since it is almost impossible to hit from inside to out. The downward momentum of the clubhead tends to upset the balance forwards and the instinctive movement is a drawing-in of the hands and arms to preserve equilibrium.

To combat this, stand a great deal nearer to the ball—you may even have a sensation of standing right on top of it. Stand so near to it that you are able to throw the weight back on the heels and to feel that you can keep it there throughout the stroke and yet still reach the ball without stretching for it. Take a rather more lofted club (a spoon, for instance, instead of a brassie) and allow for a slight slice.

The opposite kind of stance, with the ball above the level of the feet, tends to produce opposite results and demands an identically opposite treatment. Stand a little farther away from the ball, lean forwards—and expect a shade of draw.

CHAPTER XXIII

GOLF IN THE WIND

A HIGH wind is the ultimate test of the golfer. It brings out the best and the worst in his game. Perhaps that is why the average man's feeling, when he stands on the first tee with a good brisk breeze blowing, is that of the small boy who has come into class with his lesson unprepared. Nemesis is at hand.

To be brutally frank, let us admit that the week-end golfer with a double-figure handicap will never master the game in a wind (though a still, small voice suggests that he won't master it *without* a wind either); but that is no reason why the wind should, as it so often does, destroy his pleasure in the game. It should increase, not lessen, his fun; for it doubles the satisfaction of success and gives a valid excuse for failure. But he must alter his technique, however humble, to suit the occasion. The game becomes a question of strategy: it is the canny player who scores when the wind begins to blow.

The first principle of playing golf in the wind is to *swing slowly*. The natural instinct, when your balance is insecure, is to get the thing over and done with as quickly as possible before the wind has time to blow you off your feet. An irresistible but fatal temptation—for the wind can blow you off your feet in a substantially shorter time than you can make a golf swing, even if you go through the motions as quickly as George Duncan.

Compare the situation with that in which you have filled your glass too full and are trying to raise it from the bar without spilling the contents. You lift it slowly, carefully, *consciously*. Any jerk will be fatal, so you allow yourself the extra time necessary to give unbroken, deliberate attention to the question of balance. But what happens when your nerve fails you and you make that last desperate, convulsive dash towards the mouth? You may be quick, but the liquid is quicker.

Balance is always a vital consideration in the golf swing, but it becomes more important than ever when the forces of nature, as well as your own efforts to hit the ball, are conspiring to throw you over. On a calm day balance may in time become instinctive: in a wind it will always require a conscious effort. And a certain amount of extra time must be allowed in the swing for this conscious effort to be applied.

It might be possible in a strong wind to perform precisely the same movements that one makes on a normal day, but I doubt whether it is worth the effort. Frankly I think it better to bow before superior force; to admit that the wind is going to affect the performance of the swing, and make the necessary allowances for it. You may recall Æsop's fable of the Reed and the Oak Tree.

Head Wind

Here the golfer's obvious difficulty is in keeping the ball *down*, for the higher it goes the greater is the effect of the wind. A ball that goes too high in a head wind, however well hit, will always begin to 'rocket', falling at the end lifeless and perpendicular, perhaps even travelling backwards towards the striker.

For shots from the tee the advantages of a deep-faced driver have already been mentioned, but I should like just to emphasize them in passing. With this club the ball must naturally be teed high; but it is one of the apparent paradoxes of the game that, whatever depth of face your driver may have, in order to hit the ball with a low trajectory you must tee it comparatively high. To tee it lower than usual and then to keep it down by means of half topping it is a natural but unsuccessful policy. The idea is to tee it higher and hit it cleanly, with a wider, flatter movement of the club.

Acting on the principle of bowing to superior force, it is advisable to throw a bigger proportion of the weight on to the left foot, since the action of a head wind is always working towards shifting the centre of gravity backwards. A little too much weight on the right foot —and before you know where you are, the whole foundation of the shot has gone.

A good many people advise having the ball rather farther back when playing against a head wind, but for myself I am inclined to think it an unwise policy. If he begins to stand slightly more in front of the ball, the average golfer will tend to hit downwards on it, and thus accomplish exactly the reverse of his intention. Personally I am against changing the position of the ball.

The temptation to 'press' is the downfall of most people in a head wind. With nature doing its best to send the ball backwards, one may be forgiven for thinking that one has to hit it just that little bit harder in order to propel it forwards. And hitting harder, of course, means swinging more quickly. It needn't—but it always does. And so I venture to recommend this cast-iron rule—'Decide on the club with which you can reach the green—and then take the next bigger one'. The knowledge of being able to reach the target perfectly easily is a wonderful incentive towards swinging the club with a slow and easy rhythm.

They will tell you that no wind has ever touched a perfectly hit stroke. That may be true—indeed, I believe it is—but who among us hits the ball as perfectly as that? If only we had a reasonable chance of making a perfect shot, we need never bother to make allowance for any of the four winds of heaven. In that state of imperfection that is the highest to which most of us are called, we are compelled to do so.

Thus against a head wind the same distance may be covered by any one of perhaps three clubs. A high cut-up No. 2 iron, a straight No. 3, or a low, running No. 4 played with a little draw, may all travel the same distance. Circumstances, such as the presence of a bunker in front of the green, may compel you to take the biggest club and try to play the high cut-up shot, but normally the safest policy is to play not the one that looks nicest, but the one that you personally find easiest. If you have a tendency to slice—and you probably have—don't defy providence by attempting the low runner, for remember that the wind will always accentuate a golfer's faults. Say rather, ' Nothing is going to prevent my slicing this one. Hand me the No. 2 iron '. If on the other hand you are prone to the quick hook, you will probably have more chance of bringing the shot off successfully with a low, boring No. 4.

An exhilarating stroke that is rapidly dying out of the game and is now reserved for the experts is the old-fashioned push shot, played generally with the cleek or No. 1 iron. It involves standing well in front of the ball and hitting firmly down on it, but at the same time not allowing the club to dig into the turf. Only the faintest margin of error lies between perfect execution and a complete smothering of the ball. When it come off it is a joy to the eye of player and spectator alike; but it is, I am afraid, beyond the compass of most of us.

Following Wind

With a following wind the difficulty is not to keep the ball down, but to raise it sufficiently into the air. Length is achieved largely by height: once the ball is well in the air, the wind as much as the original force of the stroke may be relied upon to carry it along. For this reason a sharper, harder blow with a smaller club is indicated. As a general rule it may be said that a flat swing tends to keep the ball down, an upright swing to elevate it. So with a following wind one can safely make the swing almost vertically upright, ensuring that the club comes down on the ball in a steeply descending curve.

It is advisable to hold the weight rather farther back on the right foot, but without forgetting that in the end it must, as usual, be transferred almost wholly to the left. The forward motion of the swing, combined with the action of the wind behind, leaves very little to hit against and makes a forward sway almost inevitable. For myself I am inclined to admit the sway, and instead of trying to prevent it, simply to make allowance for it by putting the ball a good deal farther forward. For a tee shot I find, if the wind is particularly strong, that a position actually outside the left foot does not carry the principle too far, provided of course that the ball is well teed up. Notice that a following wind blows you in the *correct* direction, *i.e.* forward on to the left foot. A head wind blows you in the *wrong* direction. That is why changing the position of the ball and allowing for a sway is sound policy in the one case, but not in the other.

To put any degree of stop on a ball that is being carried along by a strong wind is difficult in the extreme, and no one need be discouraged by his inability to do it. Occasions when there is no room to pitch in front of the green, or at any rate on the short edge of it some distance in front of the flag, are fortunately rare. When there is nothing else for it but to carry some intervening hazard and stop as quickly as possible on the other side, all you can do is to take the smallest club that can make the distance and to make sure of hitting the ball a firm, descending blow with an exaggerated snap of the wrists.

Side Winds

The side winds play havoc with the average man's game. They drive him to distraction, sometimes even prevent his appearing on the course at all. Giving the whole thing up as a bad job, he stays indoors when the wind blows. Yet he should not despair, for lack of strategy rather than lack of skill is the root of his trouble.

It is a subject on which I have had many arguments with Compston. He says that every man should try to play the wind at its own game and learn to control the ball whatever the conditions. I disagree. Though I believe that most people might, if only they had the time, learn to control their ball reasonably well in a high wind, I believe that the task is too formidable for the 80 per cent. who play only at week-ends.

The fact that a man cannot make his ball play tricks to order does not mean that he cannot derive a great deal of fun from playing in a wind. Indeed, many people believe that the ultimate joy is not to be extracted from golf unless there is at least a strong breeze blowing.

Personally, having the commonplace natural tendency to slice, I find a right-to-left wind a definite asset. It is, as Bobby Jones says, a kind of cushion to hit against. I find, for instance, that one can hit the ball just that little bit harder, can put into the shot the extra vigour that usually results in a slice, and at the same time have the satisfaction of watching the wind hold the ball straight on its line. The natural hooker will welcome with equally open arms the left-to-right wind—which to most of us is a nightmare.

A right-to-left wind adds length to a draw, but it also

adds danger: a cut-up shot, on the other hand—I hesitate to call it a slice—will travel less far, but what it loses in length it will make up in accuracy.

The driver, brassie, and longer irons, provided the entrance to the green is reasonably wide, are the only clubs which may be played with a deliberate draw in a right-hand wind: the spoon, together with all the shorter approaches to the green, should, I am sure, be played with a high trajectory and a left-to-right spin to hold them on their course.

With the 'slice' wind it is perfectly logical to suggest that the position with each club should simply be reversed. So it should—if you can manage to reverse it. But how many of us, with a wind blowing us forwards on to the ball, can impart to it that right-to-left spin that is going to hold it up into the wind? Two per cent.? I doubt it. At any rate, it falls to the lot of the other 98 per cent. to make the best of a bad job. This, I agree with Compston, is an admission of defeat—but then, when you think of it, so is a handicap of anything worse than scratch.

I am a great believer *in making the wind an ally instead of an enemy*. If it wants to carry the ball away to the right, let it—but don't forget to aim correspondingly to the left. It is far easier for most of us to aim to the left of the green, do our best to hit the ball straight, and then with a malicious satisfaction watch it fade away towards the flag, than to aim straight for the flag and then hope that some intermediate miracle will prevent its fading into the bunker on the right.

All the same, though we may admit ourselves defeated by the left-hand wind, there are still certain modifications to be made in the swing and stance. This left-hand wind is tending to blow you forwards on to the ball, and any reaching for it results inevitably in a worse slice than ever. You reach out towards the ball, the wind blows, and the only way you can keep your balance is by drawing back the hands and arms, and, if not too late, the body. In actual practice you probably do all of these and still fall forwards. With a 'slice' wind, therefore, it is essential to stand really close to the ball, so that you can throw the weight back on the heels and yet at the same time hit through the ball and outwards (otherwise 'from inside out') without toppling over.

Conversely, with the wind blowing in your face as you stand to address the ball, you can stand rather farther away and reach for it, confident that as you lean forward towards it the wind will act as a sort of buttress to maintain your balance. This ability to make a long, sweeping swing without overbalancing is, of course, the reason why one can hit the ball both farther and more accurately in a right-hand wind than in a left.

The Short Game in a Wind

A great many people end their golfing career without ever grasping, or perhaps even suspecting, the existence of the one golden rule for playing the short game in any sort of wind—that is, to *keep the ball down*.

To observe this elementary principle is not a matter so much of skill in execution as skill in choosing the right club. People who have the good fortune to learn their golf at the seaside instinctively learn the wisdom of keeping the ball as near to the ground as possible, not only because they have more practice of playing in a wind, but also because the nature of the ground makes the run-up shot feasible in all weathers.

The man who is brought up to inland golf, on the other hand, learns to play the high pitch to the exclusion of the run-up, which he regards as a curious, hybrid, almost unfair type of shot. He calls it a ' scuffle ', and likes to feel, when he plays it successfully, that he has taken a rather cunning advantage of his opponent.

In a high wind this low ' scuffle ' is the most satisfactory shot for any distance up to 80 yards. For the shorter distances it is best played with a fairly lofted club, something in the nature of a mashie. Stand right in front of the ball, thus nullifying the loft on the club,[1] grasp the club firmly at the bottom of the grip, and give the ball a sharp, determined prod. See that you do not take too upright a backswing and that the club does not ' jab ' too steeply into the ground, and all will be well. Not a very pretty shot, perhaps, but a foolproof one. For shots of, say, 50 yards or more a bigger club is necessary, although the smaller clubs could cover the distance perfectly well if one played them in the normal way. One may as well, I think, go the whole hog and take the No. 2 iron, or at any rate nothing smaller than the No. 3. The principles of the shot remain the same—effectiveness at the expense of style. Cut out the frills. No turning of the body; both feet firmly on the ground throughout the shot; precious little, if any, wrist action.

As to putting, the question of what changes are necessary in a high wind depend on the way you putt on a calm day. Some people have to alter their whole method; others need scarcely make a change. Stability is the keynote—and stability comes from a crouching

[1] See Diagram 7, p. 142.

rather than an upright method. The feet should be well apart and the impression, as I have seen it well described, should be that of riding a horse and gripping the saddle with one's knees. A firm anchoring of the right forearm on to the right thigh will also be found a tremendous help. Some of the usual rhythm will have to be sacrificed and the ball given a shorter and rather sharper blow. Don't set yourself too high a standard, for putting is a precise art—and precision and a high wind simply do not go hand in hand.

CHAPTER XXIV

SOME HINTS AND TIPS

Approaching. When you start fluffing your short approaches, it is a hundred to one that you are quitting on the shot. Head up, eye off the ball, grip relaxed at the critical moment, no follow-through. Merely as a temporary measure, *take hold of the club at the bottom of the grip.* This will leave you no alternative but to give the ball a sharp, firm rap: otherwise you know you cannot make the distance. When you have become used to the idea of striking the ball firmly again, you can return to the normal longer grip and fluff no more—at any rate for a week or two.

N.B.—A good many people employ this shortened grip permanently, finding they get more regular results that way. Safety before brilliance. (Compare the picture of E. F. Storey facing page 136.)

* *

When your game is out of gear but the trouble is not confined to any specific fault, *try holding your follow-*

through for a split second at the end of the shot, as if you were going to be photographed. It may not work for the first shot, which you will probably hit on the top, through thinking too much ahead; but if you carry on for half a dozen in succession, you will find both the balance and the rhythm of your swing improved. The follow-through, let us emphasize again, is not an end in itself, but *is* a reflection of what went before. The movements leading to a good finish are more likely to be correct than those leading to an ill-balanced finish.

N.B.—Don't try to make a copy-book follow-through, which is probably unnatural to your game. Make your *own* follow-through, and hold that for a second.

* *

First shot of the day. The experts go out and hit practice shots before they start from the first tee. You don't. To make sure of opening the day with a reasonable shot, tee the ball well up, swing slowly and deliberately—*and keep your left heel on the ground throughout the stroke*. Try to get a fair body turn, but don't let that left heel move. You may be sacrificing a little distance, but it will be worth while in return for a fair start to the day.

* *

Here is a tip for checking the position of your hands at the top of the swing and the end of the follow-through. At the top you ought to be able, by turning the head to the right, to tell the time fairly and squarely by a wrist watch on your left wrist. At the finish, by turning your head to the left, you should be able to tell it likewise by a watch on your right wrist.

* *

The *right elbow*, slipping away from the body and pointing outwards and behind you at the top of the swing, is responsible for many a shut-faced shot. Very difficult to detect, too. One cure is to tuck a handkerchief under the arm and keep it there throughout the shot. That is elaborate and somewhat undignified. A better idea is to *imagine the handkerchief* to be there. It works just as well—and no one knows you are doing it.

* *

A vast proportion of errors in *putting* come from swaying the body. A sway of an inch is enough to cause the very slight change of angle required to keep the ball out of the hole—but few people can detect a sway of their own. When your putting is worse than usual, *try a stance with your feet together*, *toes and heels touching*. This is a highly sensitive stance, and the slightest sway rings the alarm bell. On a longish putt you may even lose your balance and fall over. Go on until you can swing the putter without being conscious of the least transference of weight from one foot to the other.

* *

Here is a good one for moments of stress—the final drive, the critical pitch over the yawning bunker, the last four-foot putt. Don't think the less of it for its simplicity, for it can work wonders. It is no more than—*open your eyes*. Just that. Relax the muscles in your face and open your eyes really wide. The ball will appear substantially larger : you will not only see it more clearly, you will seem to see more of it.

* *

In one of those rare moments of bliss when golf seems an easy game, check up and make a note of your stance and grip, together with the sensations you experience during the swing. You may be conscious of waiting a moment at the top, of getting the left heel well down at the moment of impact, of a particularly firm grip with the left hand—of almost anything. Write it down—for that fine careless rapture will soon be gone. Later you may like to carry the notes in your cigarette case for surreptitious reference during the game. You will be in good company—for I have seen Cyril Tolley doing it.

* *

When you have finished a round thoroughly dissatisfied with your performance, and state, in response to kind inquiries, that 'everything went wrong', a little analysis will often show that this is not, in fact, correct. The round may linger as a confused memory of bad shots; but if you go over it hole by hole, you will very often find that one fault with one particular club led to most of the trouble. This is particularly true of putting. You recall the fact that you consistently missed the hole, but it is not until you go over the round in detail that you realize that 80 or even 90 per cent. of your putts missed the hole on the same side. Thus you can narrow down what had seemed to be a general ineptitude to a single fault which may comparatively easily be cured.

PART II

CHAPTER I

LEARNING FROM THE MASTERS

HENRY COTTON: 'It may be claimed, however, that the majority of those who endeavour to learn by imitation are not mentally equipped to assimilate what they see, and consequently they do not imitate at all'.

Do these words—dispiriting, but in a sense true—mean that there is nothing to be learnt from watching the experts; that all the exhibition fourballs that take place up and down the country are in vain; that the scrambling multitude which pays to watch the open championship has come for no other purpose than to see who wins?

I cannot think so.

On the other hand, that many of the people are 'not mentally equipped to assimilate what they see' cannot be denied. Have they, then, nothing to learn?

Again I cannot think so.

It seems to me that both those who are 'not mentally equipped . . . etc.' and those who are, have a great deal to learn. Those who belong to the former class may well, as they watch, find themselves drifting imperceptibly into the latter.

Let us consider first those whose technical knowledge of the game does not permit them, as Cotton rightly suggests, to appreciate all the finer points of the game.

When I once asked Compston whether in his opinion there was such a thing as the Secret of Golf, he replied without an instant's hesitation, 'Rhythm, my boy, unbroken rhythm—legs, arms, and body moving as one'. He may not have been right in calling it the secret of golf, but this Rhythm is certainly an outstanding characteristic of the difference between the competent player and the handicap man. The one has an unbroken smoothness in the stroke (even if that stroke goes out of bounds!), the other divides his swing into a number of distinct component parts, linked together by a series of heaves or jerks.

Now, there is no man, whether he understands the finer points of the game or not, so dim of perception that he can fail to notice this smoothness of rhythm when he watches the experts in action. They may hit the ball with the gentle persuasion of Len Holland, or Harry Vardon in his later years, or they may attack it with the virile fury of that lean, athletic Frenchman, Marcel Dallemagne; they may even, if they are very lucky, achieve the deceptive lack of effort with which Alfred Padgham can knock the ball 280 yards: but in whatever manner they may play—whether their action is fast or slow, violent or persuasive—they have one thing in common: smoothness of rhythm.

The position of their feet, their grip of the club, the angle of their shoulders at the moment of impact—all these may be lost upon the novice-spectator; but he has no need to be a master of the technicalities of the golf-swing to perceive at once that these men do *not* stand motionless in the address and then whip away the club like a flash of lightning; that they do *not* bring it down from the top of the swing with the air of a man killing a snake that is about to bite him; that they do *not* make a convulsive 'dig' with the right shoulder in order to raise the ball into the air.

Another feature of their style that must soon impress itself on his mind is that, whereas he himself may finish his stroke standing on his left leg or his right leg, or even facing the hole, and whereas he may have let go impartially with either hand, these men finish every shot in a poised, balanced posture, and with the same firm grip on the club with which they began. In other words, it may be borne upon him that one of golf's many major secrets, perhaps the greatest, lies in the magic word *balance*.

Anything, too, that takes place in a state of rest should not be beyond his grasp—the position of their feet, for instance, in relation to the ball; and that of their hands and arms in relation to the rest of the body. Their general lack of strain and stress he will also notice, and the fact that they are not gritting their teeth throughout the stroke. Their whole attitude, indeed, is one which makes it appear easier to hit the ball than to miss it.

The novice may read every book in creation, including this one, and he may attend the masters in person for their instruction, but nothing in the world can teach him these indispensable elementary lessons of rhythm and balance so well as his own personal observation. And if he takes the trouble to watch good golfers in action as often as he can, he will soon find himself taking an intelligent interest in the particular, where before he had had to confine himself to the general—will find himself, in fact, becoming 'mentally equipped to assimilate what he sees'.

What is he to look for when he reaches this happy state? Well, he must be on his guard against trying to see too much at one time. You can look at the wood, or you can look at one or two of the trees; but you cannot look at all the trees at once.

It may be assumed that, by the time our friend has reached the stage where he can appreciate what he is watching, he has developed some sort of a game of his own. It may be a little crude and unpolished, but it is a game of sorts—sufficiently formed at any rate to enable him to feel clearly which parts are going to prove comparatively simple and which may be expected to give trouble. Particular problems of the stance or the grip or the swing may begin to perplex and confuse him; others he will feel to be merely a matter of practice.

The whole art of watching golf as a means of improving one's own game lies, to my mind, in an ability to dissect one's own minor problems, and then to cure them by observation of others who have mastered them.

All the same, the general impression is important, and it will be possible to assimilate something of an expert's style of play without quite knowing what that something is and without any great outward change being visible to one's friends.

Dr. Johnson, in a characteristically unjustified thrust at Garrick, defined an actor as one who 'claps a hump on his back and a lump on his leg and cries "I am Richard the Third!"'. It will do the novice no harm to make what adjustments he can detect to be necessary and cry (under his breath), 'I am Bobby Jones!'. His friends, if he be so unwise as to ask them, will be at a loss to know which of the masters he fancies himself to resemble—but the experiment, he will find, will have done him no harm.

Here is what may perhaps be a timely warning. The watcher should choose, if he can, a 'model' whom he resembles in build. The experts adhere, it is true, to certain basic principles common to all good golfers, but their style varies outwardly according to their physique. A lean, lissom man, for instance, will learn more (or at any rate more easily) from watching Padgham, Compston, or Richard Burton than from going round with W. J. Cox or James Adams.

CHAPTER II

THE PHYSICAL ASPECT OF GOLF

THE word 'training' does not mean much in the life of the average player—indeed, one of the primary attractions of the game is that it demands neither physical fitness nor abstinence in any form. Yet breathes there a golfer with soul so dead that never to himself hath said 'I wonder whether I should play this game better if I were a fitter man'? I fancy not.

Let us look into the question of training—fitness, abstinence, the daily dozen, and so forth—as it affects the experts: the more ordinary mortal may then be left, on seeing the extreme case, to judge how far he may himself be implicated.

Every one of the experts in his writings makes a point of emphasizing that some form of physical training is an essential attribute of the champion. 'Take two men of equal merit and the fitter of the two will win,' says Compston succinctly.

The strain of a big golf tournament, and particularly of its closing stages, is perhaps not apparent to the spectator. He does not realize, as he watches the solemn faces of the players, that they are suffering in their minds the tortures of the damned and in their bodies acute indigestion!

Tournament Golf

So perhaps we may be permitted to digress for a moment to consider this question of tournament golf and all it implies, for it is impossible to view physical fitness in its true perspective until the strain involved in this pedestrian game, this 'hockey at the halt', is clearly understood.

The mere act of walking 10 miles a day for a week is not, I think, so exhausting as it sounds. Indeed, the walking itself is probably more tiring for the spectator than for the player—or so I have always found. It is the constant mental strain, rising at times to peaks of the most exquisite anguish, that makes such a drain on the physical resources. Anyone who has spent three or four hours in an examination-room knows the bodily exhaustion that it entails, despite the fact that one has been sitting still.

Golfers lose a great deal of weight during tournaments, whereas they may wax fat on an identical ration of friendly rounds. Bobby Jones once found himself stripped of no less than 18 pounds in a six-day championship at Oakmont, and almost every first-class player has a similar tale to tell. It happens to the fair sex likewise; for I recall the case of a woman golfer bemoaning the fact at the end of a championship week that she could find none of her clothes to fit her for the final.

Jones, in fact, used to say that there were two kinds of golf—golf and tournament golf. Sometimes after a championship he would retire to the clubhouse with the cheers of the multitude ringing in his ears, there to be physically sick. In my humble way I once did that myself (lacking only the cheers of the multitude)—and it pulled me up with such a jerk that I have never taken the game so seriously again.

The strain of constant tournament play is well illustrated by the effect it has on the digestions of the players; Jones, Cotton, and Compston being the most notable of a horde of victims. When you see a man taking dry toast and milk for his lunch in a championship, do not be deceived into thinking that he is doing it either for the sake of training or because he likes it. He is doing it because his stomach leaves him no alternative. So much of his available store of nervous energy is being used in the tortuous business of playing in the tournament that none is left for the more mundane purpose of digesting his food. For the same reason it would be a safe wager to bet that half the field in the open championship arrive on the tee without having eaten their usual breakfast.

The strain upon the ultimate winner of the open or amateur championship is tremendous, and in no other game except, on rare occasions, 'timeless' Test cricket is it so prolonged. In the Open, having survived the two days of qualifying, he may reckon to play something between 280 and 290 strokes and to win by perhaps a margin of one. Each round will take him three hours or more: time and again he will have to wait, shifting uneasily from foot to foot and taking practice swings at the daisies, before he can play his next shot. The stakes he is playing for are high, and all the time he knows that one little lapse in concentration, one loose shot into the undergrowth, may mean the difference between the joys of a life of variety—of travel, the friendship of the famous, and an income measured in thousands—and a humble existence as a club professional.

In the amateur championship the anguish may be more severe, according to the temperament of the individual, but is of a somewhat different order. A glance at the modern drawsheet convinces the prospective winner that not only is it clearly impossible for him to win, but amid so vast a conglomeration of names impossible for *anyone* to win. Starting perhaps on Monday morning, he must act day after day, if his name is already renowned, as a kind of Aunt Sally for a succession of players, any one of whom is capable of beating him once over eighteen holes, and to whom his very name may be an inspiration to produce something a little better than their best. One 'snap' defeat and he must wait another twelve months. Any moment may be his last.

Training

And so we return to our original theme—physical fitness and training. No wonder the experts are agreed that stamina and a clear eye are indispensable in modern competition. As a man once put it to me, 'Surely you'll agree that complete fitness would make a difference of half a stroke per round?'. I agreed that it certainly would. 'Well, then', he replied, 'that makes two whole shots in the Open Championship—in other words, the difference between winning and losing!'.

Training for the tournament player takes two forms—positive and negative: things he must go out of his way to do and things he must give up doing. Of the latter, cigarettes and alcohol come to mind as the obvious examples, yet it is a fact that most of the master golfers have been heavy smokers. The outstanding example was the chain-smoking Harold Hilton; while Walter Hagen has been known before now to light a cigarette on every tee. Nearly all men who are smokers at all smoke while playing golf, some continuously, others more deliberately, reserving their pipes or cigarettes for moments of crisis. Indeed, in some cases it is a source of no little encouragement to force one's opponent to light a cigarette!

Henry Cotton, the best striker of the ball I have ever seen (which is not to be confused with a claim that he is the best the world has ever seen), recounts that he neither drinks nor smokes, principally because he 'does not like the taste of either'. It seems, however, if we may judge by the habits of the masters, that smoking and golf can, and do, go hand in hand.

As to alcohol, I should not like to get into trouble with the brewers and the wine merchants by saying that all their wares were poison to the tournament player, but I think it is fair to suggest that both during and before specific tournaments they should be used in moderation. Yet once again one must add that many of the master players have either been, or become, heavy drinkers.

The whole thing is a subject on which it is very difficult to lay down the law. I think anyone must realize that, although they may have played one or two outstandingly successful rounds when suffering from the effects of the night before, as a general rule the fitter they are the better they play. The longer the tournament, of course, the more obvious does the working of this rule become: no man may expect to walk 50 miles in a week, lose a stone in weight, endure the mental gruelling already described, and still be playing his best at the end of it, unless he has a substantial physical reserve on which to draw. The competitions in which the average golfer indulges do not, it is true, extend more than 36 holes, but they are subject to the same principle.

The Daily Dozen

The more positive side of training for golf will consist, in most people's minds, of the 'daily dozen'. There are, I believe, some physical exercises that are invaluable for the golfer, though they may vary in individual cases. Of one thing I am certain, judging both from theory and personal observation; that is, that the fellow who tries to emulate the gentlemen in the advertisements, their muscles standing out like whipcord and their bodies radiating a kind of electrical energy, is deceiving himself alive. Golf is not a game that requires all-round brute force. It needs rather a delicacy of touch combined with strength in a certain limited number of places, notably the hands and wrists. Strong hands and wrists and a long reach will hit the ball farther than bulging biceps.

I know intimately three amateur golfers who are generally reckoned to be in the top flight, two of whom have been selected to represent Britain in Walker Cup matches. All three take an extreme, and not unjustifiable, pride in physical perfection, and each is as strong as a horse. Yet none of them have succeeded in the way their talents appear to deserve.

This, in my own opinion, is simply and solely because they are *too strong*—strong, that is, in a wooden as opposed to a lissom fashion. They have the strength of the cart-horse rather than of the panther. They swing their club in the appropriate groove, they hit the ball a tremendous distance; but they do it all in a ham-handed, artificial sort of way that gives but little pleasure to the eye. A typical product of modern golf, they have only one stroke—the full shot. A sense of judgment to them means judgment of what club to take, not of what shot to play: thus when it comes to anything less than a full shot with their No. 8A, or whatever is the smallest club they carry, they find themselves unequipped for the task.

The foregoing, of course, is destructive criticism, but it may help to relieve the conscience of people who fear that they will never improve until they attain the bodily perfection of a professional pugilist.

Henry Cotton, who has an unusually happy knack of putting his ideas on paper, says, 'The best exercise for golf is the golf swing'—an opinion with which I humbly concur. On the other hand, the golf swing is not always capable of performance in the bedroom, where any such exercises usually take place. A great many men whose business calls them to the less active walks of life perform a series of exercises every morning. Those of them who are golfers may kill two birds with one stone by concentrating their attention on those which are directly beneficial for golf. The average man's principal physical handicap in the golf swing is an inability to get a full body-turn (which Jones believes to be the most important single aspect of the golf swing) without an accompanying strain that destroys the rhythm of the swing in general. Any exercises, therefore, that ease the twisting of the body, especially to the right, must benefit the golfer.

Any movement is also to be recommended that gives increased freedom to the arms. Jones was always stout and stocky, but a glance at any of the thousands of action pictures showing him at the top of the swing and on the follow-through, will show that he reaches with ease a position which the average mortal with a similar figure could not reach with the aid of a crane. Jones achieves a body-turn of such full dimensions that he can raise his left arm into an almost vertical position on the backswing and still keep it straight as a ramrod. The same applies to his right arm on the follow-through.

It is useless for a man, in order to approximate more closely to what he considers the ideal body-turn, to force himself into a strained posture, for in so doing he will automatically ruin the stroke. He should concentrate on extending the natural limit of his turn, trying by means of the appropriate exercises to increase for a few precious inches the *unstrained* arc of his swing.

I recommend most heartily to anyone remotely interested in the purely physical side of golf that they buy a miniature practice club. These clubs are about 30 inches long, and outwardly resemble a driver in everything except the length of shaft, which is about as long as a poker. The head, however, is so weighted that with the eyes shut it is virtually impossible to tell that one is not waggling a full-sized club. This instrument can be swung with immunity in the bedroom or the office, and will subject the player to exactly the same pulls and strains that he experiences on the course. It costs about half a guinea, and any professional worthy of the name should be able to make or supply one.

Club Swinging

Passing from the general question of physical fitness one comes to more specific instances relating purely to the action of swinging a golf club. I will stand or fall by the statement that the average golfer does not make a full and proper use of his left hand and arm. Since he plays the game right-handed, it is only natural that his right hand should play a consciously preponderant part. In my opinion this represents golf's major snare.

The left arm (which for the sake of brevity we will take to include also the hand) cannot play its proper part unless it is equipped for the task—a task incidentally that it is not called upon to fulfil in any of the normal walks of life. It must be given special exercises of its own, the best of which, once again, is the golf swing.

The first-class player can swing a club with his left arm alone with comparative ease; the handicap man finds it astonishingly difficult, for it opens up before him an aspect of the game whose existence he had never suspected.

In fact it occurs to me that one actually cannot perform the correct golf swing with the right arm alone. The left-handed swing will start from the correct address position, with the clubhead opposite the left heel and the hand well forward, and will describe the same arc as the copybook two-handed swing: the right-handed shot, on the other hand, will naturally start with most of the weight on the right foot and with the clubhead farther back. In the course of the stroke it will automatically illustrate nearly all the faults of the man with the 'dummy left arm'.

Still, that is a digression. The point is that swinging the club with the left hand is as good an exercise as the golfer can find for giving him extra strength where he most needs it. As an example of this, and to show that it is not only the average player who may be in need of this artificial strengthening, I may quote the case of Reginald Whitcombe, who once told me that he used to stand in his shop for as much as three-quarters of an hour at a time every morning swinging a heavy niblick with his left arm alone. He made it describe the correct arc for each shot and concentrated in particular on seeing that at the end of the shot his arm and the club were pointing directly at the hole.

Strength in the wrists is another vital consideration. In my own case I find that length varies in absolutely direct proportion to the amount of ' break ' I can achieve in the wrists at the top of the swing without letting go with the last two fingers of the left hand.

In general, therefore, any exercises calculated to strengthen the wrists and render them more supple are to be commended: in particular, I should suggest the practice of swinging two or three clubs at a time, especially for a few minutes previously to starting a round.

Each player of golf must judge the wide question of physical fitness for himself, taking into consideration his age, the nature of his other activities, the extent of his ambitions, and so forth; but everyone may rest assured that the old tag *mens sana in corpore sano* still holds good. And if ever there was a game to which *mens sana* was indispensable, that game is golf.

CHAPTER III

THE MENTAL SIDE

THE old precept that attack is the best method of defence is as true in golf as in any branch of life. The way to prevent yourself playing a bad shot is to concentrate your attention on trying to play a good one. Let your thoughts be positive, not negative.

That represents an elementary lesson in psychology

that escapes a good many people to their dying day. If you wish to accomplish any given object, you must only envisage *doing* the thing you want to do: you must not envisage *not doing* the thing you want not to do.

To take an example from everyday life—if you want to start getting up earlier in the morning, it is no good saying to yourself, 'I won't lie in bed to-morrow morning', for the only mental impression that you have thereby received is one of yourself lying comfortably in bed and thinking how unpleasant it will be to get up. On the contrary you must say to yourself, 'I am going to be up bright and early to-morrow', for then your mental impression will be of yourself leaping out of bed and enjoying it.

I believe that one of the many reasons why the Americans are better golfers than the British is the fact that they have, perhaps subconsciously, mastered this lesson. I do not believe they imagine themselves playing bad shots: they imagine themselves playing good ones.

The average Englishman, faced with a crucial stroke, says to himself, 'What a dreadful thing if I miss it! Supposing I lift my head, and fluff. I mustn't do that. But I must be careful to get under it properly, or it will run over the back. And then there's that bunker on the right—I'd better aim a little on the left and allow for a bit of a slice, just in case.'

Your American, on the other hand, confines his imagining, or so I honestly believe, to what he *wants* to do: that is, hit the ball on to the green. If he stopped to think of all the things he wanted not to do, he would probably achieve the same insignificant results as the Englishman.

This is why it is so vitally important to have a clear

mental picture of a shot before you play it. The mind, after all, directs every action of the body, subconscious as those actions may in time become. Even the lifting of a teacup to the mouth, now a spontaneous movement, was in the early days of childhood a studied, deliberate action.

When the golf swing becomes as automatic as raising a teacup (and no man has reached that state of perfection yet) it will be time to let the brain wander, leaving the body to play its part without conscious directions from the mind.

Which brings us to the subject of *concentration*. Often described as the secret of golf, it is one of the many indispensable bases of the game—and, like the rest of them, often misunderstood. So many people envisage concentration as a furrowing of the brow, a gritting of the teeth, and an expression of tense resolution. Yet the real meaning of the word is no more than *applying one's mind to the job*. The furrowing of the brow and other such manifestations are physical: concentration lies exclusively in the mind. It is physical relaxation combined with mental concentration that wins golf matches.

If ever I adopted golf as a means of livelihood, I should not confine my work to the course and the practice ground. I should at once repair to a psychologist and learn how to train my mind. Concentration, after all, is simply the ability to rivet the attention of one's mind on a given object at any desired moment. My psychologist might command me to sit and stare at an inanimate object—an inkpot perhaps—for minutes at a time, until I could focus my thoughts on it to the exclusion of all else (which is no easy matter—try it and see). But I should not mind.

At any rate, I should try to obtain sufficient control of my thoughts to ensure that, when the final putt came to be holed, I did not miss it because my mind was a turmoil of conflicting emotions, trying at one and the same time to think of the consequences of failure, the prospects of success, the spectators round the green, and the line and distance of the putt.

You remember the story of the man whose friends bet him that in one year from that day he would not hole a straight putt of one yard? For 364 days they haunted him with the prospect of this one single putt—just one—only a yard—no 'borrow'. Whenever he went to his club, people talked of his wager and pointed him out to their friends as the man who had backed himself to hole a yard putt. When the great day arrived, he gave an anxious, weak-kneed prod at the ball and it failed to reach the hole.

Why? Because he had not control of his mind. His body knew how to hole a straight putt of one yard. The flesh was willing enough. But the spirit was weak.

A friend of mine, for many years a scratch player, drew an interesting parallel in an article in *Punch* between the golfer and one of those five-barred gates that swings to and fro on its hinges until finally the latch clicks into position. The gate, he noted, had a perfect swing. It never missed. But so, for that matter, had he—sometimes. During the course of his life he had hit an utterly perfect stroke with every club in his bag, but, whereas he was constantly failing in his efforts, the gate never failed. He had a mind to contend with: the gate had none.

Should the golfer, then, be devoid of imagination? There is a lot to be said for the theory. Certainly too much imagination is a bar to consistent success. The man who can envisage all the horrid possibilities attached to every shot is not likely to stand the strain of modern competitive golf so well as one who, like Alfred Padgham of to-day or Harry Vardon of yesterday, can proceed serenely on his way, treating an open championship as part of his daily job.

On the other hand, we have the evidence of nearly every first-class golfer, in particular that of Bobby Jones, that a certain degree of nervous tension and excitement is necessary before they can produce the best of which they are capable.

The master players give no visible sign of the struggle that is going on within them. Cyril Tolley is an outstanding example. Few of the spectators who admire the almost disinterested manner in which he tramples upon his opponents know that it is but a cloak to cover a bundle of nerves, that without this pose of apparent disdain he could scarcely bring himself to make a blow at the ball at all.

The art of excluding extraneous thoughts from the mind and applying the attention to the single object of hitting the golf ball is as important to the average golfer as to the tournament player, though the consequences of failure are of course less disastrous. The man who wins is the man who can treat a putt of two feet on the last green to win the monthly medal as just another two-foot putt—and nothing more.

Allied with the question of mental concentration is that of the time one should take to play a shot. The successful golfer, you must have noticed, takes roughly the same amount of time over each of his shots; he gets into a sort of rhythm that suits his temperament, and then sticks to it. When mental rhythm breaks down, this physical rhythm goes with it.

One reads from time to time of players who fall into the strange golfing disease of 'getting stuck', particularly on the putting-green. They stand there, gazing intently at the ball as a rabbit gazes hypnotized at a stoat, and nothing on earth will induce the club to move. I suppose there is not a golfer in the world who has not once in his life, after staring fixedly at a putt for several seconds and then missing it, remarked, 'I took too long over it'. Sometimes, to counteract the malady, people walk up to the ball and hit it almost on the run.

Every man's aim, as I see it, should be to find out what degree of concentration he requires in order to achieve his best results, and then to cram that concentration into the shortest possible time. It has been estimated, I believe, by those who deal in abstruse problems of the mind, that the absolutely maximum period over which a man can maintain concentration on a given object at its highest pitch is something like six seconds. It may have been less: it certainly was not more. For myself, I find it to be between three and four.

In a golf shot it seems to me that the club can be chosen and the stance and grip adjusted and the ball addressed, before one's concentration need approach its absolute peak. They merely entail paying attention to the job, thinking of what one is doing. It is when these formalities have been completed, without much mental labour, that the real concentration begins. It can be worked up to its peak in two seconds and reasonably be maintained at that point, in the average individual, for perhaps another two. By the end of those four seconds the ball ought to be on its way. Alfred Padgham, it may be said, takes about three seconds from the moment he has finally adjusted his stance to the moment when the club starts the backswing. After four or five seconds, delay means loss of rhythm both in mind and body—and one is just as important as the other.

The subject of applying the mind to a single stroke leads one to the question of concentration in general, concentration on the whole round. It varies with the individual according to his general outlook on life. A good many people cannot give of their best unless they play in silence: they like to lock themselves up in the stronghold of their minds and not to emerge until the round is done. Interruption breaks down their mental rhythm, and they find it difficult to recapture their tranquillity once it has gone.

One of the few great players who had the strength of mind to focus his thoughts at will upon the task in hand was Walter Hagen. In the height of an open championship he remained readily accessible to friends and acquaintances, to anyone who cared to talk to him as he went round. Measured in terms of distance, it took him about thirty yards of walking to re-harness his thoughts to the business in hand. At this distance from his ball he would cease to pay attention to the conversation, and the light of determination would come into his eye as he began to gather himself together for the next shot.

Harry Vardon's supremacy, as the other members of the Triumvirate would tell you, was due largely to the fact that it was almost impossible to put him off. Long delays and the marshalling of crowds, stupid remarks by spectators that would have aggravated a lesser man, all the trivial things that are calculated to upset the sensitive player, were as nothing to him. Where others were champing at the bit, anxious to get on with the job, Vardon sat contentedly on the tee box, puffing at his pipe and gazing peacefully at the landscape.

CHAPTER IV

PRACTICE

Golf is one of the most exacting games in the world and, like many other things in this life, is subject to the rule that what you get out of it is governed very largely by what you put into it. The value of practice is dinned into the golfer from the moment that he first takes up the game; and though perhaps it is sometimes overdone, there is no possible doubt that the only road to real success lies via hard work and practice. That, to the average man, is a dismal prospect.

'All the books in the world, and instructions from the greatest professionals in the game', says Gene Sarazen, rubbing it in, 'won't teach the average man or woman how to play a first-class game of golf unless they be willing to give up a certain amount of time to practice. . . .'

Learning to play golf is, as I have remarked before, not unlike learning to play the piano, in that it involves the co-ordinated use of a great many muscles in a manner to which they are unaccustomed in daily life. And there is no way of training these muscles to perform their new function except by constant, and perhaps tedious, repetition—in fact, by playing scales.

If a beginner thinks that without practice he will ever reach anything but mediocrity, he is doomed to disappointment, unless he has the leisure to play round the

R

course every hour of every day. Indeed, I would venture to say that a golfer's progress depends almost directly on the amount of time that he is able or willing to spend in practising.

It is one of the less creditable achievements of the average English school that it teaches one to regard anything in the nature of 'work' with apprehension and distaste. Yet if you care to be honest with yourself, you must recall that a good many hours passed in the classroom were, in fact, more diverting than some of the long hours of idleness spent outside.

So it is with practising at golf. Can you deny that there have been times when you could willingly have abandoned your three comrades in a fourball and betaken yourself and your wayward game to some quiet corner of the course, there to work out your salvation with the aid of one club and a dozen balls?

'Practice', says Henry Cotton, 'is the most important thing of all to the young golfer. He must spend hours at practice play and *enjoy* every minute of the time.' That is a point well taken, for it *is* possible to enjoy practising if you go about it in the right way and the right frame of mind. But regard it as a painful duty, and the thing becomes a purgatory.

The beginner practises in order to make his muscles perform the swing, such as it may be, subconsciously: the seasoned player, having passed that stage, practises for the most part either in order to cure a specific fault or to experiment with a new trick of style. To the former, practice is essential if he is to learn the game at all: to the latter it is essential if he wishes to play it better.

Golf is like riding a horse. Once you can ride, you never quite forget. Long intervals may elapse, after which a new start may find you heavy-handed, awkward, and ungainly, and afterwards leave you stiff in the joints—but you will find, all the same, that you have not actually fallen off the horse. Thus, once you have played golf to a handicap of, say, a genuine fourteen, a period of inactivity will find your game rusty, but able to be polished up to its former state with comparatively little difficulty.

Without practice it may be safely assumed that you would never have reached this 'genuine fourteen': the snag now is that without more practice you will never improve.

These facts may as well be faced, unpleasant though they may appear. A great many golfers play the game for the exercise it gives them and for the opportunities of enjoying the company of their friends, rather than from any desire ever to see their names in the newspaper headlines.

Nor do I think that this is an outlook to be despised. A desire for pleasure and recreation is as legitimate a reason for playing games as a desire to excel; and when a man has only one day and a half per week at his disposal, it is often the sole reason—particularly if he took up the game when the first flush of youth had gone.

And so I say cheerfully that the Average Golfer, whose handicap is after all in double figures, and who has only this day and a half in which to play, has no urgent need to practise—provided, that is, that he has his ambition well under control. I would add, however, this qualification. I have but little patience with the type of man who is constantly 'off his game'. He is a tiresome type of individual and a nuisance both to himself and to his partners and opponents. If he is not prepared to accept his game as it stands, he has no excuse for declining to take steps to improve it.

The higher stages of golf illustrate the old maxim that practice makes perfect; the truth of which is still realized, perhaps, rather more keenly by the Americans than by ourselves. The expert American player practises almost as much as he plays, and to stand in solitary confinement, as it were, with a club and a bucket of balls has long since lost the air of novelty and righteousness, either to the player or the spectator, that it is still inclined to possess over here. That spirit has spread downwards, and the numerous driving ranges which litter the countryside of the United States find ready customers among the ranks of the 'rabbits'.

And that brings me to what I believe to be the reason why the average Englishman finds practising so distasteful. It is simply that he has no proper place in which to do it. New clubs are now built with practice grounds near to the clubhouse, and in some cases are even equipped with special huts: the more progressive among the older clubs are trying to find space for practising in the ground already at their disposal; but the fact remains that on most courses to-day the enthusiast who wishes to battle alone with his golfing problems must do so, as it were, on the common land, harassed by notices which forbid him to putt on the last green or hit balls from the fairways, and by fellow-players who wave him imperiously from their path. He is an outcast banished from his fellowmen.

Another feature which tends to discourage the well-meaning individual who is prepared to sacrifice an occasional round in the noble cause of improving his game, is the fact that only rarely do the beneficial results of practising reveal themselves at the time. Often as a man's arms become more and more tired and his temper progressively shorter, his game deteriorates until he may be forgiven for feeling that his last state is worse than his first. It is not until the morrow that he reaps the harvest of what he has so laboriously sown.

In this connection it is interesting to note the somewhat unusual advice of Macdonald Smith, who has recommended that one should practise with those clubs with which one is at the moment playing *best*. That suggestion strikes me as being based on some very sound thinking, the idea being, of course, that a concentration on such movements of the golf swing as we may happen to be carrying out correctly may induce those movements to find their way also into shots in which they are lacking. The main principles of all golf shots are, after all, the same.

In one department of the game, practice, I am convinced, is absolutely essential—and that is putting. And this time no one can legitimately plead lack of opportunity as an excuse for its neglect.

Every club, to my mind, should have a practice green; but where no such green exists and where the usual notice forbids you to make use of the eighteenth—well, the seventeenth cannot be more than four minutes' walk away.

CHAPTER V

WINTER AND SUMMER GOLF

SOME of my more venerable friends have told me that in their day there were no such things as winter golf and summer golf—for the simple reason that they put away their clubs at those seasons and confined their activities to spring and autumn. As to the strict truth of that statement I cannot speak, but it is probably true to say that the proportion of players who are faithful to the game for twelve months in the year is substantially greater now than it was twenty years ago.

Both winter and summer golf have their drawbacks, and each demands a certain modification of what we may call the standardized technique of the game.

The drawbacks of winter are obvious. Yet if only the ordinary golfer would take a few simple and elementary precautions, he would double his enjoyment of the game during those dark days when he plays it as much for exercise as for fun.

The first thing to do is to keep warm. Golf, despite all the talk about shifting of hips and rotation of shoulders, is a game that is played primarily with the hands. In putting and in the short game the sense of touch comes essentially from the fingers. Cold hands and golf, therefore, simply do not go together.

How to keep the extremities warm is the golfer's permanent winter problem—and his display on the links depends on its solution. Waterproof trousers, preferably of lined gaberdine, are indispensable, and should hang well down on to the shoes. That perilous gap at the ankle can undo all the good work done by the trousers. The thin rubber variety are cheaper but less satisfactory, as they split at the touch of a shoe-nail, and they 'sweat'—though this can be partly avoided by wearing them inside out. Many people only wear waterproof trousers when it rains, ignorant of the fact that these are the only true protection yet devised against a cold wind.

Most people carry one of those large, multi-coloured, and incidentally very heavy, umbrellas. For myself I do not, partly because I have now lost so many, at a guinea a time, that I can no longer afford the expense, and partly because one's hands get so cold holding the thing out in the rain that the game is not worth the candle.

So much for the attire: now for the technique. The first consideration is that, owing to the numerous extra clothes that you are wearing, you have not the same freedom of swing as at other times of the year. Take care that your jacket gives you as much room as possible, particularly under the arms, but be reconciled to the fact that your swing will not have that same sweeping grace that you like to think characterizes it in summer.

Archie Compston has announced his three golden rules for winter golf as *Open Stance—Upright Swing*—and *Be Up*. They are simple enough to understand, and if you put them into practice you will add greatly to the pleasure of the game.

Open up the stance, with the left foot as much as 6 inches behind the right, and put the ball as far forward even as to be opposite the left toe, but not too far away from the body. It is a slicer's position, as you will feel at once—but don't let that deter you. A slight slice is what you want, so aim a little to the left and allow for it. A slice, after all, is not bad *per se*—it is only the involuntary variety you need seek to avoid. Keep the action going consciously with the left hand and all will be well.

We may assume that the lies will be none too good—and here the upright swing comes in. A flattish swing is currently popular—fashions change in golf as quickly as in women's wear—but it is a swing that tends rather to keep the ball low, to impart, if anything, a shade of draw. A steeper arc is required if the ball is to be elevated from a doubtful lie. Stand near enough to the ball to hit it without 'reaching for it' and take an upright swing, but beware above all things of an instinctive temptation to let the right elbow stray away from the body. Keep it in to the side, as if you were holding a pocket handkerchief under it. Otherwise—well, we will not go into that.

The third rule, *Be Up*, is mental rather than physical. So easy to say, so difficult to do. Despite all one's good intentions, winter golf entails just one long chagrin at being short of the flag. 'It's an extraordinary thing', said Compston in a burst of mathematical enthusiasm, 'that you can get ninety-nine golfers out of a hundred to make up their minds that they really will get up to the flag this time, and yet it is a hundred to one that fifty per cent. of their shots will still be short.'

What he says is perfectly true. I can offer no solution to the trouble, for that lies with the player alone. My only contribution is the suggestion 'When in doubt, take the bigger club'. A public declaration that you will give sixpence to charity every time you are short with an approach is also a notable incentive.

A great many golfers—one hates to say it, but the fact remains—would be well advised to leave out of their bag, from November until March, the brassie and the No. 1 iron: in some cases the No. 2 iron might also be abandoned with advantage. Through the fairway a shallow-faced spoon is the safest club: this and the No. 3 iron can account for most of the longer shots between tee and green. If you have a brassie with a small head and a very shallow face, and if you can master the principles of the open stance and upright swing, then the brassie may be a useful ally: if not, it will prove to be the enemy within thy gates.

For myself I find it an enormous advantage to play with what is generally known as the 'American' ball in winter, when the lies are close. It is as heavy (1·62 oz.) as the British ball, but bigger (1·68 in. as against 1·62 in.). It is perfectly legal in Great Britain—indeed, it is possible that even while this book is being published the Royal and Ancient may decide to make it the 'standard' ball over here—and, although the difference is only ·06 in., it seems to sit up like a football.

As to length, there is nothing much to choose between the two types of ball, except that against the wind the American variety, being bigger, goes rather less far—but then, when the wind blows against you, you can put down the ordinary British ball.

In my opinion the larger ball is so much easier to hit than the smaller variety that the increased cleanness of the stroke more than compensates for any loss of distance. It is only fair to say, however, that this is a view that is not held by all my journalistic colleagues.

The problems connected with summer golf—by which I mean golf when the ground has become unnaturally hard—are more difficult of complete solution than those of winter; for the actions of the ball on a hard-baked surface become more at the mercy of Nature.

To pitch the ball well up to the flag on a sodden green is a matter of technical skill; and once this is acquired, there is an air of certainty about the result. To pitch it in a narrow gap 20 yards short of the edge of the green in summer is also a matter of technical skill—but the result is then in the lap of the gods. The ball may kick into the bunker on the right or the bunker on the left; it may pitch on a hard patch of turf and scuttle over the back of the green, or it may strike a grassy patch and stop unreasonably short.

It is this very uncertainty that so often spoils the shot. All that one can reasonably do is to strike the ball accurately and hope for the best. Provided one has looked after one's own end of the shot, there is nothing more that could humanly have been accomplished; but so often one tries to do that little bit more—to urge it on to the green, as it were, straight from the end of the club. The body sways, the head rises, the hands are in front—and all is undone. One returns to the clubhouse with a grouse about 'unlucky kicks'.

Just as in winter the style is cramped by too many clothes, so in summer it is liable to run riot on the gay abandon of shirt-sleeves. Cast-iron instructions as to how this is to be avoided are difficult to offer. When a man asks, 'What can I do to stop lifting my head?' the only just reply, short of tying him up with elastic, is '*Don't* lift your head!'. In the present case perhaps the best advice is deliberately to curtail the backswing, keeping a straight left arm and a firm grasp with the last two fingers of the left hand. You should strive above all things for an impression of compactness.

A final principle of summer golf should be pointed out. The steeper the angle at which the ball drops, and the more 'lifeless' it is when it drops, the more susceptible it will be to tiny undulations in the ground. Conversely, the lower it can be kept, the straighter it will run. In all approach play, therefore, the rule should be 'Keep it as low as you can'. If the choice lies between the run-up and the pitch or pitch-and-run, choose the run-up every time. Take as straight-faced a club as is possible, and knock it along the ground. When your friends accuse you of having topped the shot, smile in a superior manner and announce that personally you prefer to judge by results.

CHAPTER VI

WOMEN'S GOLF

In their insistence that golfing proficiency is a matter not of brute force, but of timing and precision, writers and teachers of the game are apt to forget the part that pure strength does undoubtedly play. Skill consists in applying that strength in the manner calculated to produce the optimum result.

Few of the master golfers give to the untutored spectator the impression that they are hitting the ball really hard. Many a twelve-handicap amateur, with his vice-like grip and tense expression, appears to be delivering more force in sending the ball 180 yards than does Alfred Padgham when he flicks it a mere 250. A smooth, true golf swing conceals the strength that lies behind it—but the strength is there. That is why Henry Cotton spent so much of his time in his earlier days in exercising his arms and being massaged.

A friend of mine tells a tale of how he was playing with Padgham when they saw three of the greenkeeping staff struggling unsuccessfully to shift a tree-trunk. Padgham, he says, asked where they wanted it—and then put it there. That may not be strictly accurate, but the fact remains that most of these men are enormously

GENIUS

Miss Joyce Wethered (Lady Heathcote-Amory) whom some, including Bobby Jones, hold to be the greatest golfer of all time, male or female. Her style is noticeable for its inevitable smoothness of rhythm and perfect balance. No one ever saw Miss Wethered finish a shot in anything but the copybook position.

Sport and General

'Daily Express'

Sport and General

THE YOUNGER SCHOOL

Miss Pamela Barton (left) and Miss Patty Berg. Women golfers as a rule lack power in the wrists and fingers, but Miss Barton, champion of Great Britain and the United States in 1936, has plenty in both. Notice the stability of her feet and the attitude of 'hitting past the chin'.

Miss Berg had had many major successes in the United States at the age of seventeen, and was generally regarded as the most promising young woman golfer ever produced in America.

powerful. The reason for their success is that they have learnt to harness their power.

Timing, which is said to be the secret of golf, consists in making the clubhead move at its maximum speed at the moment at which it strikes the ball, without allowing the efforts leading up to this speed to impair one's balance or shift the club from its true arc. And most of the physical force from which springs the clubhead speed is generated by the hands, fingers, and wrists.

In women golfers this vital element is lacking. Robust and brawny though some of them may look, they share one common failing: they have but little strength in their hands.

It is a failing that communicates itself to their golf in two ways, primarily in the matter of length. They cannot, without a long and rigorous course of training, induce the clubhead to move fast enough to propel the ball as far as the average male player. The latter, it is true, would lose his money if he were to stand on the tee and try to match shot for shot with Miss Pamela Barton and Miss Bridget Newell; but, then, these two ladies—the longest hitters in their own domain—would also lose their money against what are strictly speaking their male counterparts, the longest-hitting men.

Secondly, they are unable to apply, except perhaps with the mashie-niblick and niblick, that vital snap of the wrists that imparts backspin. They cannot play the high, biting iron shot that is the stock-in-trade of the professional. They cannot hit *down* and through the ball: they have to hit *along* and through it—which is a very different matter.

And so with women nothing but the best will do. Whereas a man may by sheer strength send an ill-struck ball far enough to avoid dropping a stroke, the woman player must hit it almost perfectly, or it will not fly at all. Either her shot is 90 per cent. perfect—or it is 'destructive'—in other words, it leaves her little better off than before. There is rarely a middle course. One of the few exceptions is Miss Barton, 'world champion' of 1936, who does, I think, hit an imperfect shot far enough to get away with it.

If golf were a game in which points were scored for sheer perfection of striking, the women would more than hold their own in an open championship.

I do not profess to be an expert on the technique of women's golf, but having watched a great many of their championships, I can make a certain number of observations with a fair confidence.

In the first place, I am sure that all women would be well advised to use the ordinary straightforward 'two-handed' grip. Neither their hands nor their fingers are big enough to make the overlapping or interlocking worth while.

The curtailed type of backswing practised by many of the experts is a modern fashion to be avoided by women players—though that does not say that a good many of them could not shorten their present backswings with advantage. The length of the backswing, in fact, matters a great deal more to the woman player than to a man.

If she allows it to become too short, a snatch, accompanied probably by a heave of the body, is the inevitable consequence, for her hands and arms are unable by themselves to speed up the club at the last minute. On the other hand, the lady who takes the club so far back that ultimately it bounces off her left shoulder is also a familiar sight. What her swing lacks in strength, she is trying to make up in length—the result being that as the club passes the horizontal, the hands lose control. And control of the club, once lost, is rarely regained.

The woman player should, I fancy, with all wooden clubs and with the bigger irons take the club back at least as far as the horizontal. But a longer swing, it must be remembered, is longer not only in distance but in time: it not only *is* longer, it *takes* longer. Women as a whole realize this essential truth more clearly than men; they are not so prone as men—perhaps once again because they have not the strength—to the devastating habit of snatching the club down from the top.

On the grounds that it is useless to attempt what you know in advance you cannot perform, I think that women should play their irons in precisely the same manner as their wooden clubs. If you cannot hit the ball down against the turf and force your way through, then don't try to do it. And perhaps that applies to the average male golfer as well. A perfectly satisfactory iron shot can be made with the orthodox swing used with a driver. The disadvantages of the method are only apparent in a high wind or a bad lie, or when the ball must carry an obstacle and pull up in its tracks the other side.

CHAPTER VII

GOLF AT SCHOOL

Discussion on controversies current at the moment of writing have to be treated with caution in what it is piously hoped may be a work of some lasting value;

but I am taking a chance that, whenever this book may be picked up in the future, the world will have yet to solve the problem as to whether a boy should play golf at school.

I think that he should: but, then, I am biased. The time will never come, I trust, when we see the boys drawn up in rows for their daily lesson from the golf instructor; but it occurs to me all the same that a free summer afternoon may be spent as profitably on the local golf course as in riding about on a bicycle in search of birds' eggs and surreptitious beer. There is a happy medium in all things.

Perhaps the real point at issue is 'How soon should a boy start to learn his golf?'. For more reasons than one the answer is 'As soon as possible'.

Although he has an opportunity at school of developing the various admirable qualities connected with team games, he cannot readily find twenty-one other small boys with whom to engage in combat in the holidays. Time, though he will not admit it, often lies heavy on his hands.

Secondly, if he wishes to play golf and enjoy it during his adult life, he had better lay the foundation of a respectable swing while his muscles are still young and tractable. 'I am afraid I started too late' is a phrase dismal to utter, dismal to hear.

Thirdly, pompous as it may sound, golf can teach a boy—and a man, too, for that matter—every single one of the major lessons of life. 'The game', says Henry Cotton, who owes his success in life to a schoolmaster who as a punishment forbade him to play cricket, 'can be a great builder of character; it can impart something of that peculiar quality known as personality, because it is at once most comprehensive and entirely individualistic. It can even be a selfish game. . . .'

Golf *is* a selfish game, in the best sense of the word (if that can be). Selfish motives, after all, prompt almost every one of the average man's daily actions: he works to gain himself money, he plays to gain himself recreation. Those who indulge in voluntary team games when they leave school are moved as much by a desire to gratify their own pleasure as to help their team to win.

Golf demands no physical courage; nor, save for the first-class tournament player, endurance: but it calls for a very high standard of mental courage, if it is to be played well. It demands rather the qualities of the spy in the enemy's country than those of the man who 'goes over the top'. And who shall decry one at the expense of the other?

Golf calls for a rigid and ceaseless control over the emotions: in it there is no place for 'temperament', a luxury reserved for actresses and players of lawn tennis. It demands, too, an iron concentration, coupled with a rather paradoxical easy-going philosophy that is ready to accept the rough with the smooth without losing the rhythm of its stride.

A boy with a tempestuous nature who takes up golf soon finds himself faced with two alternatives, neither of them easy. He may either learn to control his temper or he may give up the game. And commonplace human obstinacy forbids his choosing the latter. On account of its being played with a stationary ball and with no interference from one's opponent, golf promotes sensations of irritated impatience and frustration of almost unique intensity, and he will, if he is a lad of spirit, pass by easy stages from shaft-breaking to club-flinging, and from club-flinging to the traditional silver-tongued expressiveness of the thwarted golfer, emerging finally into an unruffled tranquillity that will stand him in good stead in every walk of life for the rest of his days.

A control of the outward and inward emotions is not all that is to be learnt from this extraordinary game. It teaches, for instance, more vividly than could any sermon from the pulpit of the school chapel, the old lesson that 'a battle is not lost till it's won'—another of life's platitudes that the stress of the moment is liable to make one forget. The bitter experience of losing a match from 'three up with four to play' and the sweet satisfaction of winning it from three down can teach a boy more effectively than any words of wisdom from his elders and betters that it is worth while trying until the end.

And so I think a boy should be encouraged to play golf as soon as he shows either desire or aptitude for the game. To permit him to play while he is still in his schooldays is often confused, but is by no means identical, with permitting him to play *at* school.

Charterhouse has produced a continuous flow of distinguished golfers, who win the Halford Hewitt Tournament year by year at Deal, and who for the most part had acquired sufficient skill to play for one of the Universities at the age of nineteen. Yet how many rounds were they able to play during the term? Judging from an experience of five years at that admirable institution, I should place the figure, for a boy who was exceptionally keen, at four or five in the winter term and anything up to ten in the spring and summer terms.

Every round entailed bicycling nine miles, and the number of boys who played ten rounds in thirteen weeks certainly did not, in my own day, number more than half a dozen.

Stowe is, so far as I know, the only major school that boasts its own golf course, a somewhat primitive lay-out of nine holes. The boys are permitted to play only on giving proof that they are not 'cutting' any other form of game. Even these limited opportunities, however, bore immediate fruit when five of the ten members of the 1937 Cambridge University team had come up from Stowe.

So a boy, in order to progress at golf at the age when he is most capable of learning it, does not need to waste the precious afternoons of his schooldays. P. B. Lucas was captain of football and cricket at Stowe, and yet was selected for the Walker Cup team within two years of leaving: J. D. A. Langley was captain of cricket (and generally adjudged one of the best schoolboy cricketers since the war), and was selected as one of Great Britain's ten leading amateur golfers while actually at school.

These are facts for the fond parent to bear in mind before he condemns 'schoolboy golf' out of hand. Let him forbid his offspring, if he cares, to play while he is in residence at school: but before he prevents his giving time to the game in the holidays, let him decide what better alternative he can provide.

CHAPTER VIII

CADDIES

A PROBLEM that faces the golfer sooner or later is the question of whether or not he shall employ a caddie.

Some people arrive at the answer without a second's

hesitation. For them it is 'No, I shall certainly not. Golf is expensive enough as it is.' Others reach the end of their golfing days without having made up their minds.

Just how much are the services of a caddie worth to the golfer? The first-class player, it may broadly be said, always has a caddie—and has done so since the game began. When he had a miscellaneous array of half a dozen long-headed, thick-handled mallets with which to play his primitive game, he employed a boy to carry them under his arm. Now that he possesses a battery of anything up to twenty-five steel-shafted weapons, reposing in a leather bag as big and heavy as a steamer trunk, he employs a man to stagger round with them on his shoulder.

There are still, however, thousands of golfers who never employ a caddie, and thousands more who waver on the border-line. Some waver because they are not sure that the expense is justified, others from an entirely misplaced feeling of embarrassment based on the notion that ability to play the game well is an essential qualification for a golfer to employ a man to carry his clubs. This, of course, is not so, though the underlying sentiment is a perfectly natural one. To prove it, one has only to ask a man who has come up to the club in the hopes of getting a job, whether he minds carrying the clubs of a person who does not happen to play particularly well.

If ever a man can be a guide, philosopher, and friend to his master, that man is the golf caddie. That he can also be an unmitigated aggravation is also undeniable. It depends on the characters of the two parties concerned: some golfers have made me blush for shame at the way they treat their caddies; on other occasions I could willingly have slain my own.

Caddies may be divided at once into those who know and follow the game and those who merely act as porters. It has always seemed to be one of the most outstanding anomalies in the employment conditions of any class of labour that custom should compel us to pay each kind of man identically the same wage.

After a fairly wide experience of caddies in various parts of the world, I have come to the unalterable conclusion that the way to get the best out of a man is to treat him as a partner, and not as a servant. You and he are playing your opponent and his caddie, the two of you against the two of them. If you let him feel that he is part of the firm, you will double the value of his services.

What exactly are the services you may legitimately expect him to render you, apart from carrying your clubs? The first, of course, is to put back the divots. It is his primary duty—and the one that he most often shirks. If you are anything of a man, you will not let him. It is only too easy to pretend not to notice your caddie pretending not to notice the large slab of the communal turf that you have removed—but it is a temptation to be resisted. He expects to have to put it back, he is perfectly willing to put it back: he is simply like a schoolboy, 'trying it on'. Let him know, the first time it happens, that this is not his lucky day, and the question will not arise between you again.

Another of his duties, often neglected, is to keep the ball clean. Any caddie worthy of the name will have a sponge or a wet rag or some contrivance for the purpose. What he uses should not concern you. If he chooses to spit upon the ball and then rub it, like a greengrocer polishing an apple, up and down on his overcoat, you may object in principle, but should not do so in fact. It is his business.

Then we come to the question of 'advice'—a question that contains a whole variety of pitfalls. By the Rules of Golf your caddie (and of course in matches other than singles, your partner) is the only person who is allowed to give you advice. Hence the extreme potential value of a really good caddie.

The ordinary man, I think, welcomes the advice of his caddie, for a double reason. He likes it not only for itself, but also for the opportunity it gives him for 'taking it out of somebody else' when things go wrong. It is like having the office-boy permanently handy on the golf course.

And that, of course, is where the pitfalls lie. Men expect too much of their caddies, expect almost miracles from them. Spoiled perhaps by a caddie on their home course who knows their play, they fall into the common error of expecting a man who has never seen them before to know exactly the appropriate club to hand them. Stiff and cramped in the morning, they approach their second shot to the first hole on a strange course, say 'Well, what is it?'—and expect the man to give the right answer. Probably they do not even tell him their handicap to give him a guide.

If you do not expect the caddie to be right every time (and, when you come to think of it, the very fact of your blindly taking his advice shows you to have not the remotest idea of judging for yourself), you will find him an indispensable ally. If you expect him to be an automaton, you would save money and temper by carrying your own clubs.

Other advice you may expect from your caddie concerns the line to the hole on the putting-green ; and here the position is even more generally misunderstood—this time as much by the caddie as by the player. ' A foot on the right, sir ', says the caddie or ' Just here, sir ', as he points with the flagstick to a spot between you and the hole.

Now, giving the line in this way can never, to my mind, be accurate unless there exists an almost superhuman understanding between you and your caddie. Allowing for a borrow on the green is a highly delicate proceeding. There is more than one way into the hole, as Diagram 16 shows, and the amount you must allow depends on how hard you intend to hit the putt.

Supposing, for the sake of argument, you have a fairly pronounced borrow from the right. The diagram shows three of the mathematically infinite number of ways into the hole. Putt A is a good firm stroke. It is still running freely when it reaches the hole, and the action of the slope has not yet had time to have much effect on it. If it misses the hole it will run perhaps five or six feet past, assuming the initial putt to be about five yards. Putt B is a slower one, and therefore, when it reaches the hole, is responding to the action of the slope more noticeably: it would have run something like a yard past. Putt C is a delicate ' trickler ' all up the hill and slowly down again—dying, as it were, by the hole-side: if it misses, it will always be stone dead.

Each of these three ways has its advantages. Putt A demands that you hit the back of the hole fairly and squarely; but, then, the mere fact of being able to play it firmly gives you more chance of doing so. Putt B demands a more accurate judging of the strength, but means that you should be reasonably certain of getting down in two; while Putt C demands a very delicate

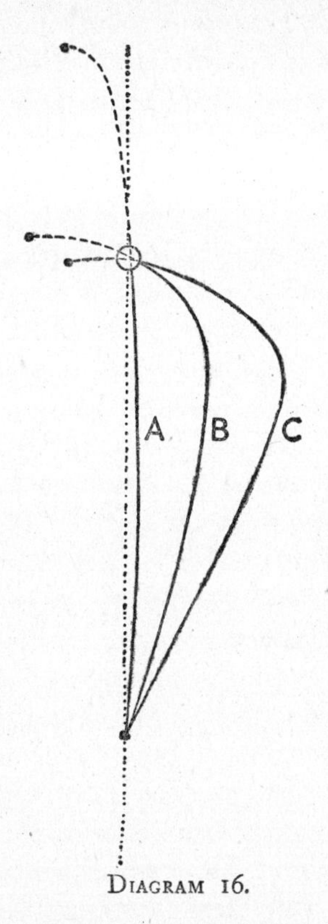

DIAGRAM 16.

touch indeed. It applies, incidentally, only to a very fast green, of the kind usually found at the seaside in summer, and is largely a 'safety' putt, to be used when the pace of the green makes a more direct approach too dangerous in case you miss the hole.

Now, the line for A, *as it leaves the club*, is perhaps a foot on the right of the hole; for B it is, say, three feet: and for C as much as six feet.

Therefore, returning to our original argument, it will be seen that it is quite impossible for the caddie to tell you the exact line to take unless he knows exactly how hard you are going to hit it—and this is a thing that is almost impossible to convey to him in words, if indeed you know it at all.

With experience comes the ability to see the line for yourself and to judge how much you should borrow, basing your judgment on the knowledge, which you alone possess, of how hard you intend to hit the putt. The advice of a local caddie who knows the green can then be reserved for the rare occasions in which you find yourself in doubt. Even then his assistance is generally limited to giving you a broad idea of the contour of the ground.

Nevertheless, if you find that experience does not, after all, bring you the necessary sense of direction, you need not despair, for you are in good company. Among the amateurs, Leonard Crawley, a Walker Cup player and past English champion, is constitutionally incapable of seeing the line for himself, and always takes it from the caddie. So little idea of the contour of the green is he able to get for himself, that I have seen him in a championship stop, when apparently about to putt, turn to his caddie and say, 'Did you say six inches to the *left* or six inches to the *right*?'.

Among the professionals you will be in even more august company, for Henry Cotton is another who trusts to his caddie. After he won his historic Open at Sandwich in 1934, Cotton gave his caddie fifty pounds, not merely as an indication of his delight at winning, but as a definite payment for services rendered. 'I could not see the line on those greens at all', he told me afterwards, 'so I decided to trust blindly to my caddie, and never once to act on my own judgment. I could not believe he was right sometimes, but he nearly always was. I putted really well all through that championship. You could not give a man less than fifty pounds for that.'

Which brings us to the question 'How much should *you* give your caddie?'. Opinions vary, but it is possible to lay down some fairly sound general rules on the subject. The thing to do is to find out first of all what tip is currently fashionable at the club at which you are playing. In provincial clubs the standard tip may be a shilling, whereupon your rule will be to pay a moderate caddie a shilling and a good one one and sixpence, unless there is a rule in the club stipulating that the tip shall not exceed a shilling. When rules are laid down in a club or a tournament, it is tempting to break them, but it is also extremely discourteous.

At a London club the fee may be two and sixpence, and the usual tip two shillings on weekdays and half a crown at week-ends. It sounds a lot of money, but if you are going to play at such a club, you must conform to its customs. You do not, after all, argue over the price they charge for your lunch. In such clubs, unfortunately, it is generally impossible to differentiate in the matter of the tip between a good caddie and a bad one.

CHAPTER IX

FOURSOMES AND OTHER FORMS OF GOLF

ONE of the outstanding charms of golf is, to my mind, the fact that it is not a team game. A schoolboy plays games primarily because he has to: sometimes he takes to them at once, sometimes he comes to like them later, sometimes they bore him to the end. An adult, however, plays games, or in my opinion is meant to play games, exclusively for his own pleasure.

A week-end in these days is a precious thing, to be expended with as much care as a five-pound note; to a good many of us the prospect of spending part of it, say, fielding to a couple of slow batsmen is little short of nauseating. We turn therefore to golf, where we may be sure of batting all the time, secure in the knowledge that a solitary bad shot—perhaps even the opening stroke of the day—is not going to put paid to all our week-end's fun.

That, I think, is a sound as well as a logical outlook. But the best of logic can be carried too far, and I believe that this passionate desire to hit their own ball all the time prevents a number of golfers from enjoying their game to the full. The average week-end golfer, for instance, never in any circumstances plays a foursome. He is prepared, when asked what is the best form of golf, to reply with the rest of the world, 'Oh, a foursome, I suppose', but he is inclined to add—either under his breath or not, according to the nature of his hearers—'but give me a fourball every time'.

The foursome as an ordinary friendly encounter is rapidly dying—is, in fact, almost extinct. It is still, however, an integral part of nearly every team match, and as such will probably live on so long as the game exists. Half of every international match, of the University match, and of almost every inter-club match in which time permits, is composed of foursomes. Such institutions as the Match Club and the Moles, whose object is to dine and wine together at intervals and challenge each other to matches, confine their activities to foursome play. In the Halford Hewitt tournament at Deal it reaches its zenith.

In the foursome lies golf's only pretence to being a team game; here alone is anything in the nature of team work possible. This is not to be confused with 'team spirit', that indefinable something of which Englishmen are so proud (despite Archie Compston's dogmatic assertion, with which I have a sneaking sympathy, to the effect that 90 per cent. of them do not know the first thing about it). Team spirit is invisible, intangible, and exists only in the mind, perhaps in the very atmosphere. Team work is the putting of that spirit into practice. The spirit can exist among ten or a dozen persons, banding them together with a common purpose that causes them to do their individual best. The work is limited to two at a time.

An aspect of the foursome that is largely forgotten is this: that all the shots you play are certain to count. This is not quite the truism that it may sound, for in a fourball all your shots assuredly do *not* count. The number that do depends on the kind of game that your partner happens to be playing.

A great deal of the fun of golf consists of trying to turn three shots into two. It is not given to most of us to hit the green consistently with our seconds, and so for most of the time we are wondering whether, despite our having missed the green, we can by hook or by crook emerge with a four. In a fourball, if your partner happens to have ' found his length ', you will find yourself denied the privilege of trying to turn three shots into two, in fact robbed of all the interest in the hole. Your partner is perhaps a mere four or five yards from the flag with his second and has already a certain four : you may finish the hole for formality's sake, but a sense of guilt reminds you that you are keeping everyone waiting.

The fourball, all the same, is a highly popular form of golf, and I should be the last to declare that there was no art in playing it. This art lies primarily on the green, where A, despite being nearer the hole, may hole out first for a safe four or five, leaving B a ' free ' putt for a three or four. Unhampered by a lurking fear of over-running the hole and taking three putts, B is able to make a bold bid for the hole, more likely to be successful than a cautious effort based on the principle of ' two putts at any price '.

Another largely psychological point that often escapes notice is this. Everyone has from time to time experienced that delightful sensation of being in a run of luck, when everything goes right. Directly you see your partner in one of these, or when you see him heading for a personal score of which he is obviously going to be proud, *let him run*. Don't interrupt the flow. If he has a 10-foot putt for a four and you are still 10 yards away in two, give him a chance to hole it, and if he does, pick up your ball with an air of ' I always knew you would '. He will begin mentally to compare himself with Walter Hagen, and will probably do the next hole in three—which again will save you a great deal of trouble.

Up to the green I do not believe that it is possible for either player to do more than simply get there in the fewest shots possible. 'You make sure of a five, partner, and I will go for a four' is a plan of campaign popular on the teeing ground. If the truth be known, I fancy that the man who is to make sure of the five is infinitely the more likely to finish the hole in four.

But perhaps the most valuable rule for fourball play is 'Never trust your partner'. Always try to keep yourself handy in reserve, in case he takes leave of his senses and three putts from 10 feet. How many post-mortems include the words 'I could have got down in two easily from there, if it had ever occurred to me that you were going to take three'!

While we are on the subject of the various forms of golf, a word concerning the threeball or 'Pawnbroker', as they used to call it in the '90's, may not be out of place. The threeball is an outcast in the golfing world—and yet I have to confess that I find it immeasurably the best form of golf. While in a fourball only half your strokes are liable to take an active part in the game, in a threeball every single one of them counts double.

There are two ways of playing a threeball, one being the normal way, each playing against the other two and reckoning by holes up and holes down. The other, and to my mind infinitely more attractive, method is by a system of points. Six points are at stake at each hole, the winner to have four, the next man two, and the last man nothing. If two halve it at the expense of the other, the scores are 3, 3, 0 respectively. If A wins it outright but B and C tie for second place, the scores are 4, 1, 1.

That is simple enough, yet many people decry the

system on the grounds of its being too complicated. They forget the score, they say. That is because they do not realize that in keeping the score the *last man must always be kept at nought.* Supposing the result of the first hole is 4, 1, 1 and the result of the second is 3, 0, 3; that gives a total of 7, 1, 4—which is the same thing as saying 6, 0, 3. The third hole may result in 1, 4, 1, the total then becoming 7, 4, 4. This at once becomes 3, 0, 0, and the whole thing retains an air of guileless simplicity. If, on the other hand, you had made the mistake of running up the entire totals, the position would now have been 8, 5, 5. At the end of the round it might have been 61, 29, 18—or something equally formidable.

The advantages of this system when properly worked are easy to see. If A wins the hole from both B and C, but B wins it from C, in the ordinary way the position would be that A would be one up on each of them. Under the points system, however, he gets full value for defeating C by more than he defeated B. On C he is four points up, on B only two. Meanwhile B is still all square in the aggregate—which represents precisely the fair position.

Furthermore, the points system ensures a full eighteen holes match between all the parties. There is no bye, and winning the eighteenth counts for exactly as much as winning the first. In other words, whereas a fourball offers you a half-share in a match that may end at the tenth hole, a threeball played by points offers you the equivalent of a full thirty-six holes.

A further form of golf which should be noticed in passing is the greensome, in which each of the two partners drives at every hole. The side then chooses which drive it will play and continues as a foursome, striking alternate shots. The greensome is popular in Alliance tournaments in the shortened days of winter, but is not a general favourite in private golf. Yet it provides an attractive game, combining many of the merits of the foursome and the fourball.

What the average golfer most desires when he says, 'Give me my own ball every time', is, in particular, his drive. He likes to have as many chances as he can of hitting the ball 10 yards farther than he has done before. And the greensome gives him that chance. He does not mind if his drive is not the one that is chosen for hole—indeed, if it is not, he has the additional entertainment of playing the second shot as well—but he does like to have the thrill of hitting it.

Finally, a word about the Stableford system of scoring should, I think, be included. It is not, like the threeball, the foursome, and so forth, a separate form of golf, but merely a form of scoring applicable to any of them. Its use is restricted almost entirely to competitions.

The Stableford system gains yearly in popularity, as more and more people come to understand its working and to realize, as they realize when they come to be familiar with the points system for threeballs, that it is not so complicated as it seems.

The system represents what is logically the fairest method of scoring known to golf. The score is kept neither by holes nor strokes, but by points. Two points are awarded for doing the hole in bogey—or, in the current parlance which I hope will disappear from the game before long, the Standard Scratch Score—and one for doing it in one over bogey. A 'birdie'—that is, one under bogey—scores three; an 'eagle'—two under bogey—scores four, while an 'albatross', as I believe it is called, scores five. But golfers who talk of 'albatrosses' are like poker players who at the beginning of the session solemnly decide upon the bonus payable on a royal straight flush.

After adding up his total points at the end, the player *adds* three-quarters of his handicap—since of course it is the highest, not the lowest, total that wins. It will be seen that a score of 36 points represents bogey.

CHAPTER X

MATCH AND MEDAL PLAY

If the question were put to all the golfers in Britain, I am sure that something in the neighbourhood of 90 per cent. would announce, and in no uncertain terms, that they preferred match to medal play. The 'card-and-pencil' complex is one from which the vast majority suffer to their dying day. The odd 10 per cent. would nearly all be low handicap players. A good many of them prefer medal play—and though it is a mean assertion, I feel sure it is right—largely because they fear humiliation at the hands of a personal adversary.

If A wins a medal competition, the world is liable soon to forget the fact that B was four shots behind: but if A beats B by 4 and 3, the result lingers on, as it seems, for eternity. The Little Man, however—the 'Tiddler', as old Mr. Abercromby used irreverently to describe him—whose successes and failures are not blazoned forth in the newspapers, has no such fear of lasting humiliation.

In any case, since he habitually plays fourballs, he is seldom exposed to individual attack.

The average mortal is afraid of a card-and-pencil because it leaves him with an impression of playing with the sword of Damocles slung permanently over his head. When will the blow fall?, he wonders, resigned to the fact that sooner or later the one bad hole must come.

From which it will be seen that his trouble in a medal competition is mental, not physical. The mistake arises, I am sure, from trying to do too much, from forgetting what his handicap is there for. Going over the course in his mind's eye beforehand, he allows himself three at the short holes—and then begins to panic when he takes fours. How much more profitable it is to go to the other extreme!

Let us take as an illustration a normal fourteen-handicap man, and let us imagine him to be playing on what we may also call a 'normal' golf course—one, for instance, which has four short holes, six bogey-fives and eight bogey-fours—scratch score 74.

For our friend, let it be at once remembered, the scratch score is not 74, *but 88*. The first thing he must do is to cast from his mind this almost mythical figure of 74 and concentrate on his own personal goal—the 88. How is he to make reasonably certain of going round in 88?

If only he can work himself into a humble, unambitious frame of mind, it can be done. Inspiration and golf rarely go hand in hand, for the game is too slow for inspired moments. Single inspired strokes, yes; inspired holes maybe—but that is all. What is wanted is a quiet caution, and the sense of calm and well-being that comes from having a situation well in hand.

Although the competition is played on handicap, our friend is to banish all thoughts of net scores from his mind. His 88 is to be his constant target. He should map out his plan of campaign in advance, starting, for the sake of argument, with the four short holes. Of these he has a reasonable hope of doing either one or two in three and the rest in four: yet his aim here will be the entirely pedestrian one of doing them in an average of four and no better. Four for each of them accounts for 16 of his allowance.

As to the six long holes, some of which he may hope to do in five, he is to assume that every one of them will take him six. That accounts for 36—and he has not yet done a single hole in bogey.

Now for the remaining eight bogey-fours. Some of them will be difficult fours, and some of them, even for him, a drive and a mashie. Of the eight he may allow himself, without being unduly ambitious, four fours and four fives, making up his total of 88. He should not try to lay down specifically the ones at which he will get the fours: he will simply take things as they come. He must, however, avoid the temptation of striving to reach a green that is beyond the compass of two shots, simply because the card says the bogey is four. He will find a 480-yards' hole much easier to do in five than one of 360 yards in four.

In this hypothetical score there are four hidden reserves. Firstly, provided he does not try for anything better than a quiet six, our friend will find himself doing some of the long holes in five. Secondly, he may hope to get a three at one or two of the short holes. Thirdly, he may hope to hole one, or on a fortunate day, two or three, good putts—good, that is, judged by whatever personal standard he cares to measure them. Fourthly, he may have at least one fluke—an approach holed or a longish shot laid close to the flag.

The emergencies against which this reserve may have to be used are various. ' One out-of-bounds ' is an ever-present threat: ' three putts ' is another: failing to get out of a bunker with the first shot is a third. Two at least, however, should be preventable in a medal tournament if proper care is exercised. If there is a dangerous out-of-bounds on the left, apply the basic principle of ' unambition ' and play safely, losing distance if necessary, to the right. Again, when trapped in a bunker, abandon all thought of distance, and make sure simply of getting under the ball.

The great art of medal play lies in taking these disasters, when they come, with a quiet mind. They are bound to come, so accept them with a good grace and remember what the reserve is for. Walter Hagen reckoned to play at least three really bad shots in a round; but, since he was ready for them, they did not worry him.

Remember, too, that if you only give them time, the breaks will almost certainly ' even out ' in eighteen holes. Some days the good ones come first, some days the bad: but they balance out in the end.

Match Play

The time-honoured axiom relating to the technique of match play is, ' Forget your opponent and play against the par of the course '. Often attributed to Bobby Jones, it was probably uttered by someone or other the very moment that bogey made its original appearance in golf. But, to whomsoever the credit is due, the fact remains that the axiom is good.

It is not, however, so easy to carry out as it sounds, for we are not all endowed with Mr. Sherlock Holmes's powers of mental isolation.

'Golf', said Compston one day, 'is like any other fight you undertake in this life. You must adopt an aggressive attitude. You can either fight your opponent, or you can say "This is a game of skill", eliminate him altogether, and beat him by golf shots. Which, of course, is the easier way to adopt, if you can do it.'

If you can do it—those are the operative words. It depends largely on individual temperament: the boy who was always fighting at school will probably grow up into a match-play golfer, the boy who would run a mile to avoid a scrap will come to prefer medal play. I am afraid I am one who prefers medal play.

To ignore an opponent who is himself of the aggressive type is a matter of tremendous difficulty to many people. To try as hard when it seems certain that he will take six for the hole demands strength of mind that is not given to most of us; yet it must be done, for bitter experience tells us that any relaxation on our part seems to bestow on our opponent not only renewed confidence, but also astounding good fortune. The ball that had vanished into the heather is found to be teed up: he puts it on the green and, inspired by the consternation he knows he will cause, sinks the putt for a 4 and wins the hole.

Yet golf, as I have tried to point out, is essentially a selfish pastime. We have our own ball to hit, our own job of work to do. Nothing that our adversary can do can have any *physical* effect on our own game: the only effect he can produce lies in our mind, and it is our business in match play to nullify that possible effect by ignoring both him and his works.

There is no panacea that can make a man into a good match player, though one or two tips may be found helpful. The most profitable scheme is to stand on the tee, survey the hole, and say, 'I set myself the task of doing this hole in five (or whatever it may be). If I do it in five, I shall be satisfied. If he can do it in less, he can have it.' To keep account of one's medal score is of course essential: if it is likely to help, one may even go to the length of taking a card and pencil and marking it down at the end of each hole. I recall seeing L. G. Crawley doing this from time to time in championships, to the amusement of those of the onlookers who knew only too well the struggle that was going on in his mind.

CHAPTER XI

BETTING

It is not the function of the writers of this series of volumes, mercifully for the reader, to preach sermons on the rights and wrongs of the games with which they deal. The present remarks on the subject of betting will therefore be informative rather than didactic.

To suggest that all betting is bad is as stupid as to hold forth against all alcohol because some persons abuse it, or against all milk because in certain cases it has been found to be infected with tuberculosis. Betting is an integral part of golf, and always has been. Since the earliest days the game has been the subject of innumerable wagers, some of them, to say the least of it, substantial, and the Minutes and Bets Books of some of the old Scottish clubs and societies make highly amusing reading.

Betting, on the other hand, is liable to be a minor evil in golf as we know it now. 'The game's the thing' has become a hackneyed phrase in Britain, if only from its long service as our excuse for sporting defeats all over the world, but it is still true. The game *is* still the thing, and there are just a few golfers who have to be told from time to time that they are overlooking the fact.

There is all the world of difference between the old-fashioned wager, made in advance and talked about in the club, and the currently popular habit in one or two of London's more wealthy clubs of finding the game not worth while at less than a fiver.

'What's your price to try really hard?' said a friend of mine to his opponent as they were fixing the stake. 'Two pounds?'

The other agreed that he would try hard for that.

'Would you try really hard for one pound?'

'Yes, I would.'

'Very well, then', said my friend, 'we'll play for ten shillings.'

That to my mind is the way to bet at golf.

Another little story may help to illustrate the point. I played in a fourball with three good players on a London course one Sunday, and in the morning, playing for ten shillings a head, we had a rousing game. Animated discussion at lunch led us, nobody quite knew why, to play for five pounds a head in the afternoon. After sixteen holes we were all square. For the past hour no one had spoken, every brow was furrowed, and an air of tension hung over the game. 'If you want to know the truth', I said, 'I am hating this. I came out for a Sunday's fun—and this is hard work.' Then of course we found that all four of us were thinking exactly the same thing—so we cancelled the bets and for two holes played the game for fun.

Perhaps that is too near to the sermon that I promised to avoid; but it does show how easily, almost unwittingly, one can be drawn into spoiling a golf game by playing for too much.

All sorts of methods of staking money on golf are in daily use. Some people like a straight bet on the result of the game, others prefer something on the first nine, something on the second nine, and something on the match—the Nassau system, as it is known in the United States. Those who are reasonably certain of completing the course may also like 'So much per shot' on their medal score.

'Syndicates', as it is generally known, provides another interesting game that admits any number of players. Each player at each hole puts the agreed fee into the pool, and the entire pool is taken by the first man to win a hole outright from all the others.

Another game that provides not only amusement but a severe test of nerve as well is 'poker' golf. Everyone puts his fee in the pool and takes his drive. Then the man whose turn it is to play last can, if he likes, increase it. They all play their seconds, and the man nearest the hole states how much it will cost the others to stay in the game and play their third shots. When it comes down to the putting, the game gives a man a wholesome opportunity of making a direct 'cash estimate' of his own ability.

The golfing bookmaker is a comparatively recent arrival. In 1898, it is true, in a professional tournament at Carnoustie, a man stood on the first tee and offered odds, but, says the *Golfers' Handbook*, 'after a few hours, whether from lack of punters or adverse public opinion, he desisted '. In 1927 a bookmaker and two assistants were ' seen off the course ' during the Open Championship at St. Andrews, but it was not until 1934 that bookmakers publicly advertised the odds for the open and amateur championships. One or two voices were raised in orthodox protest, but the layers of the odds continued to flourish, and now it is no surprise at a championship to find one's best friend touting for a bookmaker.

Whether such a state of affairs is desirable for the game it is not my function to say.

CHAPTER XII

ETIQUETTE

ETIQUETTE OF THE GAME OF GOLF

(1) No one should move or talk or stand close to or directly behind the ball or the hole when a player is making a stroke.

(2) The player who has the honour should be allowed to play before his opponent tees his ball.

(3) No player should play until the party in front are out of range.

(4) When the result of a hole has been determined players should immediately leave the putting-green.

(5) Players while looking for a lost ball should allow other matches coming up to pass them; they should signal to the players following them to pass, and having given such a signal, they should not continue their play until these players have passed and are out of range.

(6) A player should see that any turf cut or displaced by him is at once replaced and pressed down.

(7) Players should carefully fill up all holes made in a bunker.

(8) Players should see that their caddies do not injure the holes by standing close to them when the ground is soft or in replacing the flag-stick.

(9) A player who has incurred a penalty should intimate the fact to his opponent as soon as possible.

(10) Players should at all times play without undue delay.

These ten rules, expressed with admirable simplicity, are the golfer's Guide to Good Behaviour. They should be read, marked, learned, and inwardly digested by every novice; re-read in detail by anyone who has, a moment ago, skipped them on the grounds that they were familiar.

None of them demands a detailed explanation, but some, the more constantly abused, deserve a passing attention. The number of people that one meets in a lifetime of golf who deliberately disconcert their opponents by underhand methods may, happily, be counted on the fingers of one hand. The concentrated attention demanded by a golf shot can, however, be broken in the twinkling of an eye by the slightest disturbance, and to say that people are not in the habit deliberately of putting each other off is not to say that they do not from time to time do so unintentionally. And since it is inevitably a matter of some embarrassment to criticize the conduct of one's partner or opponent, these unwitting breaches of etiquette pass too often unchallenged.

(1) Glance, for instance, at this—the most universally disregarded rule. 'Out of sight, out of mind' is a good golfing precept: so long as a player cannot see you, or sense your presence, as he leans over to address the ball, it does not matter where you stand. The one place *not*

to be is behind the corner of his right eye, where the slightest disturbance spells ruin to the stroke.

The injunction to 'stand still' one would have scarcely thought necessary to the golfer, yet so many people need to be told over and over again. They think they are standing still because they happen to be motionless at the moment when the player's club strikes the ball, but that is not the moment that matters. The all-important period is the few seconds when he is contemplating the stroke—waggling his club, shuffling his feet, trying his best to pin his wayward attention down to the business in hand. The story told of Harry Vardon, Miss Joyce Wethered, Walter Hagen, Bobby Jones, and others (that they had played their stroke unperturbed by a passing train and, when questioned, remarked 'What train?') indicates a power of concentration not given to the average mortal.

(2) Breach of this is unusual: indeed, I have met only one man who habitually teed his ball before his opponent had played. It is a stupid, aggravating way of asserting one's presence, and the fellow in question has earned himself nothing but hard words.

(3) Confusion still exists in many people's minds because this rule used to read 'have played their second shots and are out of range'. The fact that a man had played his second shot never did and never will constitute grounds for driving into him. All the same, mistakes will occur, and we all drive into people sometimes. When you happen to be the sinner, wave your arms with excited gesticulations on the tee and, when you reach your victim, lift your hat and apologize. If he is then rude—

and very few people are—bow politely and retire. Two blacks don't make a white.

(4) Nothing is more irritating than having to wait to play your second shots and then to see persons practising over again the short putts they have missed. Remember this when it is you who have missed the putt.

(5) When the people in front have signalled you to go through and have a moment later found their ball, you are within your rights if you insist on passing them. Very often, however, the pace of the course in general, which is what matters, will be better maintained if you signal them to go on. They are certain to play the hole at top speed, and you will not be kept waiting long.

(6) & (7) Recall your own sensations upon finding your ball in a divot-mark or in a heel-mark in a bunker, and you will not commit the two cardinal sins to which these rules refer.

(8) & (9) No comment.

(10) This injunction was added to the list in 1933—and not before it was due. In the winter of 1937 a letter to a newspaper by Cyril Tolley renewed the controversy. He accused players of dawdling over their golf, and stated that the proposed limitation of clubs to fourteen did not go far enough. Some people naturally take longer than others to work up the concentration necessary for the production of their best efforts, but everyone should remember that any delay after the peak or optimum point has been reached detracts from the efficiency of the shot.

None of the world's great players have been sluggards. 'When I am playing well', said Sarazen to me one day, 'I am playing fast: when I am playing badly, I am playing slow'.

CHAPTER XIII

THE RULES OF GOLF

The cry for simplification of the Rules of Golf is a stock-in-trade of the journalist during the winter months. Countless words on the subject have been poured out to an ever-tolerant public, but still the long-sought simplification does not come.

The reason is not far to seek. The Rules of Golf Committee are a slow-moving body—but they are slow moving only because 'progress' is almost impossible.

Their task is similar to that which faced (and may we say defeated?) the body of eminent gentlemen gathered together for the purpose of simplifying the laws relating to Income Tax. The limit of their reasonable ambition was the simplification not of the subject, which did not permit of it, but simply of the language used. The Rules of Golf Committee have attained this, and farther they cannot hope to go.

The situations in which a couple of golfers can find themselves are so multifarious that a lengthy code of laws is necessary to cover them all. In games whose scope is confined to the narrow limits of a flat field the position is obviously different. As it is, it seems more desirable in the interests of everyone that a comparatively lengthy but fixed code should govern the game, than that a constant stream of queries should reach the

Royal and Ancient concerning problems not covered by a shorter and more simple code.

Even as it is, no fewer than 358 special decisions are set out in the volume issued in the name of the Rules of Golf Committee. This book, incidentally, should be in the possession of everyone who plays golf for anything more than physical exercise.

The Rules of Golf are like the Preface to the Telephone Directory—they look as dull as ditchwater, but they represent a whole mine of enlightening and entertaining reading.

These Rules are based, every one of them, on common sense. They represent what, when you come to argue it out, is obviously the fair course between the player and his adversary.

Some of them cover situations in which a man will not find himself once in a lifetime, others take care of the more every-day emergencies. The former he will probably know by heart, the latter will continue to escape his mind whenever they are most required!

A Few Misconceptions

It is to these latter that I wish to make especial reference here. Let us 'run through the card', as it were, clearing up a few of the more popular misconceptions as we go.

The first hurdle to be cleared lies right away at the beginning among the Definitions. It is the word 'hazard'. Just what is and what is not a hazard? The point is highly important on account of the fact that when the ball is in a hazard you cannot ground the club. In all other places you can.

The average golfer is inclined to think that the words

hazard and trouble are synonymous. Of course they are not. A hazard, officially, is any bunker, water, ditch sand, or road—and that is all. There are plenty of other positions—bare patches, tracks, paths, snow, and ice, to quote a few—which in all conscience can be described as hazardous: but they are not hazards. You can ground your club in all of them, and if any man shall say you nay, tell him to go back to his grammar and begin again at the first declension.

Now for the Rules themselves. One of the earliest, shortest, and simplest—No. 6—contains in its twenty-five words the whole essence of the golfer's catechism; the foundation on which every law and principle of the game is based. To save you the trouble of looking it up, here it is: *A ball must be played wherever it lies or the hole be given up, except as provided for in the Rules or Local Rules.* That's all.

This is not the place for a lengthy discussion on the part that luck should play in sport. Suffice to say that, undeniably, the more that luck can be ruled out of a game, the more desperately grim and serious does that game become. If you do not care to believe this statement, consider whether you would care to continue playing billiards if all flukes were barred.

At any rate, it is this little Rule 6 that has inspired all the laws of golf. The ball, once it is in play, shall be sacrosanct—a kind of sporting Untouchable. It is true that in the course of time the rule has been amended in various ways: a ball can now be deemed unplayable under a severe penalty but without the automatic loss of the hole, and there are various occasions when it can be legally picked up and dropped or placed. But basically Rule 6 remains.

Indeed, there are some people who would like to see every other rule scrapped save this one, adding one qualification that 'when in doubt, do as you would have your opponent do in similar circumstances'. But perhaps, with so much at stake as is offered by modern sport, that represents a Utopia to which we may no longer aspire.

So let us continue our casual wanderings through the Rules. No. 11, for instance, deals with Removal of Obstructions. There are some things that you can move; others that you can move away from—such things as huts and shelters, the greenkeepers' tractor, and so forth. If you can't move them, you move your ball. There are only a few of them, and the golfer will do well to remember the list.

Even the most distinguished often forget them. Had Cyril Tolley, for instance, recalled a part of this rule stating that a ball may be moved if it lies on or touching *clothes*, he might have won the 1933 amateur championship at Hoylake.

'Good heavens, I've played your ball!'. That is a remark that every golfer will utter or hear uttered many times in his life. 'What happens?' he will go on. 'Do I lose the hole? I've only played one shot with it.' The answer is that, *in a match*, he loses the hole then and there unless his opponent has played a shot with *his* ball, in which case they cancel out the errors and each finish the hole, as if nothing had happened, with the wrong ball.

In stroke play, on the other hand, you wash out any strokes you may have played with the wrong ball, add two penalty strokes to your score, and play on with your own ball.

Now, here is another highly important rule that has given rise in its time to endless discussion. It is No. 22, and concerns the whole question of the Provisional Ball. Once again, it is founded essentially on common sense, but unfortunately it does leave a loophole for the less morally scrupulous sportsman.

It is clearly in the interests of all that if you have hit your ball out of bounds or into a position in which it will probably be either lost or unplayable, you should play another ball without delay. If the ball *is* lost or out of bounds, you would in any case have to go back and play another from the spot where you are now standing, so you may as well do it without any further preamble.

Here, however, is the snag. Supposing, to make the example more lucid, you are playing your tee shot at a short hole and you slice it into a thicket at the side of the green. 'I doubt if we ever see that one again', you remark, reasonably if not grammatically; 'anyway, it will probably be unplayable if we do. I'll drive another in case.' So you drive another, and with that relaxation that is born of despair you swing in a carefree manner and lay it dead. With that ball, if you decide to continue with it, you have played three: with the other, one.

Marching forward into the undergrowth, you come upon your first ball in a highly unpleasant position. You can just get at it with a niblick—but it might take you two or three to get it out. Are you justified in deeming it unplayable and taking your certain four with the so-called provisional ball? You, after all, are the sole judge as to whether the ball is unplayable.

The answer is No. Argument still persists on this

scarcely debatable point, and the position is one that I am afraid is sometimes abused, though often unwittingly, by golfers. The answer is that you may count your provisional ball only if, on finding your first ball where it lay, you would in any case have taken the trouble to declare it unplayable, walk all the way back to the tee and play another. If you would have decided to take a hack at it and chance it, then you must do so now, and let the provisional ball and its certain four go hang. It may be hard, but at least it's honest.

And now we come to Hazards again, mentioned in Rule 25. You must not, as you know, ground your club in a bunker, nor move anything lying in it. If a ball is sacrosanct in the course of ordinary play, it is doubly so in a hazard. But supposing there is a little island of grass in the bunker or, since all Greens Committees cannot be perfect, a few odd tufts of grass, or even weeds. You may not be able to prevent your club touching them, or the side of the bunker itself, on the backswing. It does not matter. You may do so, so long as you do not in any way improve the lie of the ball or make the shot any easier.

Another thing in connection with bunkers is worth remembering. Very often you will find that they have steps leading either into or out of them, or planks or duckboards to assist you in walking through them. If you are near enough to any of these to make the stroke embarrassing, you may move the ball and place it—still in the bunker, of course—in a similar lie or position.

So much for hazards: now for casual water. And if ever a subject were misunderstood, it is casual water. Yet really it is all so simple.

If your ball lies in any casual accumulation of water that is not normally there, in the rough or on the fairway, you may pick it out and drop it, without penalty, either behind or (if that is not possible) not nearer the hole.

If it lies in casual water in a hazard, you may pick it out and, for a penalty of one stroke, drop it either in a dry part of the hazard or behind it—just as you like. Learn this rule by heart, and you will win half-crowns in the clubhouse every time the course is flooded.

Hitting the flagstick is the source of a lot more unnecessary trouble. The rule is different in stroke and in match play, for reasons that appear obvious. In match play *either side may have the flagstick held at any time*. If you think your opponent is going to hit the flag with his brassie and so stop near the hole, you can cause him to wait while you send your caddie forward to hold it: alternatively, if something tells you that you are going to hole your own brassie, you can wait while a caddie goes forward to take out the flag and let the ball drop in.

Actually trouble only arises on and around the green. If there is nobody holding the flag and you hit it, it does not matter how far away you were. If you hit the flag when there is someone holding it, that side loses the hole. If it is your opponent's caddie, he loses the hole: and if it is yours, you lose it.

What causes the muddle in so many people's minds is the special qualification in the rule as applied to *stroke play*. 'Isn't there something about 20 yards?' they always ask. There is. In a stroke competition it does not matter who is holding the flag, or indeed if no one is. If you hit it from anywhere that is technically on the putting-green—namely within 20 yards—you add a penalty of two strokes. From beyond 20 yards you can do what you like.

As to the special Stroke Rules, only a few of them give any trouble. No. 2, concerning Discontinuing Play in Bad Weather, is sometimes a cause of discussion. As usual, the law is extremely simple. In a medal competition you must not discontinue play for any reason whatever, either meteorological or otherwise. If you do, you are disqualified. On the other hand, if you are held up by the couples in front and you are compelled to wait in any case, there is no reason why you should not take shelter. Yet there are still people who will stand out in the rain in what they fancy to be a righteous obedience to Stroke Rule 2.

Practising on the day of a tournament is another point of contention. The truth is that you may practise shots all over the course, but you must not deliberately play them either on a putting-green or to any of the holes. If you slice one on to a green by mistake, you are forgiven.

A great many people must have suffered the aggravating experience of being disqualified for handing in a Card Wrongly Marked (I do not mean deliberately). The rule is simply that if you return any figure lower than that which you actually accomplished, you are disqualified; if higher—well, that is your own fault. If you like to be careless enough to pass a four as a five, you may at least be sure of the thanks of your fellow-competitors.

On the other hand, the *addition* of the card is not, as it were, your pigeon. The Committee is responsible for that. It is your duty simply to see that the figures themselves, hole by hole, are correct.

CHAPTER XIV

WHAT IS AN AMATEUR?

DEFINITIONS OF PROFESSIONAL AND AMATEURS

AN official statement issued with the revised Definitions stated that the Championship Committee of the Royal and Ancient Golf Club had been considering the conditions of professional and amateur status, and after hearing the views expressed by the Joint Advisory Council, the authorities controlling golf in the British Dominions Overseas and the United States Golf Association, the following definitions were issued to be in operation as from January 1st, 1934.

PROFESSIONAL

A professional golfer is any player who has played for a money prize or has received payment for playing or teaching the game.

Note.—The Championship Committee of the Royal and Ancient Golf Club of St. Andrews rules that the following come within this definition :—

Those who teach golf for remuneration either by personal demonstration, or by lecturing, or by allowing themselves to be filmed.

AMATEURS

The following shall not be eligible to play in any amateur competition:—

1. Professional golfers.
2. Those who have carried clubs for hire after attaining the age of 18 years.
3. Those who exploit their skill at the game or allow their skill to be exploited for profit.

The following are some examples of those who would come within the provisions of Clause 3:—

A—Those who for remuneration allow their names or likenesses to be used for the advertisement or sale of any goods except in the usual course of their business as dealers in, or manufacturers or inventors of such goods.

B—Those who for remuneration permit their names to be advertised or published as authors of books or articles on golf of which they are not actually the authors.

C—Those who for remuneration and under their own names, or under a description from which they can be recognized, report a golf competition or match in which they are taking part if journalism is not their usual and recognized vocation.

D—Those who either accept as presents or are given facilities to buy at prices below those usually charged golf balls, golf clubs, or other merchandise, when such presents are made or facilities granted for the purpose of advertisement.

E—Those who, being employed by firms, companies, or individuals interested in the manufacture or sale of golfing goods, play in golf tournaments or competitions with the object of furthering their employers' interests.

HENRY GULLEN,
20th November, 1933. *Secretary.*

Note 1.—In reply to a letter from the Joint Advisory Council asking if the new Amateur definition would prevent Amateurs accepting samples of golf balls for testing purposes, Mr. Gullen wrote on January 13th, 1934, 'I have to state that it is not the intention of the Championship Committee to remove the permission given to Golf Ball Manufacturers to present to Amateurs two golf balls'.

Note 2.—The following letter, dated March 14th, 1934, has been sent to the Joint Advisory Council with reference to the payment of Amateurs' travelling and hotel expenses: 'Dear Sir,—I beg to inform you that the Championship Committee of the Royal and Ancient Golf Club of St. Andrews has adopted the following note to the Conditions of Amateur Status:—"Without forfeiting their Amateur Status, players may receive their travelling and hotel expenses when representing their Country, County, Club or similar body in Team Matches provided such expenses are paid by the body they represent; or when representing their Country in a Tour overseas provided such expenses are paid through the Authority controlling Golf in their Country". Yours faithfully, Henry Gullen, Secretary.'

Amateur Status

Here is a thorny topic indeed!—one that has led to bitterness, rancour, loose thinking, and loss of temper wherever, as the novelettes say, it has 'reared its ugly head'.

The average golfer, to whom the present volume is primarily addressed, may be forgiven for suggesting that this is a subject with which he is not unduly concerned. The motion-picture magnates have not scrambled for the film rights of his swing; the editors of Fleet Street have not fallen over each other to secure his descriptions of 'competitions in which he is himself taking part'; he has not even been offered a box of balls.

Nevertheless, the subject does concern him—and the chain of connection that links him with the pseudo-amateur is clearly defined. The welfare of a game depends to no small degree on its freedom from controversial unpleasantness of the type usually associated with questions such as amateur status. Rules and definitions can be laid down; but with whatever diligence and skill they may be drawn, there remain always a few loopholes by which an enterprising fellow with a controlled conscience may evade them. The real arbiter of what is and what is not truly an amateur is Public Opinion. And Public Opinion is represented, as to about 90 per cent., by the average golfer.

The welfare of the game lies ultimately in his hands: it is incumbent on him to be aware of his responsibilities.

This query 'What is an amateur?'—or, if you prefer it that way, 'What is a professional?'—produces a variety of answers. The printed word exists, it is true, but it is subject to a variety of interpretations. It is not my function here to give my own. What follows is confined to the acknowledged facts of the case.

The 'shamateur' can thrive only in those sports where sufficient financial opportunity presents itself to the unscrupulous. Illicit rewards of skill in the game of darts are, we may presume, insignificant, since the cash value of the winner having used darts of so-and-so's manufacture cannot be high. In a game like lawn tennis, on the other hand, with its tremendous commercial background, huge sums may depend on the fortunes of a single amateur player. If he is a world champion, he may be worth upwards of £20,000 per year in gate receipts to his national Association: his use of so-and-so's rackets may mean hundreds to the firm in question: local tournaments may depend on his presence for their success. If any of these parties deem a scrupulous adherence to the rules and traditions of the game to be unnecessary, they have it in their power to place a grave temptation before an individual player—one that is the less easily resisted if it represents an income in excess of what he could earn in other walks of life.

I am not stating that illicit rewards are offered or accepted either in darts or lawn tennis: I take the two games simply as representing the two limits of opportunity and as illustrating the circumstances of the case.

Golf, perhaps, falls somewhere between the two. There are illicit rewards to be had in plenty (I am writing this in the year 1937), but they are not for the most part sufficiently big to provide a decent income for a bogus amateur, whatever his skill at the game. Perhaps the most depressing aspect of the situation is the number of people who shut their eyes to Clause 3, Section D, and receive either a dozen a month, two dozen a month, or even an unlimited supply, of free golf balls. The fact that they are for the most part people who could well afford to buy balls anyway, makes their conduct the more reprehensible.

As a matter of fact, the whole definition of amateur status could just as well be summed up in the eleven words 'You shall not "cash in" on your skill as a golfer'. If only people could be counted upon to interpret it fairly, the rule could be left at this and a whole lot of trouble saved to a great many people. But life is not so simple as that.

Skill—that is the operative word in all the five sub-sections of the vital Clause 3. Let us glance through them and see. The first, A, means to say, reasonably enough, that the amateur champion may not issue to the world, stamped with his image and superscription, copies of the magic clubs to which he owed his victory—at least, he may not do so for profit. Mr. Gordon Selfridge, on the other hand, may, if he likes, sell clubs bearing his name (*a*) because it is in 'the usual course of his business as dealer in . . . such goods', and (*b*) because his personal skill as a golfer can scarcely be said to have swayed the decision of his customers to buy their clubs at his store instead of at their local professional's shop.

For those whose conscience is fairly elastic, there is a loophole here, in that the amateur champion might claim to be the 'inventor' of a set of clubs bearing his name. It is to be hoped, however, that none of our champions will, by taking any such action, compel St. Andrews to alter the letter of the law to conform with what already exists as its spirit.

B is simple and straightforward, but a most necessary provision. As any practising journalist is aware, there are only one or two professionals who write a word of the articles and books that appear under their names : in some cases one cannot but suspect, from reading them, that the so-called writers have not even read the proofs. The professional, however, is avowedly in the game to make his living—besides which, we ourselves are anxious for the benefit of his instruction, written as lucidly as possible.

C, I think, needs neither explanation nor justification, but the pitfalls in D are as thick as the quills on a porcupine. These are hard times, and we must not blame the manufacturers overmuch if, in their efforts to sell their products, they regard golf as an industry rather than a game surrounded by tradition. But the fact remains, to take an impartial view, that the jiggery-pokery connected with the sale of golf balls is a serious threat to the good name of golf as a truly amateur sport.

A certain amount of success can be obtained from advertisements claiming that such-and-such a ball goes 10 yards farther than any of its rivals and suggesting that it 'putts well' (irrespective, of course, of the ability of the striker); but the fact remains that most people know that it doesn't, that not one golfer in a hundred could tell the difference between one ball and another if he could not distinguish it from the name or the marking. In the end the most successful way of popularizing a brand of golf ball is to be able to publish legitimately enough an impressive list of championships and tournaments that have been won with it. And, unfortunately, human nature being what it is, the surest way to make a man play with a given brand of ball is to give him a free supply.

The amount of first-class players who, at the moment of writing, habitually receive illicit supplies of golf balls is quite extraordinary. Just as a man who manages to evade the payment of some of his Income Tax would view with pious horror the suggestion that he was stealing money from the Government, so do these fellows view the suggestion that they are cheating at golf. The fact remains that they are.

The final provision, E, does not concern the average golfer. It fell hardly upon one or two notable amateur players whose knowledge of the game and those who played it made their services valuable to golf-ball manufacturers as salesmen, but it is only fair to say that they accepted it in good part as being for the general good of the game, and that no trouble has arisen from its application.

PART III

RETURNING TO GOLF

When I wrote this book in 1937, I was well steeped in golf. I earned my living by writing, and to a minor extent broadcasting, about it. I attended the championships and all the main tournaments; heard, discussed, and sometimes instigated, the theories and controversies of the day. I knew all the leading professionals and amateurs, read their books, dissected their methods, and dug deep down into the psychological aspect that makes golf, to the student of human fallibility, the most intriguing game in the world. I played frequently—though, I like to claim, exclusively for amusement—and in the summer allowed myself the luxury of performing in the continental championships.

So I do feel, on looking back, that I was at least qualified to express an opinion—to put it no higher—on how a difficult game might with the least difficulty be played by the average club player.

In those days I was a player addressing himself to other players. Now in the autumn of 1943, when the publishers call for a reprint of this book, times have changed and so has the relationship between writer and reader. It is on account of these changes that I take the opportunity to present about an eighth of the book in new form. Nothing much has been lost in the process, as I have been able to find the necessary space by eliminating the rules of golf, which are of purely academic interest now and in any case were in the early editions for reference only.

Our new relationship is that of one ex-golfer addressing

himself to a lot of other ex-golfers, all renewing their acquaintance with the game and re-tasting, with dishevelled clubs and broken-down balls, the delights of a golden age we were beginning to think we had lost for ever. At least, that is my assumption. I write at a time when the result, but not the duration, of the war is known with reasonable certainty. It is equally certain, judging by the intensity of the interest which people seem to have retained in golf during the bleak and barren years, that they will return to it with the enthusiasum that was snuffed so suddenly in 1939.

I gave my qualifications for writing the book in the first place as a golfer to golfers. May I now give my qualifications for writing as an ex-golfer to ex-golfers?—with occasional pauses by the wayside for semi-instructional observations that may be of use to both sides.

Having talked and thought and read and written golf for about seven years—incidentally almost to saturation point—I shut up my golfing shop in September, 1939, and the game vanished from my life.

After the address from which I wrote this book in the first place, and the address before it, and the one after it, and myself as well, had been blown up in the raids on London, the army took me to Blackpool, where I taught sundry soldiers to drive dilapidated, impressed civilian lorries, rose to the rank of temporary supernumerary probationary acting assistant unpaid lance-bombardier Long'urst, and came no nearer to playing golf than being billeted in one of the row of houses overlooking the little course attached to the Cleveleys Hydro.

The Norbreck Hydro also had a 9-hole course attached, with a pleasant little clubhouse which could generally be relied on to provide refreshment when the local pubs had run dry. It housed in the locker room during the mornings the regimental barber, and I recall leaning over the fence one day, waiting my turn and idly watching some holiday makers duffing their way to the home green.

'Can't see nothing to a game like this, meself', said the youth beside me. And so far had I too sunk by that time, that, with one ear alert perhaps for the crowing thrice of a distant cock, I replied 'No more can I'.

Later I repaired of an evening to the North Shore club, where the exhortations of various members, the scent of the old atmosphere that had been so much a background to my former life, and the luring aspect of the course stretched out below the clubhouse in the evening sun, persuaded me at last to try my hand again for the first time since the war began. I borrowed six primitive, ill-assorted clubs and, attired in a collarless army shirt and plimsoles, in which the advertisers of expensive golfing shoes could in the old days have proved it impossible to play golf at all, I set out to play nine holes.

The par of these nine was not a stroke under 36, and of course I did them in 34. As this is an experience which is likely to happen to the reader renewing his career as a golfer after the war, we may appropriately pause for one of the instructional halts I mentioned earlier.

I do not say you will do your first nine holes in 34—but I do say that you will play with immeasurably greater success than you had ever dared to hope. And, as you meditate contentedly in the clubhouse afterwards, you may conclude, as I did, that you took the game a lot too seriously in the old days; that your mind was confused with a multitude of 'secrets', tips, and theories; and that you would have done better to recognize, as you recognize now, that golf is only a question of catching an implement in two hands and making with it a simple forward movement at the ball.

People make the game too complicated. If, instead of wondering one day where their left heel is at the top of the backswing, and the next day which way their right little finger is pointing at the end of the follow-through, they bore in mind the old adage that 'the ball maun be hit' and got on with the job, everyone would be a lot better off.

I remember thinking along these lines after my brilliant 34, which impressed so greatly all those who came to hear about it. Being out of practice, I had not tried for great length and, after all, it is easy enough to hit the ball on to a broad fairway if you don't try to knock the cover off it at the same time. Pitch shots, with a No. 5 downwards, were the easiest part of the game anyway. Long seconds were always difficult, but by keeping your head down and taking it quietly, you could perfectly well get down in two more if you happened to miss the green. As for putting, if you level the club up behind the ball and give it a firm, smooth blow at right angles to the clubhead, it should, and *does*, go in.

By this time you will have suspected the sequel. If I could hole the long outward half at North Shore in 34 with six rather miserable borrowed clubs and army plimsoles, what miracles could I not perform with my own familiar instruments and the shoes with the nails set out at an angle, thus ensuring a firm stance and the maximum etc., etc.? So I sent for my clubs, and the answer turned out to be 'Approximately 41'.

Why should this be? Are the causes physical or psychological? A bit of one and a bit of t'other, perhaps, but to my own way of thinking largely psychological. And here I must be allowed to continue taking myself as the example, for, while we may observe what the experts do with their hands or feet or hips or chin or whatever portion of their anatomy the current teaching may be focussed upon, we cannot tell what goes on in another man's mind.

It all links up, I think, with the curious fact that you play better on a strange course the first time than in the next few succeeding rounds—illustrating, incidentally, a secret of psychology which applies to every branch of human endeavour. I am sure from long experience that suggestion plays a profound part in golf—and indeed in every game. See yourself playing well, and you play well. See yourself playing badly, and sure enough you are right. Apply it to individual shots, especially in the more crucial stages of the match, and the conception is brought into stronger relief. You are standing, let us say, on the seventeenth tee, with a broad fairway stretched out before you and a railway line running down the right-hand side—and you are trying very hard.

I suggest that your ball will go where you *see* it going. Not where you *hope* it will go, but where the picture in your mind shows it to be going. If there never enters your head an image other than that of a ball sailing down the fairway, in nine times out of ten that is what it will do. But supposing the uneasy alternative has already printed its picture on your mind—the railway line, stroke and distance off the tee, collapse, confusion, and the match thrown away? Why, then, one of three things will happen: either you will slice it over the railway; or, lifting your head quickly to see whether you have sliced it over the railway, you will top it into the rough in front of the tee; or, determined at all costs not to slice it over the railway, you will hook it at what the caddies call 'left angles' into the rough. Can you honestly say that any of these three things would have happened if, in the first place, it had *never occurred to you* to slice it over the railway?

How often you hear people saying 'Funny, but I *knew* I was going to hit that one!' or 'I *knew* I was going to hole that one!' Of course they did—because they never had any mental image of themselves doing anything else. Is it to be supposed that they would have holed it if they had been saying to themselves 'I may push it out to the right, I may pull it round to the left, I may leave it short, or I may hit it into the hole'?

That is what happens to people when they play for the first time on a strange course, and what happened to me at Blackpool. For many months I had not seen, played, talked, or written about golf. So I occupied my mind exclusively with what I was trying to do and there was no room left to think of avoiding what I wanted not to do. Mind you, I am not quoting this to show what a clever fellow I am. I only thought it out afterwards—but it's right.

It worked particularly well with the short game. You can see the shape of shot you want, and where it ought to pitch, and, *if you think of nothing else*, there is no great difficulty in pitching it there. And the same with putting. There really is no great difficulty in moving a club six inches and bringing it back in the same direction—if that is all you are thinking about.

But what a confusion of thoughts, theories, memories, and ambitions arose with the arrival of my own clubs! The very 'feel' of the things brought surging back the tips, secrets, and other mental paraphernalia with which one's game is clouded in more leisured days. Each one of them, it seemed, brought back its own individual style of play, instead of a single workmanlike style serving for the lot. Worse, they brought memories of their fallibility—not only the good times they had given me but the villainous strokes they had sometimes made. As for the putter, I had no sooner entwined my fingers affectionately round it than a small voice reminded me that I used never to be quite safe from four feet.

So the first careless rapture was lost and the spell was broken. Complications had set in. From then onwards I tried to 'think' my way back into being a golfer.

That little shot from just off the green, for instance. It had been so simple. Instead of a single nondescript mashie-niblick, I now had as wide a selection of pitching clubs as a dentist has of those curiously similar instruments on his tray. Which one should it be? All sorts of shots were 'on'. So they were—but when I came to play one of them, I was still thinking of the others.

So the ball finished fifteen feet away instead of three, and the very touch of the putter recalled to me that, though I had been known to hole out from fifteen feet, there had also been times when I took three putts!

The brassie, too, as I waggled its little black head in the first practice swing, reminded me not only how much more easily it used to nip the ball out of a close lie than the modern shiny-headed, deep-faced article, but also how, like the great Hagen, I was always prone, suddenly and for no reason at all, to hit one slap on the head.

Things went from bad to worse, and in perhaps half a dozen studious rounds I never succeeded in doing the first nine holes in 40. Then came a break and we marched away to camp for a fortnight under some trees opposite the entrance to the Green Drive club at Lytham. Here was a most tantalising state of affairs, for it fell to my lot to be on guard on Sunday morning. Stooge-like, I stood at our gateway opposite the club, contemplating the infinite, as sentries do, and occasionally sloping my arms and taking a stroll to the end of the wall and back. A small child collected pebbles from the gutter and placed them trustingly in my palm; a kindly citizen left a cigarette on the wall. Then, exquisite torment, the members began to roll up in cars for their Sunday golf.

I watched them vanish into the club and emerge later, clad as free men, to take their practice swings round the first tee. As the bad payers drove up, the caddy boys darted away to hide in the wood beside me, where I heard them making adult observations on men who gave only 'arf a dollar. I reflected a little sourly that my own fee at the time was three farthings an hour.

Eventually I managed to get a few games at this hospitable club, but I will not risk your rising from your seat with 'This is where I came in', by describing the painful business again. Suffice to say that I borrowed some clubs and played very well. Someone—confound the fellow—remarked once or twice 'That was a long one!' So the voice of temptation whispered 'If you can hit them that far with those clubs, how much farther could you not hit them with your own?' So I persuaded a driver to bring them over one day, and the answer this time was 'About twenty yards less far, and not so straight!'

The hazards, boundaries, ditches, ponds, and spinneys which I had not noticed in my first round, *because I wasn't looking for them*, obtruded themselves upon the attention and I found my mind engaged in the negative process of trying to avoid them instead of the positive purpose of hitting the ball down the middle. To make it worse, the battery commander went round in 68.

The free and easy summer at Blackpool was succeeded by a chill winter spent on a barrack square near Chester, teaching unenthusiastic gentlemen (and myself in the process) the intricacies of the Bofors gun, a period relieved by nostalgic weekly visits to the house with the black-and-white gables beside the second fairway at Hoylake, from which I had watched the last championship before the war. We need not at this stage pause for any golfing reflections, for I was induced to play only twice, and in the process only learnt what I knew very well before—namely, that, whereas Hoylake always was a merciless course, with borrowed clubs and out of practice in a perishing wind it is quite impossible.

Nevertheless, I shall not forget those games. I never thought to live to see the 'Alps' wired off with great red notices declaring to the members of Royal Liverpool 'DEATH. Explosive minefield. Keep out'. Balls lay tantalizingly in the open, often almost within reach, and there they stayed till the Sappers chose to collect them. A big crater marked the extinction of a retriever which a member had allowed—I won't say 'sent'—through the wire. Incidentally, I suppose they *will* remember where they buried these things, and how many? All the same, it will be some years before I search for balls in the rough of most of our seaside links without a certain amount of misgiving.

Apart from these incidental outings at Hoylake, it was thirteen months before I played golf again. The army caused me to spend the spring and summer in the Vale of the White Horse, for which I bless it, and then set me down in August, for which again I unreservedly bless it, a few miles from Aberdovey—a name with which readers of my distinguished colleague, Bernard Darwin, will no doubt be familiar. I remember how we crowded to the windows as the train wound its way along the single track beside the estuary of the Dovey, with its little bays and rocks and tunnels so like a softer edition of the Côte d'Azur, and the feelings with which I caught my first glance of the links on the flat expanse between the railway and the sea, which the Almighty designed so obviously for golf and nothing else.

Here was the real old-fashioned golf again, little changed since the days when Darwin's uncle had laid out the course with flower-pots for holes. Crisp turf, wild flowers, sandhills, a breeze off the sea, and from the back tee at the fourteenth (make a note of it in case you find yourself one day at Aberdovey) a stupendous view of golden sands, rollers of surf, mountains, and the two farthermost tips of Cardigan Bay.

But I must not let the delights of Aberdovey carry me away from the main theme. It was the same old story—the borrowed clubs, the strange simplicity of the game after the long absence, the comparatively flawless round (74 from the back tees), the inflated estimation of one's ability, the letter summoning one's clubs to be put on the train, the joyous anticipation, the steady decline, and the ultimate wretchedness. So once again we will pause for reflection.

Aberdovey, being 'the real thing', made it worth one's while to *try*. The undulating seaside turf, the big sandhills, and the close-cut greens threw out a personal challenge to prove that one wasn't 'past it' after all. I began to play for the figures, instead of playing the shots and letting the figures look after themselves (' look after the shots and the figures will take care of themselves ' is a good maxim for golfers) and a sense of caution crept back into the game. A five-foot putt was no longer the simple business of rolling a ball along into a hole. It was ' this for a 3 ' or ' this for a 4 ' or whatever it might be, or, worse, ' this to avoid a 6 '. Putts took on all sorts of previously non-existent twists and borrows.

Gradually I began to creep about the green, like some of the leading amateur players before the war, removing little bits of dried grass and such like which would no more deflect a golf ball than they would a croquet ball: and eventually, of course, I turned into quite a bad case of putting paralysis. As it reached its peak at Aberdovey, survived a further six months absence from the game, and emerged undiminished when I began to play again, and as at this moment I believe I am now at last off the danger list, I may as well write of it now.

You will recognize the symptoms, of course. You stand brooding over the ball as though paralysed. You grip the club till your knuckles are white, painfully levelling it up at right angles to the line and at the same time working out schemes as to how you may avoid pulling it, like the one ten minutes ago, or pushing it out to the right, like the one on the hole before. You make a mental note that you hate the whole business, at the same time cursing yourself for not leaving the previous shot nearer or farther away—anything but five feet.

Your meditations are interrupted by the small voice saying, ' You can't stand like this for ever—you've got to hit it some time '—so, with a last resolution that the whole essence of putting is a slow, smooth motion, you move the club slowly and smoothly to the rear, keeping it carefully square to the intended line. You start it on its downward journey. . . . A moment later you are reaching angrily for the ball to try the putt over again.

Holding the inquest as you trudge to the next tee, you find you have no conscious recollection beyond starting the club on the down swing. At that point your hands turned to water (your knees, too, in bad cases), the ball faded unaccountably from view and the brain went numb. For an instant the hands clutched feverishly at the club, twitching the ball to right or left of the hole—or a foot short of it—and again lost their senses. At this point you regained consciousness and started reaching out for the ball. Agreed?

I suffered agonies with this ridiculous, degrading ailment. It has this in common with golf's most humiliating stroke, the socket, that you stand there knowing perfectly well that you are going to do it, yet powerless to prevent it. For weeks, even in practice putts, which is surely the last stage of demoralization, I 'blacked out' just before the moment of impact. The ball might have been filled with explosive. You may see a splendid glimpse of the 'black out' in process in the picture of Arthur Lacey (page 177) which alone should make this book worth the money to the handicap golfer.

That's all very well, you may say, but how do you cure it? Well, I am afraid I have no guaranteed remedy. Personally I worked my way through it, but, looking back, I can see a number of things that helped.

It is abundantly worth while to consult someone who knew you in the days before you became a putting paralytic, who will remember roughly what you used to look like on the putting green. He will pick out the difference. You don't remember what you did then:

you can't see what you are doing now. The particular crony to whom I exhibited the wreck of my own putting said at once, 'You never used to scoop it with your right hand like that'—so I started using two hands again instead of one. He detected that in the old days, when I was as good as the next man with a putter, I used to swing it roughly one third as fast, and hold it with an appearance of 'touch', like a violinist, instead of like a man trying to grip an eel.

Soon he had retrieved quite a nice style for me—on the carpet. But when, next evening, I tried it on the lawn in front of the Mess, I was hypnotised again. Truly it is an extraordinary sensation! I remember staring at the hole and staring at the ball and then at the thread-like path which seemed to join the two, and reflecting how manifestly impossible it was to strike a ball with such hair's breadth precision.

At last, however, I worked my way through to salvation, and to curtail the agony of any reader who may be thus afflicted, I may as well set down what happened. To convince myself that the ball *would* go into the hole (it sounds ridiculous now, but I was thoroughly convinced that it wouldn't), I solemnly knocked in several dozen putts of twelve and fifteen inches. Don't laugh at this: you may be reduced to it yourself one day. An air of confidence returns with the merry 'plip plop' of ball after ball bouncing round the bottom of the hole, and eventually you suspect that what can happen so often from fifteen inches must happen occasionally from three feet. Warily you increase the distance, and sure enough it sometimes does.

Next, our old friend 'Swing slowly' or, as I prefer, 'Swing quietly'. Simple enough, you would think, if you put your mind to it. What takes so long to realize is that any fool can take his club back quietly. What matters is the return journey to, and through, the ball. The old tag 'Slow back' is a snare and a delusion. It is 'Slow *down*' that matters. It is quite astonishing how smoothly, and how far, you can hit the ball by moving the putter quietly into and through the ball. Indeed, it almost seems to hang for a second on the face of the club. You don't have to hit it hard: you need only hold the club with a firm, gentle grip in the fingers. And, whatever the length of putt, make the follow-through longer than the backswing.

Of course I tried stiff wrist and loose wrist, and all sorts of artificial stances before I recalled what I have always known to be the nearest thing to a single universal 'secret' of golf (which I shall be emphasizing again later) namely that if you let the *hands* lead the way, all the rest will follow in natural sequence. Think and feel through your hands. Hold the club like the violinist, set it down squarely behind the ball, and, if you do nothing artificial to stop it, the rest of your body—arms, shoulders, hips, legs, feet and the rest—will flow into their natural position. And there, to my mind, you have the perfect putting stance.

Stiff wrist or loose wrist? As usual, a quiet compromise between the two. Your hands, if you let them, will tell you the way they find easiest. It is when you start conscious interference that the trouble begins.

Well, so much for putting. To return to my story. The Army, still kind, sent me from Aberdovey to the little grey town of Haltwhistle, in the valley of the South Tyne midway between Newcastle and Carlisle. Hadrian's Wall was our horizon on the north, purple grouse moors and square clumps of forest rolled away into the distant south, and everywhere cock pheasants gleamed in the autumn stubble. A grand countryside, and folk to match. The roads over the moors had tall poles beside them to mark the track in the snow, which lay, we were told, feet deep for months at a time and cut off whole towns from civilization. But the sun shone all through the winter that year and it was not until May that Northumberland had a fall of snow.

No one worries about golf in such surroundings and for six months the game hardly entered my head, till suddenly I was cast into a static existence hard by the Grims Dyke club in Middlesex. At first I used to walk over for an evening pint on the terrace, betting odd shillings on the matches coming up the eighteenth, but it was not long before the usual summons went out for my bag of clubs and I settled down to a steady series of evening rounds that enabled me to experience in advance the processes of golfing re-adjustment which less fortunately posted warriors will not enjoy till the war is over. This happy state prevails as I write but, knowing the exigencies of service life (and the evenings are beginning to draw in anyway) I set down my reactions while they are fresh in the mind.

The summons for a reprint of this book, together with the addition which you are now reading, came at the one period of the war when I could call myself temporarily a golfer. I wrote the book in the first place from the inside, looking out. I have now been able to re-read it, as it were, from the outside, looking in. On the whole I like to think it stands up pretty well to the passing of time. Some of it is, of course, more theoretical than you will be prepared to stomach on your immediate return to the game after a long period of stagnation, so I propose, if you will bear with me, to refer to the passages which I, as the advance guard of the army of returning golfers, have found to bear most directly on the problem.

First things first. At the risk of boring you, I return to a subject I have only just left. I am glad to see that I started the short discourse headed 'Hands' (page 52) with the words 'I stand or fall by this chapter'. I do still. You have to think of *something* while you make, and prepare to make, a golf swing: and you can think of only one main thing at a time. You can, if you like, bear one or two other minor points in mind, mostly of the 'Don't' variety, but these negatives can be only accessories to the main theme, which *must* be positive. A single thing you are aiming to do is worth more than a dozen you are trying not to do. Harry Vardon called the hands the 'chief point of concentration' in the golf swing, and I cannot put it more succinctly than that.

Your hands and fingers are, after all, your only direct contact with the club. You can move your shoulders or your feet or any part of the body without necessarily affecting the club: but any movement of your hands and fingers is reflected directly by the club. Shut your eyes and you can feel, through your fingers, the exact position of the clubface three feet away. Through your hips, legs, feet, and what not, you can feel nothing.

I suggest that, in returning to golf, you will by-pass an astonishing amount of trouble, irritation and downright bad temper if you stick to this single conception of thinking at all times through your hands, making them, in fact, your ' chief point of concentration '. The navvy driving a wedge into the ground never makes a bad shot. He does not know where his left heel or his right elbow is at the top of the swing. He keeps his eye on the ball (without being told to), and lets his hands wield the hammer while the rest of his body passively follows. We shall do well, at golf, to do the same.

If your experience resembles mine, you will find this very successful at first and be delighted at so short a cut to golfing prosperity. Then, as enthusiasm gets the better of you, you will become ungrateful, and forget. Surely it would go a little farther if you hit a little harder—got a little more ' body ' into it? No, sir, it would not. When you have proved this by painful trial and error and are beginning to get disgruntled at the game in general and swear to high heaven that it is all the fault of the Germans and how can a man expect etc., etc., just whisper the magic word ' Hands '. Relax those muscles in your back and let your hands quietly take charge again. They won't lead you astray.

Next I should like to touch on a couple of points from my own experience, each of which are related to what I have just written. The first is stance. I know that the accepted masters do not all stand to the ball in the same fashion and that a precedent can be found for almost any kind of stance. What I am concerned with is to find that which is the most generally acceptable. The game is difficult enough in all conscience. Let us at least look for the least difficult way of playing it.

Whatever theories you may hold on the way to play golf, or if you hold none at all and swear by letting Nature take its course, you must agree that the golf swing is a combination of a backhand shot with your left hand and a forehand shot with your right. Now if you try these two shots independently (and I invite you to do so—it won't take more than ten seconds) you will find that they have something in common. The natural line of both is across and *outwards* from the body. The power is not exerted along a line parallel with the body, *i.e.*, the line drawn between the tips of your toes. The power is exerted at an angle veering outwards from the body. Make a further experiment and you will find that the harder you hit, the more 'outwards' the angle becomes.

Indisputably this line, not the line of your body, is the one which should be pointing to the hole. The ball will travel (we hope!) in the direction along which you apply the blow to it, not along the line of your feet. Thus your stance must surely be of the 'open' variety, with the left foot slightly behind the right. That is the theory of it and that is how, in my experience, it works out in practice. It is also, incidentally, how nearly all the professionals do it.

How is all this related to the previous sermon on letting your hands take charge? Why, because, if you let your hands be the guiding influence, leading the rest of the body into what they sense to be the appropriate position in relation to the line of play, you will find that your feet, without being asked, will take up a stance that is slightly 'open'. Try it and see.

The second point I want to mention is even more closely related. This time I refer you to previous observations (page 63) on 'Body turn'. It is manifestly impossible, if you stop to think of it, to apply power in the direction of the hole without a 'winding-up' movement on the backswing. I cannot improve on the example I gave of trying to make a blow with your hips locked in parallel bars. It just isn't 'on'. Bobby Jones, as I recorded, rated a full body turn the hall mark of the accomplished golfer.

With due respect I agree with the master. But it is my own opinion that, either as a beginner or as a 'returner' to golf, you will not achieve a respectable turn without a certain amount of effort. If you are particularly lissom by nature, you may have no trouble, but most of us, including your humble servant, are not as lissom as we were. Mind you, I persist doggedly that if you leave it to your hands they will try to guide you naturally into a full body turn, but I think that alone they may not succeed. I can still hear Fred Robson saying, 'You're getting in your own way, Mr. Longhurst, you're getting in your own way!', and I believe most of us tend to get in our own way in the backswing unless we take steps to get out of it.

Nor is the stiffening-up of advancing years the only influence which restricts the turning of the body, at least in my own case. One's early efforts to recapture past form are liberally spattered with wild, eccentric strokes. One is inclined, as the Americans nicely put it, to 'spray' them. And there comes upon the mind an unworthy, creeping desire to poke them at all costs up the middle—a desire, I may add, that is strongly fortified by the shortage of golf balls.

As I have said, you cannot tell what goes on in another man's mind, so I can merely report that in my own mind, when I try to poke them up the middle, there comes the temptation not to turn away from the hole at all in the backswing, for fear that I never get back into the right direction again! This is absurd. I know it is absurd, but I often find myself doing it, and it takes quite a little resolution to get out of the habit when I see a narrowing fairway. Nor have I any patent remedy against this failing. You just have to overcome it, that's all.

The golf swing can never be a matter of certainty. Two men may go through apparently similar motions and yet one of them feel himself to be doing something quite different from the other. I am glad to feel, on re-reading it, that at no point in this book can I be accused of laying down the law, of committing the now world wide sin of confusing, either deliberately or unconsciously, opinion with fact. On the other hand, while no one may point to a golfing method and declare it to be the 'right' one, I had, when I wrote this book, come to a few conclusions as to methods that are 'wrong'. Between that time and September, 1939, when my clubs went up into the attic, I had another two and a half years of increasingly mature association with the game. I saw Cotton, Whitcombe, and Burton win their championships; I saw a new star rise in the firmament in the shape of young Bruen, whose future may remain for ever a matter of clubhouse speculation; I saw the miracle come to pass at St. Andrews when at last we won the Walker Cup. That period hardened some of my conclusions into certainties.

One of them I have already laboured to death, namely that your hands must be the guiding agents of your swing (revive in your mind a picture of Padgham in the good old days and you will see at a glance what I mean). Another, equally sure and equally universal, I wish to re-emphasise now. I refer to what Compston calls the 'dummy left arm'—or, as I think he might have said, 'dummy left side'.

The conclusion that this is one of the 'certainties' of golf comes partly from my own experience, largely from observation of others. Let me start by quoting an extreme specimen upon which I chanced the other day—a strong, athletic-looking fellow who shaped as though he ought to play well and in fact played quite exceptionally badly. He did not hook or top or slice consistently: he just scored all round the wicket with a fine, all-embracing variety of execrable strokes. It turned out—to give away the secret—that he was a tennis player.

His golf swing, of course, was merely a forehand drive in disguise. He did, as a concession to golfing custom, hinge his left arm on to the club, but it played a purely nominal rôle. I say without exaggeration that he would have done better to join the one-armed golfers' society and keep his left hand in his trouser pocket. This is not a matter about which we need become deeply theoretical. There is no argument about golf being a two-handed game: the question is, What part should your left arm play? I suggest that it has a double function.

In the first place it makes a blow on its own account. So does the right, and the two combined make your two-handed golf shot. I do not think there is anything complicated about the blow with your left arm—it is nothing more than the blow you would make in a one-handed practice swing. But when you combine the two, it has a vital job in providing the resistance to the force you put in with your right hand—something, as it is normally described, 'for the right hand to hit against'.

(Experts on stresses and strains and the application of force by one object upon another might prove that, technically speaking, there is no ' resistance ' by the left hand, since both are making a blow in the same direction, but any golfer will know what I mean and I shall continue to use the term.)

In my tennis-playing friend this resistance was literally non-existent (I said he was an extreme specimen). The whole of his left arm crumpled and retired from the stroke at the moment of impact. He let go with his last two fingers; his left wrist ' broke '; his elbow doubled back on to his stomach; and the force of the blow with his right hand swung his whole body round till it was facing the hole. He was the embodiment *par excellence* of the dummy left side.

The average golfer does not descend to this level—often. He does not qualify to join my friend in the golfing chamber of horrors by committing all the sins at once. But he commits them one by one, on and off, nearly all the time. Certainly I do myself. I have to watch constantly for the resistance to crumble at the critical moment, even on the putting green—where it leaves you with that miserable sensation of having hauled the ball limply round to the left of the hole, probably short. I am always doing it. Look at the pictures of Locke (page 32) or Cotton (page 56) caught at the moment of impact and see how *not* to let the left arm crumple. They are hitting hard, agreed, but they have something to hit against. Supposing their left elbow had ' given ' at this instant?

It is this firm, straight left arm at and immediately after the moment of impact (not to be confused with our old friend, the straight left arm throughout the swing) that characterises the good player, or for that matter the good shot by the ordinary player. It is the absence of it which sets strong, fit, healthy men of ten handicap wondering why the hell they are outdriven by pipsqueaks who are plus one—and which causes, despite a great display of energy, those infuriatingly ineffective shots that a friend of mine caps by crying 'Good shot, Gladys!'

There are dangers in this advice, of course. Overdo it and you might find yourself playing something like a forward stroke at cricket—all straight bat and left arm. I do not invite you to keep your left arm *stiff* at the moment of impact. I invite you to keep it *straight*, which is a very different thing. Indeed, there is quite an art in this business of straightness without stiffness. The impression is one of hanging the club on the end of an arm that is lissom yet straight. You see a good example of this in Cotton, who contrives to grip the club like a leech with the last two fingers of his left hand, so that to all intents and purposes the club is merely an extension of his arm, yet at the same time keep his wrist pliable and the muscles in his arm relaxed.

Now for another conclusion that has hardened into the most positive of the few that I am prepared to back as 'certainties'. Namely that no golfer—plus, average, or otherwise—can afford to ignore the assistance of the club erroneously described on page 196 onwards as a blaster, correctly known, I now understand, as a sand-iron. The longer your handicap, the more assistance this club will give you. It offers the only pretty-well foolproof short cut to proficiency which in a long experience of golfing disillusionment I have come across.

Diagram 14 on page 197 tells the story. There is no need for further description. Unfortunately, in describing the club I had in mind as a blaster, I led several trusting readers astray. They were sold great bludgeon-like instruments, heavy as sledge hammers and often with rounded soles, and of course the results they obtained did my judgment no credit. I now make plain certain points which characterize the genuine article. First, it must have a flat, not rounded, sole. It must sit quite noticeably on the back edge of its base, as in the diagram. Secondly, it must be no heavier than your niblick—or No. 8, if you have sunk to the level of so describing it. Thirdly, it must be, if anything, a shade shorter than your niblick (I estimate the maximum range of this club to be 30 yards). In fact, far from being a bludgeon, it is the most 'delicate' club in the bag, except the putter.

They will try to sell you a bludgeon, of course. 'Must have a bit of weight behind it, sir!' They will tell you that a rounded sole is just as good. Almost inevitably the shaft they offer will be longer than your niblick. Pay no attention. All that matters when you buy the club is the flat sole. When you have found it, shorten the shaft to about one inch less than the length of your niblick and have enough weight filed off the back of the head (where they stamp the maker's name) to make it slightly lighter than the niblick.

All that remains is to grasp, and by trial and error to prove, the principle that the club will do the work. You do *not* have to loft the ball. The club will to that. All you have to do is to quietly, almost nonchalantly, bounce the back edge of the club on to the ground or sand just behind the ball and let it skid forwards. Quietly, slowly, firmly. 'Good shot!' they say. So it would have been —with a sharp niblick!

Finally, before passing to more general observations, I want to draw your attention to a conception of golf which I applied in the first instance to putting (page 158) and which I now wish to extend to all strokes. I have found it of much value as a mental re-approach to the game. I refer to the comparison between putting and the act of firing a rifle; the suggestion that anything you put into the shot must be applied at *this* end, not at the target end.

The truth of it will hardly be challenged, but how often it is forgotten! The idea needs no long description. Briefly, it can be summarised that your primary aim is not to 'hole out', but to make a perfect blow with the putter in keeping with the line and strength you have decided on. The holing-out is only a consequence, not part of the main business. Similarly, your object on the tee is not to hit the ball on to the fairway, but to make your standardized stroke with a driver—as a consequence of which you hope the ball will finish on the fairway.

You may say that this is an obvious and elementary conception of golf. I reply that it may very well be, but the constant overlooking of it leads to many of the bad results in golf and every other game. Compare a man trying to convert a try or score a penalty, the simplest procedures in either brand of football, pure mechanical formalities you might say, and the only occasions on which he is given a free hand by the opposing side. I do not believe that an accomplished footballer would ever fail with a penalty or a try (except, of course, from angles which make it technically difficult) if his whole mind were given to the mechanical process of kicking the ball. He misses because, instead of confining himself to the primary object, he is thinking of the consequences. One might add that when things are going right, he is thinking of the goal he is going to score (and is therefore the more likely to score it), and when they are not, he is thinking how deplorable it will be if he misses it (so he does). In either case he would have done better to give his full attention to his job—applying his boot to the ball.

This applies more intensely to the golfer on account of the wide variety of the terrain on which he plays. One football pitch is the same as another and it is only the 'occasion' which intimidates. In golf the very ground intimidates—slopes, bunkers, trees, 'out-of-bounds', lakes, ditches, and all manner of other hazards conspire to divert the attention which one ought to be confining to making the same old shot with the same old club and the same old ball that one has made hundreds of times before.

As a golfer returning from the wilderness I have found this conception of reducing a golf stroke to a question of 'going through the motions' to be of most use in shots to the green with, say, a No. 4 upwards. They always were the most difficult in the game; now they are more formidable than ever. Very few of us are gifted with the art of hitting 100 per cent shots with the longer irons consistently—that is why we are so often short with them: we dare not take a bigger club in case, for once, we catch it fair and square—and the sight of a narrow opening or a cross bunker or a plateau green makes them more difficult still. We try to play one 'specially straight' or 'specially high' to meet the circumstances, whereas of course all that is needed is the ordinary standard product.

I am sure, for instance, that a green sloping away to the right tends to make you slice—merely from picturing the ball falling away to the right. How much easier it becomes when you realize that all you can do at *this* end is to aim a perfectly orthodox straight stroke to the left edge of the green and then let nature take its course.

Next time you are faced with a long iron shot to what looks like the eye of a needle, try saying to yourself, 'Of course it is impossible, so I will simply line myself up to the green and go through the ordinary standard motions of an iron shot'. You will be surprised how often this comes off. Notice the different result when you try from *this* end to guide it consciously through the eye of the needle at the other.

So much for the practical side. Before we part company I should like to offer a few more general observations, hints, tips, and miscellaneous etceteras which I like to think may ease your return to pre-war golf.

For instance, you are bound to make some pretty fearful shots—but there *is* a limit! After the first two or three rounds I decided that, whatever else I might fail in, I would at least eliminate what we may call the B.F. shot. I don't care what your standard is, there are some shots that even *you* need not have played! You can eliminate them because you know them for B.F. shots before you play them as well as when you have seen the result. You *know* it is a B.F. shot to take a spoon out of the rough in these days when even in 1938 the odds would have been against you. You *know* it is a B.F. shot to take a sharp niblick when a pitch-and-run with some flat-soled club would be perfectly adequate. You *know* . . . but then you know them as well as I do. All I can say is—a great deal of irritation can be saved by resolutely cutting them out.

Again, for your peace of mind you may as well recognize once and for all that you are not as long as you used to be. A small voice may add 'And never will be'. Never mind. The game is just as good—may even be better. You used to reach this green with a No. 4? Very well, take a No. 3—or a No. 2, if you like. Never mind your pride. Reaching the green is what counts—not what club you reach it with.

A thing that soon began to bother me in returning to golf, and for that matter still does bother me, is the state of mind which I see I described, in a quotation from Gene Sarazen, on page 53. He said, you will observe, that the average golfer stands on the tee thinking of fifty different things at once. '*His brain bothers him. It is congested with ideas.*' I remember that I was a little surprised when Sarazen so unhesitatingly quoted this as the main difference between the accomplished and the indifferent player, but in these past few weeks, when I have become a golfer again (of a sort!), I have come to realize only too well what this perceptive little man was driving at. I know just what it is to have the brain 'congested with ideas'.

Don't think that I am advocating a pure hit-or-miss technique to regain your pre-war golfing form. Not at all. No one can improve without giving a good deal of thought to it, without 'ideas'. But ideas must be kept in their place. In other words, do your thinking *before* you set about the shot, not while you are making it.

'You look so serious when you address the ball', a lady observed to me the other day. I denied it with much protest, but reflection showed it to be true. Heaven knows how many different things I was thinking about. However, the effect was good. I had a thorough mental spring-cleaning, and instead of standing over the ball with a lot of meditative waggling of the club, sorting out ideas from one another and in the process ensuring that the rhythm and flow of the stroke was lost, I started saying to myself, in effect 'Made your mind up? Right. Then go and hit it.' The game becomes a great deal simpler in this way.

While we are on the subject of the mind and its relation to the golf swing, let me mention a final point. I am sure you will agree that at the times when you were playing really well—if you can cast your mind back that far—your concentration, or attention (call it what you like), was at its highest during the moments when the club was just coming into the ball, hitting it, and passing through it. The backswing, if you remember, seemed to look after itself, and the follow-through just arrived as a matter of course. It was at the striking of the ball that your attention reached its peak.

Now that the old familiarity of the game is not what it was, I find this distributing of the attention to have become distorted. I find myself thinking intensely at the moment when the club starts to go back—all studious and deliberate. Concentration comes to a peak at the beginning of the down-swing—all sorts of points to be watched here—and from that moment evaporates. By the time the ball is being struck it has pretty well vanished, when of course it ought to be working to its climax. This happens to me time and again. I look back on a half-foozled shot and can honestly say that I have not the slightest recollection of doing anything at all after the first downward movement. I remember gazing fixedly at the ball in the first place, starting the backswing in the approved manner, and even beginning to bring the club down. Beyond that I remember nothing till the shot is over and spoilt.

It is one thing to be aware of one's faults, another to cure them. In this case I have made progress by hammering into my head the idea '*Finish* the shot!'. Never mind where it goes: at least let it be a whole shot, not half a shot or two-thirds of a shot.

Well, there you are. Time, or rather space, has now expired and we must part company. If you find yourself tied up in knots, don't blame me. I warned you that I was a non-golfer. But we shall not quarrel, for we have in common an enchanting road stretching out ahead.

INDEX